NATURAL LAW AND TOLERATION IN THE EARLY ENLIGHTENMENT

PROCEEDINGS OF THE BRITISH ACADEMY · 186

NATURAL LAW AND TOLERATION IN THE EARLY ENLIGHTENMENT

Edited by
JON PARKIN & TIMOTHY STANTON

Published for THE BRITISH ACADEMY
by OXFORD UNIVERSITY PRESS

Oxford University Press, Great Clarendon Street, Oxford OX2 6DP

Oxford New York

Auckland Cape Town Dar es Salaam Hong Kong Karachi
Kuala Lumpur Madrid Melbourne Mexico City Nairobi
New Delhi Shanghai Taipei Toronto

With offices in
Argentina Austria Brazil Chile Czech Republic France Greece
Guatemala Hungary Italy Japan Poland Portugal Singapore
South Korea Switzerland Thailand Turkey Ukraine Vietnam

Published in the United States
by Oxford University Press Inc., New York

First published 2013

British Library Cataloguing in Publication Data
Data available

Library of Congress Cataloging in Publication Data
Data available

Typeset by
New Leaf Design, Scarborough, North Yorkshire

Printed and bound by CPI Group (UK) Ltd, Croydon, CR0 4YY

ISBN 978–0–19–726540–6

Contents

Notes on Contributors

Thomas Ahnert is Senior Lecturer in History at the University of Edinburgh. He is the author of *Religion and the origins of the German Enlightenment: faith and the reform of learning in the thought of Christian Thomasius* (New York, 2006), essays on Hutcheson, Pufendorf, and Isaac Newton, and editor (with Susan Manning, University of Edinburgh) of *Character, self and sociability in the Scottish Enlightenment* (New York, 2011). He is currently completing a book entitled *Saving grace: religion and morality in Enlightenment Scotland* for Yale University Press.

Maria Rosa Antognazza is Professor of Philosophy and Head of Department at King's College, London. Her research interests lie in early modern philosophy and in the philosophy of religion. She is the author of *Leibniz on the Trinity and the incarnation: reason and revelation in the seventeenth century* (New Haven, 2007) and *Leibniz: an intellectual biography* (Cambridge, 2009). She has published a number of essays on early modern philosophy in collective volumes and journals, and has edited texts by Leibniz, Grotius, and J. H. Alsted.

John Dunn is Professor Emeritus in the Department of Politics and International Studies at the University of Cambridge and Fellow of the British Academy. He is the author and editor of twenty books, including *The political thought of John Locke* (Cambridge, 1969), *Western political theory in the face of the future* (Cambridge, 1979), *The cunning of unreason: making sense of politics* (London, 2000), and *Setting the people free: the story of democracy* (London, 2005). In 2011 he gave the Henry L. Stimson Lecture on World Affairs at Yale University, entitled 'Beyond the Democratic Maze'.

Knud Haakonssen is Professor Emeritus of Intellectual History at the University of Sussex and Honorary Professor of History at University College, London. He works on moral and political thought, especially natural law, 1600–1800. He is the author of *The science of a legislator: the natural jurisprudence of David Hume and Adam Smith* (Cambridge, 1989), *Natural law and moral philosophy: from Grotius to the Scottish Enlightenment* (Cambridge, 1996), and *Enlightenments and religions* (Athens, 2010), editor of *The Cambridge companion to Adam Smith* (Cambridge, 2006) and the *Cambridge history of eighteenth-century philosophy* (2006), and general editor of the *Edinburgh Edition of Thomas Reid* and of *Natural Law and Enlightenment Classics*. In 2012 he was the Lim Chong Yah Professor of Political Science at the National University of Singapore.

Ian Harris is Lecturer in Early Modern History at the University of Leicester. He is the author of *The mind of John Locke* (Cambridge, 1994, 1998) and editor of *Edmund Burke: pre-revolutionary writings* (Cambridge, 1991). He is currently editing the *Cambridge reader in western political thought* (with Professor Geraint Parry, University of Manchester) and *Two treatises on government* for the Clarendon edition of the Works of John Locke.

Ian Hunter is Emeritus Professor at the Centre for the History of European Discourses at the University of Queensland and Fellow of the Australian Academy of the Humanities. He is the author of *Rival enlightenments: civil and metaphysical philosophy in early modern Germany* (Cambridge, 2001) and *The secularisation of the confessional state: the political thought of Christian Thomasius* (Cambridge, 2007). In collaboration with Thomas Ahnert (University of Edinburgh) and Frank Grunert (Martin Luther University Halle-Wittenberg), he has edited Thomasius's *Essays on church and state* (Indianapolis, 2007).

Petter Korkman is a researcher at the Helsinki Collegium for Advanced Studies. He is the author of essays on Jean-Jacques Burlamaqui, Vattel, and Locke amongst others, and editor of Burlamaqui's *Principles of natural and political law* (Indianapolis, 2006) and (with Virpi Mäkinen, University of Helsinki), *Transformations in medieval and early-modern rights discourses* (Dordrecht, 2006).

Jon Parkin is Fellow and Tutor in Modern History at St Hugh's College, Oxford. He is the author of *Science, religion and politics in restoration England* (Rochester, NY, 1999) and *Taming the Leviathan: the reception of the political and religious ideas of Thomas Hobbes in England 1640–1700* (Cambridge, 2007), editor of Richard Cumberland, *A treatise of the laws of nature* (Indianapolis, 2005), and the joint editor of this volume.

Timothy Stanton is Senior Lecturer in Politics at the University of York. He was Beinecke Fellow at Yale University in 2008 and Balzan-Skinner Fellow in Modern Intellectual History at the University of Cambridge in 2011. He is the author of a number of essays on Locke, Hobbes, and issues in intellectual history, and the joint editor of this volume. He is currently bringing to completion a critical edition of John Locke's unpublished 'Defence of non-conformity' (1681–2).

Simone Zurbuchen is Professor of Modern and Contemporary Philosophy in the Department of Philosophy at the University of Lausanne. She is the author of essays on Pufendorf, Vattel, republicanism, and toleration in the early Enlightenment, and editor of Samuel Pufendorf, *The divine feudal law: or covenants with mankind, represented* (Indianapolis, 2002) and *Of the nature and qualification of religion in reference to civil society* (Indianapolis, 2002).

Acknowledgements

This volume emerges as a product of the conference 'Natural Law and Toleration in the Early Enlightenment' held at the British Academy in London on 13 April 2007, convened by Susan Mendus, Jon Parkin, and Timothy Stanton. We should therefore begin by thanking all the speakers, discussants, and participants at that conference whose contributions ensured a high level of debate and a productive exchange of ideas. We are also glad to acknowledge the assistance of the British Academy for hosting the conference and providing the generous financial assistance that made it possible. Further thanks are owed for the support received from the same source, which facilitated public discussion of the themes identified at the conference, again at the British Academy, in October 2007. Finally we should like to record our appreciation of the cooperation, patience, and flexibility of the contributors to this volume and the publications committee of the British Academy, which has greatly assisted our task in bringing it to completion.

Jon Parkin and Timothy Stanton

Preface:
Rethinking Toleration via Natural Law

JON PARKIN

THE EARLY ENLIGHTENMENT period has been hymned in much recent historical writing as the period in which the most significant philosophical defences of toleration in the western tradition were first developed and advanced by right-thinking and forward-looking persons.[1] John Locke frequently assumes pride of place in these histories, his *Letters on toleration* providing the paradigmatically liberal philosophical arguments for religious freedom which (so the story goes) would go on to inspire tolerant and enlightened thought across Europe. The same arguments (the story continues), revised and enlarged in the works of later liberal writers from Paine, Humboldt, Constant, and Mill to Rawls, delivered those benefits—religious freedom, diversity of belief, tolerance, and the protection of individual rights—which are the chief characteristic marks of liberal society and desirable features of any polity.[2]

Such histories have dramatic power and a (self-) gratifying narrative arc. But their plot is driven by character and that plot lays certain requirements *upon* character. Not least it requires early Enlightenment thinkers to appear, however inexplicitly, as pioneering proto-liberals. This casting inevitably distorts the historical detail of what is being represented dramatically. One especially insinuating distortion is that discussions of toleration in this period embody a transition from a 'religious' to an essentially 'secular' understanding of human relations. The classic western theories of toleration, we are told, arose in response to, and rejection of, the murderous religious violence

[1] For general treatments of the development of tolerationist thought during this period (not all of which are uncritical of this view), see Wilbur K. Jordan, *The development of religious toleration in England* (4 vols., Cambridge, MA, 1932–40); Henry Kamen, *The rise of toleration* (London, 1967); Ole Peter Grell and Robert W. Scribner, eds., *Tolerance and intolerance in the European Reformation* (Cambridge, 1996); John Christian Laursen and Cary J. Nederman, eds., *Beyond the persecuting society* (Philadelphia, 1998); Ole Peter Grell and Roy Porter, eds., *Toleration in Enlightenment Europe* (Cambridge, 2000); Perez Zagorin, *How the idea of religious toleration came to the West* (Princeton, 2003); and John Marshall, *John Locke, toleration and early Enlightenment culture* (Cambridge, 2006).

[2] For critical discussion of this conventional account, see John Christian Laursen and Cary J. Nederman, eds., *Difference and dissent: theories of tolerance in medieval and early modern Europe* (Lanham, MD, 1996), pp. 1–5.

Proceedings of the British Academy, **186**, x–xxi. © The British Academy 2011.

unleashed by the Reformation.[3] For many influential modern commentators that response entailed a necessary move away from religious and communal reasoning about social coexistence to the more enlightened secular and individualist arguments of modernity.[4] Locke is taken to exemplify this move, offering a theory in which religion becomes the private business of the individual whose beliefs are his or her own affair and have a claim to be tolerated by right.[5]

Many commentators feel very much at home in the company of this Locke. Pausing now and again to note the strangeness of some of his preoccupations, the burden of their attention is nevertheless claimed by preoccupations shared in common with him and by the views about freedom of belief, equality, and the rights of the individual that apparently fall out of them.[6] A cursory inspection of the pages of any late seventeenth-century or early eighteenth-century writer, including Locke, quickly reveals that what claims *their* attention more often than not is not problems of individuals and their religious rights but questions about the relationship between God and His creation and its implications for human life and the institutions through which it is lived. This revelation ought to give pause to readers in search of the origins of liberal individualism. A closer look into the substance of these writers' views would bring perturbation besides, for having embraced Locke as a contemporary and confederate they will be brought up short by the fact that he, and many of his contemporaries, denied toleration to Roman Catholics and to atheists.

This fact invites comment, but the returns have not always been very satisfactory. Most modern Locke commentators have quickly decided that Locke's theory does not in itself require such unpalatable commitments and have proceeded to conclude either that he was not *really* committed to making these exclusions or that, if he was, they were functions of the fundamentally unreasoned prejudices of his time, from which the currents of history and our

[3] This is not to say that no human association in the West (or elsewhere) before the Reformation had confronted questions of religious difference and disunity or developed distinctive responses to those questions. Neither is it to deny that the Reformation in many ways fashioned the world in which virtually all human beings now live and in which we now seek to make sense of those questions for ourselves. For the difficulty of avoiding being carried away in either direction to conclusions about toleration that tack between vacuity and self-deception, see Jon Parkin and Timothy Stanton, 'Toleration, past and present', *British Academy Review*, 11 (2008), pp. 12–14.

[4] See for example the influential historical sketch in John Rawls, *Political liberalism* (New York, 1993), pp. xxiii–xxvi.

[5] This account captures a range of common interpretations of Locke's toleration theory which are systematically debunked by Ian Harris, see Chapter 4, pp. 59–105.

[6] See Jeremy Waldron, *God, Locke, and equality: Christian foundations in Locke's political thought* (Cambridge, 2002), p. 16 and compare pp. 240–3.

own happy experience have delivered us.[7] Where Locke fails to meet our expectations, the failure is to be expurgated or exonerated. But the failure is *ours*, a failure to do justice to the integrity of early Enlightenment arguments about toleration. The hostility towards atheism expressed in these arguments, as many of the chapters in this volume emphasize, was not an excrescent feature of their proponents' thinking. It flowed from a complex of theistic assumptions that framed discussions of toleration during this period.

The frequent exclusion of Roman Catholicism from the scope of toleration, for example, had less to do with empirical generalizations about the trustworthiness of particular individuals than with divine requirements for the relationship between the religious and civil spheres (however those requirements were construed). In order to understand how arguments about toleration worked it is necessary to move away from a mirror in which we find images of ourselves reflected, and to look again at those features of early Enlightenment thought that we may find less familiar, and in many respects alien or unsettling.

The need to think harder about the intellectual matrix surrounding and suffusing discussions of toleration in this period is what prompted this collection of essays, on the relationship between natural law and toleration. One of the most obvious defects of the view that theories of toleration were articulated in an essentially secular and individualist mode is the simple fact that some of the most important discussions of toleration emerged from writers who were committed to a structure of assumption and belief in which natural law was foundational. Although in the case of Locke this has been known (in some quarters) for some time,[8] the consequences of this fact for his theory of toleration have not (until now) been systematically investigated. The relative paucity of work in this area is not surprising, for reasons that have already been adduced. If natural law thinking involves theological prepossessions—that God has bound his creation according to laws that are accessible to rational human beings—such prepossessions have, on the face of it, very little to contribute to thinking about toleration in the secular mode which has interested most commentators.

It is true that the role of natural law thinking has not passed unnoticed in stories of the development of the idea of toleration, but its role is usually

[7] On the question of the intolerability of Roman Catholics, see Jeremy Waldron's strategy of exoneration in *God, Locke, and equality*, pp. 218–23 and John Rawls's remark that presumably 'a greater historical experience and a knowledge of the wider possibilities of political life' would have convinced Locke that he was mistaken, in John Rawls, *A theory of justice* (Harvard, 1971), p. 216. For a contrasting view, see John Dunn, *Locke* (Oxford, 1984), and, at greater length, Chapter 4 by Ian Harris in this volume.

[8] At least since the publication of Locke's *Essays on the law of nature*, ed. Wolfgang von Leyden (Oxford, 1954).

circumscribed to the creation of the conditions under which secular theories of toleration emerged. The tension between the theological commitments of natural law thinkers and the supposedly secular results of early Enlightenment thought are much more easily reconciled if we regard natural jurisprudential thinking as preparing the ground for the emergence of secular thought, rather than as something constitutive of it. One thinks immediately of Samuel Pufendorf, whose natural jurisprudence was formally separated from his moral theology, the one being confined within the orbit of this life and the other concerning the expectations of human beings for the life to come.[9]

There is something to be said for this line of thought generally. It is undeniable that much natural jurisprudential thinking during the seventeenth and eighteenth centuries represented a dialectical response to the intractable confessional conflicts of the ever present past. Uncovering the essential structures of natural law allowed natural lawyers to map relationships between groups and individuals in ways that avoided the disruptive effects of revealed theological dispute and scriptural bickering. Discussion of the natural rights and duties of the individual and the political associations and institutions that arose from consideration of those rights and duties gave natural law theory a distinctively 'modern' secular feel.[10] It is easy, under these circumstances, to assume that the development of natural law arguments emancipated discussion of political and social relationships from what had become a lethal conflation of theology and politics, with the rise of an autonomous realm of natural reason prefacing a shift in orientation away from an idea of religious uniformity and unity drawn from revelation towards an idea of toleration based upon the inalienable natural rights of rational individuals to choose how to believe and worship for themselves. Natural lawyers, on this view, acted as sometimes unwitting midwives at the birth of the modern secular idea of toleration.

This view has its champions and its charms. But it fails to capture the whole story of the relationship between natural law and toleration. To believe

[9] See Kari Saastamoinen, 'Liberty and natural rights in Pufendorf's natural law theory', in Virpi Mäkinen and Petter Korkman, eds., *Transformations in medieval and early-modern rights discourses* (Dordrecht, 2006), pp. 225–56.

[10] See Richard Tuck, 'The "modern" theory of natural law', in Anthony Pagden, ed., *The languages of political theory in early-modern Europe* (Cambridge, 1987), pp. 99–120. For general discussion of the modern natural law tradition see Knud Haakonssen, *Natural law and moral philosophy: from Grotius to the Scottish Enlightenment* (Cambridge, 1996); T. J. Hochstrasser, *Natural law theories in the early Enlightenment* (Cambridge, 2000); Ian Hunter and David Saunders, eds., *Natural law and civil sovereignty: moral right and state authority in early modern political thought* (Basingstoke, 2002); T. J. Hochstrasser and Peter Schröder, eds., *Early modern natural law theories: contexts and strategies in the early Enlightenment* (Dordrecht, 2003). For a case study, see Kari Saastamoinen, 'Pufendorf on natural equality, human dignity, and self-esteem', *Journal of the History of Ideas*, 71 (2010), pp. 39–62.

that natural law was self-effacing and ultimately self-consuming lends a certain ease, especially to those who have no use for natural law today, but it remains a mistake to think that the theological architecture that sustained it provided nothing by way of support to the discussions of toleration that emerged from it.[11] Perhaps this is truer of a Locke, for whom duties to preserve oneself and others in natural law were matched by a duty to worship, than of a Pufendorf—it is for readers of the chapters in this volume to judge.

One theme that recurs in these chapters is the ambiguous status of religion in relation to natural law and toleration. Some general remarks about this relationship may be in order, to set the scene for what follows.

Natural law writing, almost by definition, eschews extended discussion of revelation. But the practice of revealed religion could not be ignored by natural lawyers, both because religious observance by individual believers and churches impacted inexorably upon the world of social institutions with which natural law was concerned and because natural law arguments seemed a promising way of resolving disagreements about revelation through natural reason. Natural law could neither adjudicate directly between conflicting scriptural claims nor play trumps. But it could be useful in establishing through natural reason the general forms of external conduct God found acceptable and so in placing side-constraints on the forms of worship that might or might not be appropriate.[12]

In playing this role natural law could and did cut both ways. In most natural jurisprudence religion both came under the jurisdiction of civil authority and it did not. The practice of religion took place *within* the state and had effects in and for the state but its concerns were not the earthly concerns *of* the state. The situation, in other words, was complicated, and it could be interpreted in different ways by different writers. In practice this meant that natural law could license both toleration and persecution, sometimes even within the terms of the same theory. As it happens, early modern natural jurisprudential arguments more often than not served to bolster the authority of states as instruments of natural law, capable of realizing its ends of self-preservation and sociability better than individuals were capable of doing without it. Natural reason suggested that a civilized social existence was best secured by an omnicompetent civil sovereign whose responsibility for civil order entitled it to jurisdiction over the external actions of churches and

[11] Consider the discussion in Rawls's *Political liberalism*: natural theology could be dissolved into moral discussions of the toleration due to individuals qua human beings endowed with an array of indefeasible rights that ought to be encoded legally and politically.

[12] As in Hobbes. See Jeremy Waldron, 'Hobbes on public worship', in Melissa S. Williams and Jeremy Waldron, eds., *Toleration and its limits* (New York, 2008), pp. 31–53, at pp. 34–7.

believers, a position that could have tolerant *and* intolerant consequences for subjects simultaneously.[13]

The idea that magistrates should regulate the conduct of believers so that they did not subvert the ends of the state licensed a natural jurisprudential defence of a national church.[14] Perhaps inevitably, the results were not always congenial to the toleration of worship outside that church: most preferred to contemplate the relaxation of the doctrinal conditions attached to membership of national churches than to permit dissenting voices to go their own way.[15] If toleration was considered, it was usually as a grudging capitulation to political realities rather than as a matter of principle.[16]

Natural law, then, could be used to inflate civil authority. But it could also have more radically *de*flationary implications for the authority of states. It was an agreed datum in most natural jurisprudence that the authority of temporal magistrates was limited to the ends required of them by natural law. If those ends were restricted, as they could be, to self-preservation and sociability, then what went beyond these ends—for example religion—would be none of their concern. Thus the idea that natural reason and natural law required such limits to be observed became one of the most powerful arguments against the coercive authority of the magistrate in matters of religion. It underlay Pufendorf's complaints against French persecution of the Huguenots after 1685, while something like the idea figured centrally in Locke's writings on toleration at around the same time.[17]

Sometimes, as has been said, natural law cut both ways within the same theory. Pufendorf's work embodied a pragmatic theory which could be both tolerant and intolerant. At the same time it offered principled condemnations of Louis XIV's violation of the proper limits of magisterial action. Locke's

[13] Hobbes's *Leviathan* offers one more example of sovereign authority that is both potentially coercive and at the same time creates space for a prudential account of toleration. See Thomas Hobbes, *Leviathan, or, the matter, forme, & power of a commonwealth ecclesiasticall and civill* (London, 1651), II.xxix.171–2, III.xxxiii.199, III.xlii.309. The various ways that natural law discourse subjected questions of toleration to reasons of state and the ambiguous consequences of pragmatic reason of state-based positions for toleration are discussed by Zurbuchen, Ahnert and Hunter in Chapters 1, 2, and 5, respectively, in this volume.

[14] See Michael Seidler, 'The politics of self-preservation: toleration and identity in Pufendorf and Locke', in Hochstrasser and Schröder, eds., *Early modern natural law*, pp. 227–55.

[15] In the English context, natural law writers typically preferred comprehension to toleration. See e.g. Richard Cumberland, who besides being the author of *De legibus naturae disquisition philosophia* (London, 1672) was bishop of Peterborough. For discussion see Jon Parkin, *Science, religion and politics in Restoration England* (Rochester, NY, 1999), pp. 26–32.

[16] As the chapter by Thomas Ahnert, this volume, indicates in the case of Pufendorf, but similar points could be made with regard to English latitudinarian writers, including Cumberland and Samuel Parker.

[17] See the work of Timothy Stanton (Chapter 3) and Ian Harris (Chapter 4), in this volume, for the fuller complexities of Locke's view.

natural law theory, too, combined tolerant and intolerant outcomes on the basis of similar distinctions between those things that were legitimate concerns of magistrates and those that were not. In both cases understanding the natural law foundations of the theory helps to explain what otherwise seems baffling, baffled, or wrong-headed—one more reason for placing natural law and toleration in juxtaposition. It could be added that the treatments of jurisdiction one finds in the natural law theorists of the period may well, on more than one of the accounts presented below, contain useful lessons to bring home to modern thought.[18]

The chapters presented here are organized roughly chronologically and focus on some of the more important thinkers within the European natural law tradition in the early Enlightenment. Inevitably the selection is biased towards the northern European Protestant tradition which produced the most influential discussions of both natural law and toleration during this period. The volume begins with two chapters on the German jurist Samuel Pufendorf. Traditionally seen as a *Staatskirchler* whose reading of natural law underpinned claims for the necessity of a sometimes intolerant national church,[19] more recent work has begun to explore the complexities of Pufendorf's approach to questions of toleration. Pufendorf was, as intimated above, a severe critic of the Revocation of the Edict of Nantes, and some of the grounds for his pro-toleration stance lay in arguments about natural law and natural religion. Pufendorf perfectly exemplifies the Janus-faced character of natural law arguments and this characteristic of his work is explored in Chapter 1 by Simone Zurbuchen and Chapter 2 by Thomas Ahnert.

Zurbuchen starts with the thought that a nuanced account of early Enlightenment natural law theory may have something to offer modern debates still caught between a liberal emphasis on individual rights and a communitarian emphasis upon group rights. An exploration of the sources of toleration within Pufendorf's work reveals that his natural law theory embraces two connected ways of thinking about toleration. On the one hand, his theory underpins the power of the magistrate to tolerate pragmatically for reasons of state. On the other, his account of natural religion defines a sphere that cannot be invaded legitimately by the state. Zurbuchen indicates that Pufendorf's distinction between churches (as voluntary associations) and

[18] See the chapters by Simone Zurbuchen and Ian Harris in this volume. Although we might consider the diverse effects of natural law discourse one if its weaknesses, there are reasons to think that its capacity to offer complementary conceptualizations of religious and secular relationships might have been one of its practical strengths, from which we might still have something to learn today. Zurbuchen's chapter in particular pursues this thought.

[19] See Friedrich Lezius, *Der Toleranzbegriff Lockes und Pufendorfs* (Leipzig, 1900), pp. 60 and 75. For discussion of the deficiencies of this view, see Seidler, 'The politics of self-preservation', p. 228.

states (as guarantors of individual rights) offers resources for rethinking contemporary discussions that struggle to balance claims by religious communities to maintain their identities with the claims of their vulnerable members not to be oppressed.

Zurbuchen recognizes the limited practical scope of Pufendorfian toleration. As she observes, Pufendorf's appeal to natural religion necessarily precludes the toleration of atheists, idolaters, and blasphemers. Thomas Ahnert's chapter focuses on the place of intolerance in Pufendorf's natural law theory, highlighting one way in which natural law discourse could underwrite intolerant outcomes. For Pufendorf, natural law did not require intolerance towards anyone who lived up to the fairly undemanding standards of natural religion; but the Pufendorfian sovereign was under no requirement to tolerate them either: intolerance just as much as tolerance could be justified pragmatically on natural law grounds. While Pufendorf was explicitly opposed to religious coercion as an illegitimate use of state power, he supported the Swedish king's refusal to take in Huguenot refugees. As Ahnert explains, what makes sense of this seemingly paradoxical position is Pufendorf's broader religious agenda, so often lost from view. Toleration, for Pufendorf as for some other natural law writers, was not a good in itself, but the first pragmatic step towards establishing a properly constituted church-state in tune with both natural law and true religion.

These discussions of Pufendorf's work alert us to the contextual complexities and ambivalences of early Enlightenment natural law theory. In turning to John Locke, Timothy Stanton, and Ian Harris offer accounts of the manner in which Locke's theory of toleration, and his selective intolerance, flowed from, and was structured by, his natural law theory. For reasons canvassed above, the role of natural law in shaping Locke's account of toleration has not been studied closely, and yet, as both Stanton and Harris demonstrate, one cannot properly understand the nature of Locke's arguments about toleration independently of the natural jurisprudential resources from which he drew. Their chapters, taken together, not only demonstrate the defects with the traditional approach to Locke's theory of toleration, they also renovate our understanding of its founding principles.

Stanton's chapter provides a meticulous reconstruction of the steps that Locke took to establish the terms of his famous tolerationist arguments: firstly, his rejection by 1667 of the idea that the magistrate had any right to impose conformity to the national church, and second, his recognition by 1685 that the magistrate also lacked the ability to impose any rites or ceremonies in any church. The first move, argues Stanton, entailed the rejection of the idea of an authoritative conscience in favour of the authority of an identifiable natural law, a position that defeated the claims of dissenters and the magistrate alike to impose their beliefs on others. The second move explored the implications of natural law theory for human existence. In particular Locke came to the realization that each area of human life was bounded by laws that governed its scope. On this account civil society existed for temporal ends, whereas the concern of religious societies was future bliss. Churches should therefore not impinge on states or vice versa, a view that heralded the themes of his *Two treatises of government* (which conspicuously excluded discussion of churches and their attendant ends) and the *Epistola de tolerantia*, which make clear that the magistrate has no business in matters of religion. Indeed, as Stanton points out, this means that Locke is not, in the normal run of things, a toleration theorist at all: he simply denies that the magistrate possesses the right to tolerate, or not to tolerate, religious belief.

If Stanton's chapter establishes the steps by which natural law came to shape Locke's response to the problem of toleration, that by Ian Harris explains the full extent to which Locke's tolerationist arguments relied upon natural law. In so doing it completely transforms our understanding of the *Epistola*. Harris notes that the effect of the standard view of the *Epistola* is to make Locke 'a simulacrum of John Stuart Mill or John Rawls', who claims that religion is the business of the individual, and that individuals possess a right to choose their own way of settling it. Religion is thus private and is to be tolerated by the state. This simulated Locke does not believe in coercion, but his theory is marred by a curious and regrettable denial of toleration to Roman Catholics and atheists.

Harris's interpretation offers a wholesale reassessment of this Locke, and does so by shifting the terms in which the real Locke's theory is understood. Harris argues that Locke sees public worship as a duty prescribed by natural law. Religion is therefore neither private nor optional and is a matter of duty rather than right. Locke's focus on law directs human beings towards jurisdictions, ecclesiastical and civil, each of which, as Stanton also shows, has its own end, connected with providing the means for people to obtain the ends of natural law. Church and state are thus free from each other's direction. For Harris, toleration enters the picture because natural law requires that people love one another, and Locke takes this requirement to mean that people (including magistrates) should tolerate other people's manner of worship.

Conversely the state, because its jurisdiction is to enforce natural law in the interests of citizens, has a duty to coerce actions of any sort and the beliefs that animate them where these undermine civil interests. Locke believed that coercion should be applied to Roman Catholics who put allegiance to the Pope above their civil allegiance because this amounted to a rejection of the independence of the state from direction by a church that threatened its ends. Atheists should be coerced because they deny the being of God, and therefore the validity of natural law, both of which are fundamental to any civil jurisdiction. Locke's attitude to Roman Catholics and atheists, so far from being a blind spot, blip, or blot, is therefore an integral feature of his thinking, one established by the terms of his natural theology and natural jurisprudence. Harris argues that this means in practice that for Locke the boundary of free worship is theism, consistent with civil interests. Theism and what follows from it—natural law, its duties, an account of jurisdiction, free worship, a duty of mutual toleration—are fundamental to the *Epistola*. Natural law also requires the protection of civil interests, and the state protects these against inroads even where the latter are religiously inspired or irreligiously inspired. One of the many striking outcomes of this treatment is to show that the traditional account of Locke as a proto-liberal is exceedingly wide of the mark.

Ian Hunter's chapter is more sympathetic to that traditional account in the course of its comparative treatment of Locke's position about toleration and that of Christian Thomasius, rooting their contrasting approaches in the contextual circumstances of their struggles against confessional states. For Hunter, Thomasius's version of toleration went beyond Locke's. Instead of taking as his starting point the capacities of natural reason, Thomasius used scepticism about those capacities in matters of religion to disarm the coercive pretensions of churches and states. Such a position required mutual toleration amongst Christians, but formal rights of toleration only for magistrates, who could choose whether to tolerate or not for the sake of the public peace, in accordance with natural law. Thomasius's approach ultimately allowed him to contemplate the toleration of Roman Catholics and atheists in a way that Locke, committed as he was to a substantive natural theology, could not. On Hunter's account, it is this more sceptical use of natural law arguments that opens the way for more secularized conceptions of toleration.

Leibniz is not usually regarded as a thinker who had a substantive theory of toleration, but Maria Rosa Antognazza's chapter elegantly pieces together the scattered evidence to suggest otherwise. Antognazza argues that Leibniz did have a doctrine of toleration after all, which operated on philosophical, theological, and pragmatic levels as part of his project for religious reunification. The structure of Leibniz's philosophical arguments reflected his dependence on an idea of natural law that, while very different from the arguments encountered in writers like Pufendorf and Locke, nevertheless acted to support conceptions of toleration that were by some measures far more inclusive. By reference to the primary, inalienable moral qualities of human beings, Leibniz was able to suggest, for example, that the coercion or punishment of individuals for almost any form of sincere belief was fundamentally illegitimate. There were limits to Leibniz's toleration, fixed by his natural law arguments—doctrines against natural law were emphatically not to be tolerated—but their effect was to create a surprisingly wide and inclusive doctrine of toleration.

Petter Korkman's chapter discusses another seminal figure in the history of natural law doctrine, and one who, as a Huguenot refugee, had much to say on the topic of toleration. Jean Barbeyrac's translated editions of the masterpieces of seventeenth-century natural jurisprudence were for many eighteenth-century readers their main conduit into the Protestant natural law tradition. For Barbeyrac, natural law offered a secular rationalist principle of morality that could be used in the battle against Catholic persecution—and toleration was its decisive weapon. As Korkman explains, Barbeyrac took from his seventeenth-century predecessors the natural law idea that the state was an essentially secular body and used that idea to license a much more thoroughgoing form of toleration than either Pufendorf or Locke had envisioned. If the state had no religious competence, then even atheism could be permitted, because it did not *eo ipso* constitute an injury to the civil peace. Barbeyrac's radical account of natural law and toleration made substantial modifications to the arguments of his predecessors and in doing so shows us another way in which natural law moved beyond the theological constraints that structured the defining work in the genre to open alternative possibilities to the future.

If Barbeyrac shows how natural law discourse could be transformed in a more radical direction, Knud Haakonssen's discussion of Francis Hutcheson locates Hutcheson's theory of toleration and related discussions of the right of free conscience in a more traditional set of religious assumptions. Although Hutcheson was nominally committed to an account of an inalienable right of conscience and the rejection of intellectual coercion, such apparently 'modern' and 'liberal' tolerationist sentiments were chaperoned by a more conservative natural law theory that determined the exercise of such rights. If natural law granted the state extensive prudential rights over the organization of religion, Hutcheson's rights of conscience were constrained by the requirements of the common good and a moral pedagogy designed to ensure that they were exercised in the appropriate fashion.

That Hutcheson's account of toleration bore the imprint of a theologically motivated account of natural law serves to underline another recurrent theme of these chapters considered as a whole. Although natural law theory operated in diverse ways, it played a vital role in structuring and constituting the ideas of toleration with which it was associated. As all the chapters presented here make clear, unless we grasp the formative character of natural law arguments for our conceptions of toleration, we will gravely misunderstand some of the central works of the western toleration tradition and badly misrepresent their (and our own) history. A careful reassessment of that history shows that the development of the idea of toleration was a far more complicated story than is usually written or read. Tolerationist thinking emerged from distinctive contexts in which the intellectual presuppositions and the political and religious questions and answers were very different from our own. It owed a great deal to the theological traditions we often suppose it to have superseded, and gained its strength from its roots in those traditions. The conceptual innovations which have brought in their train the views of toleration we fondly and familiarly admire today often did not come from the thinkers whom we venerate as their inventors.

These salutary facts should make us at least more cautious than we tend to be of assuming that the story of toleration marches in step with, and triumphantly vindicates, the conclusions that right-thinking and forward-looking persons favour nowadays. The pressing need to recognize and reckon with these facts is articulated by John Dunn in his 'Postface'. Dunn offers a timely meditation on the importance of understanding the complexity of the history of toleration in the West for any adequate view of its past, its present, and its prospects. His chapter is a fitting conclusion to the present volume, for this is the ongoing task to which it makes its own modest contribution.

1

Religious Commitment and Secular Reason: Pufendorf on the Separation between Religion and Politics

SIMONE ZURBUCHEN

Liberal concepts of toleration, which prioritize individual liberty over communal attachments, have increasingly been questioned. A number of authors, in dealing with the issue of toleration in contemporary multicultural societies, have suggested that the concept of religious toleration that developed in Western societies in the aftermath of the Reformation and the subsequent wars of religion took on a very distinctive form: religious communities are protected from oppression through the separation of church and state.[1] This concept removes religion from the public agenda, leaving adherents of competing doctrines free to pursue their beliefs in private. Although it is still possible for the individuals to express their faith in community with others, the church is relegated to the status of a private association.

Critics of a liberal concept of toleration recall that peaceful coexistence between religious communities—or, more generally, between groups of people with different histories, cultures, and identities—can take on very different political forms. Michael Walzer, for example, distinguished between five 'regimes' of toleration: multinational empires, international society, consociations, nation-states, and immigrant societies.[2] In this chapter I shall focus on just one specific version of imperial toleration, namely the 'millet system' of the Ottoman Empire, as it was put to work in one early modern thinker's argumentation about religious difference and accommodation.

[1] See, paradigmatically, John Rawls, *Political liberalism* (New York, 1993), pp. xiii–xxx and compare Will Kymlicka, *Multicultural citizenship: a liberal theory of minority rights* (New York, 1996); Michael Walzer, *On toleration* (New Haven, CT, and London, 1997); Robert Audi, *Religious commitment and secular reason* (Cambridge, 2000); Amy Gutmann, *Identity in democracy* (Princeton, NJ, 2003), esp. ch. 4; Andrew R. Murphy, *Conscience and community: revisiting toleration and dissent in early modern England and America* (University Park, PA, 2003); Perez Zagorin, *How the idea of religious toleration came to the West* (Princeton, NJ, 2003).
[2] Walzer, *On toleration*, pp. 14–36.

Proceedings of the British Academy, **186**, 1–14.

I

The 'millet system', which describes the scenario of peaceful coexistence of religious, self-governing communities, is often cited as an example of an alternative to liberal concepts of religious toleration. For Will Kymlicka the 'millet system' is the most developed example of a group-rights model of toleration, in which each religious community is granted official status and a substantial measure of self-government.[3] This model need not recognize any principle of individual freedom of conscience, because it allows each religious community to base self-government on religious principles and to enforce religious orthodoxy. Thus, under the 'millet system' not only the dominant Muslim community but also the Jewish and Christian communities could punish heresy and apostasy and impose severe restrictions on individual freedom of conscience. As Kymlicka notes, the 'millet system' of toleration is, in one respect, the perfect opposite of the liberal regime of toleration that has come to predominance in the West, 'because it unites, rather than separates, church and state'. Although Kymlicka admits that the 'millet system' was 'a deeply conservative, theocratic, and patriarchal society', he considers it 'a viable alternative form' of religious toleration.[4]

The main reason for taking the group-rights model of toleration seriously is that the conception of the person as a free or autonomous chooser of his or her ends, on which the liberal concept of toleration is based, is extremely controversial. According to the communitarian conception of the person, the final ends one pursues are not chosen, but constitutive of one's identity. In so far as people's religious affiliations are constitutive of their identity, they will have an overriding interest in protecting and advancing their communal beliefs and practices, and they have no interest in being able to stand back and critically assess their deeply held beliefs and traditional practices.[5] If one accepts this conception of the person it follows that religious communities cannot and should not be understood as purely voluntary and private associations. Rather, they represent exemplary cases of what have variously been described as 'identity groups', 'encompassing groups', and the like.[6] If we

[3] Will Kymlicka, 'Two models of pluralism and tolerance', in David Heyd, ed., *Toleration: an elusive virtue* (Princeton, NJ, 1996), pp. 81–105.

[4] Kymlicka, 'Two models', p. 83 n.

[5] See Michael Sandel, *Liberalism and the limits of justice* (Cambridge, 1982), pp. 58–9, 152–4, 179, and Charles Taylor, 'Atomism', in his *Collected papers 2: philosophy and the human sciences* (Cambridge, 1985), pp. 187–210, but compare Will Kymlicka, *Liberalism, communitarianism, and culture* (Oxford, 1989), ch. 2.

[6] See Gutmann, *Identity in democracy*, ch. 1; Iris Marion Young, *Inclusion and democracy* (Oxford, 2000), ch. 3; Avishai Margalit and Joseph Raz, 'National self-determination', *The Journal of Philosophy*, 87 (1990), pp. 439–61.

acknowledge that religious ends are constitutive of people's identity, we can understand better why communal self-government is often seen to be of greater importance than individual liberty. From this perspective, the liberal concept of toleration undermines rather than protects religious communities. As Michael Walzer puts it, '[v]irtually all the tolerated religions aim to restrict individual freedom, which is, for liberals at least, the foundation of the very idea of toleration. Most religions are organized to control behaviour. When we require them to give up this end, or to give up the means to this end, we are requiring a transformation whose end product we cannot yet describe.'[7]

In this chapter I wish to suggest that this opposition between a liberal and a communitarian model of toleration is misconceived.[8] I will argue that the separation between state and church, as it was advocated by the first proponents of a liberal concept of religious toleration in the early Enlightenment, can serve both to protect individual liberty of conscience and enable religious communities to maintain their distinct identity. I will develop my case on the basis of Samuel Pufendorf's writings on religious toleration. Pufendorf is not commonly considered a central figure in the story of the birth and subsequent rise of the liberal concept of toleration. While some scholars have maintained that Pufendorf's religious commitment to the Lutheran faith led him astray from secular reason on the issue of toleration, I have argued that Pufendorf, because of his concern for religious unity in the state, weakened his own arguments in support of freedom of religion, and that he ultimately defined toleration in terms of 'reason of state'.[9] This allowed him, on the one hand, to defend the legal rights of religious minorities who had obtained their freedom of religion through contracts and agreements with the ruler and, on the other hand, to uphold the right of the ruler to grant or withhold toleration according to interests of state.

[7] Walzer, *On toleration*, p. 71.

[8] This point is not in itself new, of course: it is the setting in which it is developed that distinguishes it from alternative versions of the suggestion it embodies. See e.g. Shlomo Avineri and Avner de-Shalit, eds., *Communitarianism and individualism* (Oxford, 1992), and Elizabeth Frazer and Nicola Lacey, *The politics of community: a feminist critique of the liberal-communitarian debate* (Hemel Hempstead, 1993), for other settings and lines of development.

[9] For the former interpretation, see Detlef Döring, *Pufendorf-Studien: Beiträge zur Biographie Samuel von Pufendorfs und zu seiner Entwicklung als Historiker und theologischer Schriftsteller* (Berlin, 1992); idem, 'Samuel von Pufendorf and toleration', in John Christian Laursen and Cary J. Nederman, eds., *Beyond the persecuting society: religious toleration before the Enlightenment* (Philadelphia, 1998), pp. 178–96. For the latter, see Simone Zurbuchen, 'Samuel Pufendorf's concept of toleration', in Cary J. Nederman and John Christian Laursen, eds., *Difference and dissent: theories of toleration before Locke* (Lanham, MD, 1997), pp. 163–84; idem, 'From denominationalism to Enlightenment: Pufendorf, Le Clerc, and Thomasius on toleration', in John Christian Laursen, ed., *Religious toleration: 'the variety of rites' from Cyrus to Defoe* (Basingstoke and London, 1999), pp. 191–209.

This position is neatly summarized in the posthumously published tract on the reunion of the Protestant confessions, the *Jus feciale divinum*, which appeared in 1695.[10] In this work Pufendorf defines toleration as a means to allow those who disagree on matters of faith to 'live together as if there were no Dissention among them', so that 'at least one Party does not hinder those of another from the publick Profession of their different Opinion, or from Worshipping God after their own Manner'. Speaking of 'political' as opposed to 'ecclesiastical' toleration, he states more precisely that the subjects of a commonwealth who differ in religion 'may have their Liberty to do so Two manner of Ways; either in their own Right, or by the Concession and Favour of those who have Possession of the Government'.[11] The former applies wherever liberty of religion is granted by contract. Pufendorf points to the examples of the Lutheran, Calvinist, and Catholic communities in the German Empire, whose rights were guaranteed by the Peace of Westphalia (1648). He also stresses that when in any state a prince departs from the publicly established religion (as was the case in Brandenburg-Prussia and in England under James II), both he and the people enjoy liberty of religion in their own right. The Huguenots in France, whose liberty of conscience had been granted by the Edict of Nantes (1598), provide another example. Commenting on these cases, Pufendorf states, 'those who in this manner enjoy the Liberty of their Religion, cannot properly be said to be tolerated.'[12]

Toleration in the proper sense of the term applies only to those communities that have their liberty granted 'by the concession of the Government',[13] as in the case of foreigners of a different religion admitted into a state or that of a minority which rejects the established religion. In general, toleration should be granted only when the tolerated party adheres to religious principles that are conducive to public peace and safety. Here, as elsewhere in his works, Pufendorf made clear that these reservations applied especially to the Roman Catholic party and their priests, who 'hold many Opinions which are greatly to the Prejudice of the Civil Magistrate. The Fountain and Source of which Opinions is this, that they feign the Church to be a peculiar and distinct State, altogether Independent, and no way Obnoxious to the civil Government.' Similar reservations, aired elsewhere, applied to Muslims, Arians, and

[10] Samuel Pufendorf, *Jus feciale divinum, sive de consensu et dissensu protestantium* (Lübeck, 1695). I will refer henceforth to the English translation of this work, Samuel Pufendorf, *The divine feudal law: or, covenants with mankind, represented*, ed. Simone Zurbuchen (Indianapolis, 2002).

[11] *Divine feudal law*, p. 16.

[12] *Divine feudal law*, pp. 16–17.

[13] *Divine feudal law*, p. 18.

Anabaptists.[14] Hence, Pufendorf advocated a fairly limited concept of toleration that looks more like that of an open-minded Lutheran than of a modern liberal.

In what follows I have no intention of questioning these findings. Rather, I wish to show that Pufendorf proposed an altogether different solution to the problem of religious toleration, when he dealt with the relation between religion and politics in a pagan state. In this connection it is useful to recall that Pufendorf's major work on toleration and related themes, the *De habitu religionis christianae ad vitam civilem* (1687), is divided into two major parts.[15] In the first part of the work Pufendorf examines how state and church are related, when no state religion is established. In this context he refers back to the situation of the Christian church in the Roman Empire. In the second part of *De habitu* he raises the question of how the relation of church and state changed 'after Princes, whole Kingdoms, and States did profess the Christian Religion'.[16] In this context he elaborates the limited concept of toleration I have just described.

The remainder of this chapter will be concerned with the relation of church and state as it is discussed in the first part of *De habitu*. In the next section I will discuss how Pufendorf interpreted the regime of toleration in the Roman Empire. As we will see, he suggested that it was quite possible to uphold individual freedom of conscience without precluding the possibility that the various nations were able to maintain themselves as distinct societies. However, he also insisted that peaceful coexistence of various nations and religions crucially depended on the separation of church and state. In the third and last section of the chapter I want to suggest that Pufendorf's interpretation of the imperial mode of incorporating religious difference is more helpful in thinking about problems of toleration in multicultural societies than modern accounts of the Ottoman 'millet system'.

I turn now, therefore, to Pufendorf's view of toleration in a 'pagan' state.

II

Pufendorf's investigation into the proper relation between state and religion in *De habitu* was motivated by the Revocation of the Edict of Nantes in 1685.

[14] Samuel Pufendorf, *De habitu religionis christianae ad vitam civilem* (Bremen, 1687). This is Pufendorf's main work on toleration. I refer henceforth to the English translation of this work: Samuel Pufendorf, *Of the nature and qualification of religion in reference to civil society*, ed. Simone Zurbuchen (Indianapolis, 2002). For the noted reservations, see *Of the nature and qualification of religion*, p. 106.

[15] See previous footnote for details.

[16] *Of the nature and qualification of religion*, p. 91.

In the face of this latest act of intolerance and persecution it seemed important to him 'to know exactly, what bounds ought to be prescribed to the Priestly Order in Ecclesiastical Affairs; as likewise to determin[e], how far the Power of Sovereigns extends it self in Ecclesiastical Matters: For, if either of them transgress their Bounds, it must of necessity prove the Cause of great Abuses, Disturbances and Oppressions, both in Church and State'.[17]

The scholarly controversies over the proper interpretation of this work can be explained by the fact that, in it, Pufendorf does not speak with one voice. He varyingly adopts the personae of a philosopher, who argues on the basis of reason, and that of a Protestant theologian, who relies on the Scripture. In the latter persona he is deeply entangled in confessional polemics. In fact, the bulk of the work consists of a harsh critique of the Catholic understanding of the church. As already mentioned, Pufendorf expressed strong qualms about the toleration of Roman Catholics, except where they had already been granted religious freedom by contracts, as was the case in the Treaty of Westphalia for instance. This fact has encouraged some modern commentators to conclude that Pufendorf's concept of toleration rested on theological grounds. Although it is not easy to categorically distinguish the religious arguments he makes in his works from the purely rational ones, I will try to show that Pufendorf aimed at settling the boundaries between church and state on rather different grounds.

In the preface to his *De officio hominis et civis* of 1673, which functioned as a kind of compendium of and companion to the massive *De jure naturae et gentium* of the previous year,[18] Pufendorf famously argued that men derive knowledge of their duties from three springs, namely from the light of nature, from the laws and constitutions of countries, and from divine revelation. From the first source derive the duties of man 'that constitute him as a *sociable Creature* with the Rest of Mankind',[19] from the second source derives the duties of man as a member of a particular city or commonwealth, and from the third derive the duties of a Christian man. From these sources there proceed, so Pufendorf continues, three distinct sciences, the first of which is of the law of nature, common to all nations, the second of civil or municipal law specific to each country, and the third, moral theology.[20]

Pufendorf highlights two crucial differences between natural law and moral theology. First, natural law is limited to the affairs of this life and thus

[17] *Of the nature and qualification of religion*, p. 11f.

[18] Samuel Pufendorf, *De officio hominis et civis juxta legem naturalem libri duo* (Lund, 1673), and idem, *De jure naturae et gentium libri octo* (London, 1672). I refer henceforth to the English translation of the former work: Samuel Pufendorf, *The whole duty of man, according to the law of nature*, ed. Ian Hunter and David Saunders (Indianapolis, 2003).

[19] Pufendorf, *The whole duty of man*, p. 16.

[20] *The whole duty of man*, p. 16n.

informs man how to live in society with the rest of mankind. Moral theology teaches man how to live as a Christian, how to regulate his life in expectation of the reward for his piety after this life. Second, the law of nature is limited to regulating the outward actions of men, while moral theology aims at forming the mind, and its internal motions, so as to be agreeable to the pleasure of the divine being.[21] For present purposes it is important to note that the science of natural law, which derives from human reason alone, is addressed to all men, regardless of their religious faith. As Pufendorf avowed in his controversies with orthodox Lutherans, he conceived of natural law as a philosophical doctrine valid for all men, whether they were Christians, Jews, Muslims, or pagans.[22]

Pufendorf did not argue that religion was entirely beyond reason. 'Natural' religion derives—just as natural law—from the 'light of nature' and is thus common to all men, while 'revealed' religion is based on particular revelation. In *De habitu* he stresses from the outset that he wishes to trace the 'very Original' both 'of Religion in General' and 'of the Christian Religion in Particular', 'so as to examine both their Natural Qualifications in reference to Civil Society'.[23] Accordingly, the first sections of his work, which claim that state and religion are established for wholly different ends, are explicitly addressed to men as rational creatures whose knowledge of divine worship derives from the 'Light of Nature' as opposed to 'Revelation'. Pufendorf takes it for granted that not only Christians but 'most of the Pagan Philosophers' agree that 'there is a Supream Being, the Author and Creator both of the Universe, and especially Mankind, which ought to be acknowledged and worshipped as such' by men as rational creatures. To demonstrate the truth of natural religion is deemed superfluous, 'since, scarce any body, that is not beyond his right Wits, can be supposed, now a days, to make the least Doubt' of it.[24]

Once we acknowledge that for Pufendorf natural religion was accessible by reason, it becomes clear that the notion of 'secular reason', which I use in the title of this chapter, needs further qualification: it is meant to characterize arguments that are derived from universal human reason as opposed to revelation. From today's perspective the truth of natural religion rests on contested metaphysical or rational theological assumptions that cannot claim universal validity.

[21] *The whole duty of man*, pp. 19–21.

[22] Samuel Pufendorf, *Eris scandica und andere polemische Schriften über das Naturrecht*, ed. Fiammetta Palladini (Gesammelte Werke, 5, Berlin, 2002), pp. 6–8.

[23] *The whole duty of man*, p. 12.

[24] *Of the nature and qualification of religion*, p. 12.

Speaking of religion in general, Pufendorf insists that religion is part of man's natural freedom that cannot be delegated to the state. Here, he relies on two arguments.[25] He first claims that religion consists in the care of the soul, which, unlike the care of the body, man can carry out only for him- or herself. The religious duty of worshipping God cannot be performed by a deputy but only by a person for him- or herself. As religion originates in the relation between man and God, it need not be exercised in community with others. As rational creatures men in the state of nature were obligated to worship God but free to exercise religion either according to the dictates of reason alone or according to divine revelation. They were equally free to dispose of the outward form of worship, without being accountable to anybody but God. Pufendorf's second argument, developed at length by Locke, is that the internal consent that accompanies true knowledge can never be obtained by force. Thus 'a Prince may force a Subject to make an outward Confession by way of Mouth, to comply in his Behaviour, with his Commands, and to dissemble his Thoughts or to speak contrary to his Belief; but he can force no body to believe contrary to his own Opinion'.[26]

Since in the state of nature religion could be exercised by a few as well as by many, in a small as well as in a large congregation, Pufendorf concludes that men did not enter into civil societies with the purpose to establish and exercise their religion more conveniently.[27] Because states were not founded for the sake of religion, the patresfamilias, when first submitting themselves to civil government, were not obliged to surrender their religion to the sovereign in the same way as their lives and fortunes. For the purpose of civil society consists exclusively in the security of the citizens. Although Pufendorf does not speak of freedom of religion as a natural right, he nevertheless acknowledges that respect for religious freedom is a duty of the sovereign. He argues that the sovereign transgresses the limits of his power if he extends his rule to religion. The persecution of subjects on religious grounds can no longer be considered an act of legitimate rule but is an unjust, hostile, or tyrannical act.[28] This is Pufendorf's fundamental objection to the Revocation of the Edict of Nantes.

[25] *Of the nature and qualification of religion*, pp. 13–15.

[26] *Of the nature and qualification of religion*, p. 15. See, by way of comparison, John Locke, 'An essay concerning toleration' (1667), in *An essay concerning toleration and other writings on law and politics, 1667–1683*, ed. J. R. Milton and Philip Milton (Oxford, 2006), pp. 269–302, at p. 272, and idem, *Epistola de tolerantia / A letter on toleration*, ed. Raymond Klibansky and trans. J. W. Gough (Oxford, 1968), pp. 69–71.

[27] *Of the nature and qualification of religion*, p. 17.

[28] *Of the nature and qualification of religion*, p. 18.

Nevertheless, Pufendorf accepts that the sovereign's duty to respect individual freedom of conscience has its limits. Since social order ultimately depends on the citizen's respect for God as founder and provider of natural law, Pufendorf defends the right of the sovereign to control opinions and doctrines. As atheists and those having false ideas of God's role and properties are considered incapable of morality and sociability, they may legitimately be prevented from publicly denying the existence of God and his providence or worshipping fictitious gods or the devil. Natural religion thus serves as a basis for excluding atheists, idolaters, and blasphemers from the scope of toleration.[29]

The relation between state and religion, however, has a second aspect, stemming from the fact that religion does not merely consist in individual faith and worship but is established as a worldly organization. I have already mentioned that Pufendorf's analysis of the nature of the Christian church is deeply entangled within confessional polemics. How, then, does Pufendorf aim to settle the disputes about the proper nature of the church and the power of ecclesiastical authorities? Michael Seidler has suggested that Pufendorf had recourse here, once again, to the state of nature, arguing that 'like religion itself, churches antedate the state and are functionally distinguished from it'.[30] This, however, is not quite how Pufendorf saw it. Instead, he assumed that the public exercise of religious worship originated in revelation and could take different forms.[31] As the example of the Jews had demonstrated, revelation could be addressed by God to one particular nation instead of to all men impartially. Pufendorf argues that in this case God himself 'established at once, both their Civil Government and Religion … and this in such a manner, that there was always to remain a strict Union betwixt their Religion and their State'.[32] Unlike the Jewish religion, the Christian religion 'was introduced after Civil Societies were erected throughout the World'.[33] This is precisely why it was necessary to examine 'whether by its establishment a new sort of Government, separate and independent from the Civil Power, has been introduced?'[34]

Pufendorf's answer to this question is twofold. Speaking as a Protestant theologian, he first argues at length that according to Scripture no ecclesiastical sovereignty ought to be exercised by priests. Having established that the

[29] *Of the nature and qualification of religion*, p. 103.
[30] Michael J. Seidler, 'Pufendorf and the politics of recognition', in Ian Hunter and David Saunders, eds., *Natural law and civil sovereignty: moral right and state authority in early modern political thought* (Houndmills, 2002), pp. 235–51, at p. 240.
[31] *Of the nature and qualification of religion*, p. 22.
[32] *Of the nature and qualification of religion*, p. 24.
[33] *Of the nature and qualification of religion*, p. 17, p. 112.
[34] *De habitu*, p. 27.

Christian church is not a state, he then investigates 'onto what kind of moral Bodies the Churches have the nearest relation, as they were in primitive Times under the Pagan Princes'. Here, he is not specifically concerned with the Christian religion, but with the nature of churches in a more general sense. He believes that 'they were of the nature of Colledges, or such Societies, where a great many are joined for the carrying on a certain Business, under this limitation nevertheless, as not to be independent from the Civil Jurisdiction'. He deems it 'well worth our most particular Observation, that such Societies as were erected for the exercise of Religion were by Publick Authority allowed of in the antient *Roman* Empire'.[35] Quoting Athanagoras' *Apology for the Christians*,[36] Pufendorf praises the benefits of a regime that allowed 'several Nations [to] live according to their own customs and Laws, and every one, without being controuled by any Penal Statutes, freely exercise the same Religion in which he was educated'. It may be worth emphasizing, with an eye to modern prepossessions, that when praising the benefits of the Roman regime of toleration, Pufendorf did not advocate religious diversity as such. For he went on to argue that this 'Liberty of Conscience' was, among other things, 'the true cause, why the Christian Religion in so short a time did spread it self all over so vast an Empire'.[37] It is, nevertheless, interesting to see how Pufendorf analysed the regime of toleration under imperial rule. As we shall see, his account of the imperial mode of incorporating religious difference and facilitating peaceful coexistence between various nations differs sharply from what modern authors describe as a group-rights model of toleration.

According to Pufendorf, peaceful coexistence under imperial rule crucially depended on the assumption that churches were like colleges or private societies that 'have not any Power or Jurisdiction over their Members, unless what is absolutely requisite for the obtaining the true end of each Society, or else has been granted to them by their Sovereigns'. Despite these precautions, the churches had various powers at their disposal, which allowed them to influence their members' convictions and to control their behaviour. Not only did they have the power to nominate teachers and to make statutes, but they were equally allowed to apply church censorship. To the extent that churches were granted the right to inflict punishment upon their members, they possessed a powerful means to enforce uniformity among them. Why, then, did Pufendorf believe that the power to apply church censorship went 'without the least prejudice to the Civil Government'?[38]

[35] *Of the nature and qualification of religion*, p. 86f.

[36] For this work see *Athenagoras: Legatio and De resurrectione*, ed. W. R. Schoedel, with translation and notes (Oxford, 1972).

[37] *Of the nature and qualification of religion*, p. 87.

[38] *Of the nature and qualification of religion*, p. 90.

The answer can be found in his comments on the various modes of punishment. He specifically mentions 'private Admonitions', 'publick Reprimands', 'Church Penances', and 'Excommunication', by virtue of which 'a Member of the Church was either for a time deprived from enjoying the benefit of the Publick Worship, or entirely excluded from being a Member of the Church'. Although Pufendorf was aware that excommunication was a harsh mode of punishment, indeed the 'utmost [remedy], onto which a Colledge can pretend', it was nevertheless warranted, since it 'did not alter the Civil State or Condition of a Subject'. As long as churches kept to the status of private societies, excommunication entailed no loss in the subjects' 'Dignities, Honour, Rights or Fortunes'.[39]

Pufendorf further suggests that churches were constituted by the 'free Choice and Consent' of their members. Churches, like any other private societies that may exist in a state, are therefore voluntary associations. One would naturally assume that the voluntary character of these societies does not, in and of itself, determine their internal organization. Depending on their particular end, one might imagine, their constituent members might equally opt for a hierarchical structure as a more egalitarian one: they would will whatever they judged the best means to the end in view. This, however, is not how Pufendorf saw it. He believed that all of these societies contained 'something resembling a Democracy, where such Matters as concern the whole Body of the Society are to be dispatched by common Consent', and where no particular person 'can claim any further power over the rest, than what he has received by their joint consent'.[40] This neatly coincides with the results of Pufendorf's theological analysis of the true nature of the Christian church. In the polemical part of *De habitu*, where he spoke as a Protestant theologian, Pufendorf argued at length that according to Scripture the Christian church needs to be understood as a kind of college or private society. He insisted that the original meaning of the word *ecclesia* implies not statehood but democratic governance. Elders or deputies always depended on the common consent of the congregation.[41] Hence Pufendorf's claim that membership of the Christian church did not change man's status as a subject of civil government.

It now becomes obvious that Pufendorf's concept of toleration under imperial rule cannot be understood as a 'neutral' historical account of what he praised as a model showing how different nations could live together according to their own customs and laws and freely exercise their religion. It was clearly adapted to a Protestant understanding of the Christian church.

[39] *Of the nature and qualification of religion*, p. 90f.
[40] *Of the nature and qualification of religion*, p. 88.
[41] *Of the nature and qualification of religion*, p. 59f.

Walzer was certainly right to conclude that 'Seventeenth-century toleration was first of all a mutual accommodation of Protestants.'[42] I also agree with Walzer that this concept of toleration cannot be treated as self-explanatory and self-evident, but needs, rather, to be explained and vindicated. This is the task I perform in the next section of this chapter.

III

As I mentioned near the beginning of the chapter, it is frequently argued today that religious communities cannot be understood as purely voluntary associations. Given that Pufendorf assumed that churches were like colleges or private societies, it would seem that his interpretation of the imperial regime of toleration is of little relevance for addressing the problem of religious toleration in contemporary multicultural societies. It is worth recalling, however, that Pufendorf had a more complex idea of membership of a religious community than his understanding of churches may initially suggest. In the first place he assumed that parents have a duty to educate children in the religion they profess.[43] He further explained that the Christian faith is only obtained through God's grace.[44] As Pufendorf saw it, becoming a member of a religious community could certainly not be explained as a voluntary act, as, say, was the case with someone joining a society of merchants. Why, then, did Pufendorf nevertheless insist that churches were like private societies? The reason must be that the way one enters a community is quite different from the way in which one belongs to it. The fact that community attachments are not originally chosen, but given, does not imply that membership cannot be voluntary.[45] The latter simply means that members are not forced to belong without their consent or against their own will. This is precisely why Pufendorf argued that the church is no state and it is also why modern liberals insist that no legal powers be delegated to religious associations so as to enable them to enforce their own systems of law.

Against Pufendorf's portrayal of churches as democratic organizations, modern liberals would object that religious communities understood as voluntary associations need not be organized in a democratic way.[46] Walzer was certainly right to observe that most religions aim to restrict individual

[42] Walzer, *On toleration*, p. 67.

[43] *Of the nature and qualification of religion*, pp. 15–17.

[44] *Of the nature and qualification of religion*, pp. 15 and 57.

[45] See Brian Barry, *Culture and equality: an egalitarian critique of multiculturalism* (Cambridge, MA, 2002), pp. 147–9.

[46] And so, by implication, unjustly. See Ian Shapiro, *Democracy's place* (Ithaca, NY, and London, 1996), p. 112: 'democracy is essential to ordering social relations justly'.

freedom and to control behaviour in one way or another. Few religious communities, Brian Barry observes, have democratic decision-making procedures; many of them are hierarchically organized, with key decisions taken by officers who are not responsible to the congregation. Equality of the sexes is denied by communities that reserve the ministry to men. In order to maintain themselves as distinct communities, all of them need to define strict rules of admittance and retain the power to excommunicate dissenting individuals who are branded as 'heretics' or 'apostates'.[47] Although most religious communities aim to control the beliefs and practices of their members, they have to be tolerated by the state, on the crucial assumption, however, that they are private associations that do not have any power to enact their own systems of law. To protect the most vulnerable members of 'non-liberal' religious communities (most often women and children), the state needs to make sure that they have a realistic option to leave their communities if they wish to do so.[48] This can only be achieved when the distinction between the individual's role as a religious believer and as a citizen is strictly maintained. Pufendorf's comment on the right of excommunication is perfectly in line with such a distinction. As we have seen, he approved of the church's right of excommunication on the grounds that it did not alter an individual's 'civil' standing. On the liberal account, liberty of conscience enables individuals to maintain their communal attachments, but it also protects them, by the same measure, from intra-group oppression by making exit options available to them.

IV

The main issue today, it seems, is not whether the liberal concept of religious toleration ought to be replaced by any kind of group-rights concept of toleration modelled after the 'millet system' of the Ottoman Empire. As supporters of the latter are themselves ready to admit, there is no doubt 'that any form of group rights that restricts the civil rights of the group members is … inconsistent with liberal principles of freedom and equality'.[49] There can thus be no question that the separation between church and state, advocated by the first protagonists of a liberal concept of religious toleration in the early

[47] Barry, *Culture and equality*, p. 155f.
[48] On the 'exit option' see Barry, *Culture and equality*, pp. 148–54,187–93. See also Susan M. Okin, 'Multiculturalism and feminism: no simple question, no simple answers', in Avigail Eisenberg and Jeff Spinner-Halev, eds., *Minorities within minorities: equality, rights and diversity* (Cambridge, 2005), pp. 67–89, and Jeff Spinner-Halev, 'Autonomy, association and pluralism', in Eisenberg and Spinner-Halev, eds., *Minorities within minorities*, pp. 157–71.
[49] Kymlicka, 'Two models', p. 95.

Enlightenment, remains of fundamental importance. Today the central problem is rather how claims by religious communities to maintain their distinct identity ought to be balanced against claims by their most vulnerable members not to be oppressed by their leaders. Given that both claims are based on individual freedom of conscience, they clearly remain within the horizon of a liberal concept of toleration. It is, however, beyond the horizon of this chapter to decide how these claims ought to be adjudicated in contemporary multicultural societies.[50]

[50] I have elaborated such a proposal in Simone Zurbuchen, 'Universal human rights and the claim to recognition of cultural difference', in Beat Sitter-Liver, ed., *Universality: from theory to practice. An intercultural and interdisciplinary debate about facts, possibilities, lies, and myths* (Fribourg, 2009), pp. 259–89.

2

Samuel Pufendorf and Religious Intolerance in the Early Enlightenment

THOMAS AHNERT*

THERE ARE STRONG GROUNDS FOR RELATING IDEAS of religious toleration in the early Enlightenment to early modern theories of natural law. From the time of the Reformation onwards Western Europe was divided into a variety of rival Christian churches, and the religious disagreements between them contributed to the growing political tensions that culminated in the Thirty Years War between 1618 and 1648. It is often argued that the experience of the destruction caused by religious controversy persuaded an increasing number of jurists and philosophers towards the end of the seventeenth century to abandon previous ideas of a political order that was designed to promote religious orthodoxy and impose it on the population. They accepted the inevitability of religious differences, advocated the toleration of other beliefs, and turned to a secular theory of natural law, as an alternative, non-confessional foundation for politics and morality. The German jurist Samuel von Pufendorf is often considered a classic representative of such a development. He was undoubtedly one of the most influential theorists of natural law of the early Enlightenment, whose main work, the *De jure naturae et gentium* of 1672,[1] had a huge impact on European natural law theory, while his shorter *De officio hominis et civis* of 1673 had, by the early eighteenth century, become a standard textbook at Northern European Protestant universities.[2]

Describing this early modern natural law as 'secular' does not mean God no longer played any role in political and legal argument. In the case of Pufendorf's theory, for example, the precepts of natural law were binding on humans precisely because they were divine commands: 'the obligation of the

* Arguments in this chapter have been presented at several conferences and seminars. I am particularly grateful to participants in the British Academy workshop on 'Natural Law and Toleration in the Early Enlightenment', the School of Historical Studies seminar at the Institute for Advanced Study in Princeton, and the 'Enlightenment 2.1.3' conference at the University of California at Berkeley for their suggestions. I should also like to thank Dr Hannah Dawson for comments on an earlier draft.

[1] Samuel Pufendorf, *De jure naturae et gentium libri octo* (Lund, 1672).

[2] Samuel Pufendorf, *De officio hominis et civis juxta legem naturalem libri duo* (Lund, 1673).

natural law is from God Himself, the Creator and supreme governor of the human race, who by virtue of his sovereignty over men, His creatures, has bound them to its observance.'[3] But they were 'secular' insofar as they, and God's role as legislator, were known from natural reason, to all humans, no matter which particular set of Christian (or even non-Christian) religious beliefs they subscribed to: Calvinists, Roman Catholics, Lutherans, and even pagans could, in principle, all agree on the validity of natural law, regardless of their disagreements over, say, church government, the importance of good works in salvation, or the nature of religious faith generally. The religious truth that underpinned natural law was based on a 'natural religion' that was derived from reason, not on a specifically Christian revelation; it was thus, in principle, accessible to any human being. Natural law, it is argued, thereby permitted the separation of political thought from theological controversies among Christian confessions, and prepared the deconfessionalization of politics, in the interests of temporal peace and security.[4] It seems plausible to argue that some measure of religious toleration would follow from such a development.

Pufendorf did, indeed, write extensively on religious toleration. The two works in which he addressed this question most fully and directly were the *De habitu religionis Christianae ad vitam civilem* (*On the relation of Christian religion to civil life*) of 1687 and the posthumously published *Jus feciale divinum,* a title best (though rather freely) translated as *Divine feudal law*, which first appeared in 1695.[5] The *De habitu* came out shortly after the revocation of the Edict of Nantes by the Edict of Fontainebleau in 1685, when Louis XIV of France deprived French Huguenots of the remaining, limited toleration they had been enjoying since 1598. Pufendorf, in *De habitu*, was reacting to these events, although he had been reflecting on the place of religion in the political order for some time, as is evident, for example, from his dissertation 'De concordia verae politicae cum religione Christiana' ('On the harmony of true politics with Christian religion') of 1673.[6]

[3] Samuel Pufendorf, *De jure naturae*, II.3.20. See idem, *The political writings of Samuel Pufendorf*, ed. C. L Carr , trans. Michael Seidler (New York and Oxford, 1994), p. 155.

[4] See, for example, Simone Zurbuchen, *Naturrecht und natürliche Religion: zur Geschichte des Toleranzbegriffs von Samuel Pufendorf bis Jean-Jacques Rousseau* (Würzburg, 1991), pp. 6 and 38.

[5] Samuel Pufendorf, *Jus feciale divinum, sive de consensu et dissensu protestantium* (Lübeck, 1695). The *jus feciale* in ancient Rome was a set of laws governing the relations with other nations, which was applied by certain priests, the so-called *Fetiales*. It is not clear whether the term *feciale* in the title of Pufendorf's work refers to the relationship between the two main Protestant confessions, Lutheran and Calvinist, or to that between God and Christian believers, as is implied by the term 'feudal law' in the English translation of the title. See Detlef Döring, 'Einleitung', in Samuel Pufendorf, *Jus feciale divinum*, ed. Detlef Döring (Berlin, 2004), pp. xxx–xxxi.

[6] Samuel Pufendorf, 'De concordia verae politicae cum religione Christiana', in *Dissertationes academicae selectiores* (Uppsala, 1677), pp. 428–58.

The *Jus feciale* contained Pufendorf's proposals for reuniting the two main Protestant confessions in the Holy Roman Empire, Lutherans and Calvinists. This plan for Protestant reconciliation was motivated strongly by Pufendorf's concern over the political and military resurgence of Roman Catholicism in the last quarter of the seventeenth century. In the Holy Roman Empire high-profile princely conversions to Catholicism had taken place or seemed imminent.[7] In the Palatinate, where Pufendorf had held the first chair in natural law between 1661 and 1667, the Calvinist line died out in 1685 and was replaced by a Catholic, so that the Protestant estates in the empire lost one of their votes in the electoral college that chose the Holy Roman Emperor.[8] At the same time, Louis XIV had not only revoked the Edict of Nantes, but had also embarked on a series of ambitious military campaigns which conjured up the prospect of a European 'universal monarchy', under a French Catholic ruler.[9] In Britain, James II had been openly working towards re-Catholicizing his realm, until he was removed by parliament with the help of William of Orange.[10] As late as 1707, the Union of parliaments between Scotland and England was justified by the need for Protestant states to stand together against the political threat of Roman Catholicism.[11]

In principle, Pufendorf would have welcomed a project for religious reconciliation between Protestants and Roman Catholics, but he was nearly always very doubtful about the likelihood of its success, because the Roman Catholic faith, he believed, was so closely tied to the self-interest of the papal clergy that any attempt to agree on a common understanding of religious truth was likely to be thwarted by the Catholic side. Already in the *De concordia* of 1673 he had stressed that Roman Catholicism was not a genuine system of religious belief, but a pretext for the papacy to extend its power over secular states. At one point Pufendorf had been encouraged by the writings of the Roman Catholic scholar and later bishop Pierre-Daniel Huet (1630–1721) to hope that Roman Catholics might be amenable to being reunited with Protestants. In a letter to his brother Esaias in February 1681, for example, Pufendorf enthusiastically praised Huet's *Demonstratio evangelica* (1679),[12]

[7] Volker Press, *Kriege und Krisen: Deutschland 1600–1715* (Munich, 1991), p. 304.

[8] Matthias Schnettger, 'Kirchenadvokatie und Reichseinigungspläne: Kaiser Leopold I. und die Reunionsbestrebungen Rojas y Spinolas', in H. Duchhardt and G. May, eds., *Union—Conversion—Toleranz: Dimensionen der Annäherung zwischen den Christlichen Konfessionen im 17. und 18. Jahrhundert* (Mainz, 2000), pp. 139–69, at p. 157.

[9] See Franz Bosbach, *Monarchia universalis: ein politischer Leitbegriff der frühen Neuzeit* (Göttingen, 1988).

[10] Jonathan Scott, *England's troubles: seventeenth-century English political instability in European context* (Cambridge, 2000), pp. 205–10.

[11] Christopher A. Whatley, *The Scots and the Union* (Edinburgh, 2006), pp. 1–7.

[12] Samuel Pufendorf, *Briefwechsel*, ed. Detlef Döring (Berlin, 1996), pp. 122–7. Compare Pierre-Daniel Huet, *Demonstratio evangelica ad serenissimum delphinum* (Paris, 1679).

but by the mid-1680s his confidence that the divide between Protestants and Catholics might be overcome had disappeared, mainly, it seems, in response to the political events since the beginning of the decade.

Religious toleration was a possible response to confessional disagreements. It is also true that natural law theory occupied a very prominent place in Pufendorf's thought. And yet, as will be suggested in this chapter, the contribution of secular natural law to Pufendorf's theory of religious toleration was quite limited. It is arguable that he did not regard natural law as the best possible foundation for politics and morality, but continued to be guided to a very considerable extent by a strong concern with restoring and preserving Christian religious orthodoxy. Important parts of my argument throughout rely on recent research, especially the work of the German historian Detlef Döring.[13] But I also intend to supplement these existing interpretations in a way that makes it possible to answer a puzzling question, namely, why Pufendorf often seems to be such an inconsistent advocate of religious toleration, who condemns religious intolerance in one instance, and appears to approve of it in another.[14]

This apparent inconsistency in Pufendorf's thought had already been noted in the early eighteenth century. The author of the preface to the 1719 English translation of the *De habitu religionis Christianae ad vitam civilem* commented that

> It must be own'd, that amongst all the excellent Thoughts contain'd in this Treatise, there are some Things too weak to bear the Tryal, and which make the Book not so much of a Piece, nor so consistent with itself in all its Parts, as one could wish.[15]

In particular, Pufendorf appeared to allow the magistrate a 'power of establishing *Forms and Confessions of Faith, Creeds and Articles of Religion*', as well as of forcing clergymen to conform to these, while at other times he argued for 'an *universal Toleration*, of all who differ from one another, provided they behave themselves in a quiet and peacable manner'.[16]

Simone Zurbuchen has also argued that there is an irresolvable tension in Pufendorf's thought between two approaches to the question of religious toleration. The first is that of 'classical republicanism', with its emphasis on the primacy of the public good before that of the individual. Using this tradition, Pufendorf 'defends the Christian religion … as a means to make subjects

[13] See, for example, his *Pufendorf-Studien: Beiträge zur Biographie Samuel von Pufendorfs und zu seiner Entwicklung als Historiker und theologischer Schriftsteller* (Berlin, 1992).
[14] See Simone Zurbuchen, 'From denominationalism to Enlightenment: Pufendorf, Le Clerc, and Thomasius on toleration', in John Christian Laursen, ed., *Religious toleration: 'the variety of rites' from Cyrus to Defoe* (Basingstoke and London, 1999), pp. 191–210, at p. 191.
[15] Samuel Pufendorf, 'Preface', in *Of the relation between church and state* (London, 1719), p. vii.
[16] Ibid. (emphasis original).

obedient to the sovereign, disposed to fulfil their duties, and ready to subordinate their private interests to the common interest'. Here Pufendorf 'is not concerned with the protection of religious freedom, but with the maintenance of peace in internal politics and the balance of the European powers in external politics'. The other language on which he draws, however, is that of natural law, which, it is argued, denied the sovereign the right to impose religious beliefs on his subjects, because the original contract on which the political community was based did not permit the transfer to another of the right to choose one's own religious beliefs. Zurbuchen concludes that Pufendorf failed to formulate an intellectually coherent concept of toleration.[17]

Detlef Döring has similarly commented on Pufendorf's apparent inconsistency and has suggested that this reflects Pufendorf's willingness to adjust his position on religious toleration to specific circumstances. While Pufendorf was, for example, very critical of the revocation of the Edict of Nantes by Louis XIV, this did not prevent him from supporting the decision of the king of Sweden to refuse Huguenot refugees from France permission to settle in his territories. According to Döring, Pufendorf's inconsistent attitude is best explained by the fact that he was then an employee of the Swedish king and therefore under an obligation to justify his ruler's actions.[18] And yet, while Pufendorf's views need not have been intellectually consistent at all times, it can be shown that his position on religious toleration is not as incoherent as it may at first appear to be. I shall first examine the relationship between Pufendorf's theory of natural law and his natural religion, and the significance this has for his arguments on religious toleration, before turning, in section II, to the place of religious *in*tolerance in Pufendorf's theory. Finally, I shall discuss the great importance Pufendorf attached to orthodox Christianity, rather than any secular political and legal theory, as the foundation of a just, virtuous, and flourishing state.

I

At the beginning of *De habitu* Pufendorf states that humans know of the existence of God from natural religion, which is based on human reason:

[17] Simone Zurbuchen, 'Samuel Pufendorf's concept of toleration', in Cary J. Nederman and John Christian Laursen, eds., *Difference and dissent: theories of toleration in medieval and early modern Europe* (Lanham, MD, 1996), pp. 163–84, at p. 166. See also Horst Dreitzel, 'Gewissensfreiheit und soziale Ordnung: Religionstoleranz als Problem der politischen Theorie am Ausgang des 17. Jahrhunderts', *Politische Vierteljahresschrift*, 36 (1995), pp. 3–34, at p. 14. Dreitzel there says that Pufendorf's secularization of the state was incomplete.

[18] Döring, 'Einleitung', in Samuel Pufendorf, *Jus feciale*, ed. Detlef Döring, pp. xxxvii, n. 155.

> we … by true Ratiocination deduced out of the Light of Nature, may be Convinced of those Sentiments we ought to have of God, and what Reverence is due to him from us Mortals.[19]

Revelation is not needed for such knowledge, although it supplements the findings of natural reason and is compatible with them, for 'some Matters, being beyond our Apprehension, by the bare Light of Nature, are by God's special Command Revealed to Mankind'.[20] Natural religion allows humans to recognize that they owe their existence to an omnipotent Creator. It makes them acknowledge his authority and power over humanity, the existence of his providence, and the debt of gratitude they owe to him. Since natural law, according to Pufendorf, is the product of the divine will, to the extent that it is known to human natural reason, its binding force depends on natural religion. A person who does not accept its basic truths will also refuse to be bound by the secular duties of natural law. On these grounds the magistrate has the right to coerce and punish those subjects who deny the truths of natural religion. Indeed, without such a natural religion

> [t]he internal cohesion of states would be perpetually insecure … fear of temporal punishment would certainly not suffice to keep the citizens to their duty, nor loyalty pledged to their superior, nor the glory of being faithful to their allegiance, nor gratitude that his sovereign power protects them from the miseries of the natural state.[21]

At the same time, however, Pufendorf's theory of natural religion also seems to restrict the ruler's right of religious coercion within rather narrow limits. Natural religion allows the ruler, for example, to punish atheism, because atheism denies the existence of God or, at least, essential properties of God that are known from natural reason; he can prohibit idolatry, because it is the worship of beings other than the deity known from natural religion; he can also punish blasphemy, because it indicates a lack of respect for divine authority. Natural law, however, does not grant the magistrate the right to punish subjects for any religious beliefs as long as these meet the rather limited requirements of natural religion, which is the case for the main Christian confessions. The result would seem to be a theory of religious toleration, which includes Lutherans, Calvinists, and, in principle, Roman Catholics, and in which natural jurisprudence and natural religion are of central importance.[22]

[19] Samuel Pufendorf, *Of the nature and qualification of religion in reference to civil society*, ed. Simone Zurbuchen (Indianapolis, 2002), §1, pp. 12–13.
[20] Ibid., p. 13.
[21] Samuel Pufendorf, *On the duty of man and citizen*, ed. James Tully, trans. Michael Silverthorne (Cambridge, 1991), I.4.8, p. 43.
[22] Zurbuchen, *Naturrecht*, ch. 3 ('Das Toleranzproblem'), esp. p. 55.

Yet it is possible to say that Pufendorf's theory of natural religion was not intended to provide a general justification of religious toleration: strictly speaking, Pufendorf in the *De habitu* is only stating that natural law on its own is insufficient to justify intolerance towards religious beliefs that fulfil the minimal requirements of natural religion; and that is true of a wide variety of religious beliefs that need not even be Christian (though Pufendorf does not mention Jews, Muslims, or pagans).[23] Natural religion and natural law do not, however, impose a duty on the secular ruler to tolerate all such religious beliefs, for Pufendorf's argument does leave open the possibility that religious intolerance might be justified on grounds other than natural religion or natural law. When Pufendorf discusses natural religion, it appears that he is making a point about the weakness of natural reason as a source of religious truths, especially those concerning the all-important issue of salvation, rather than defending a principle of religious toleration. What he is saying is that the truths of natural religion are very limited, even if they are adequate as a religious foundation for natural law: ''Tis true, Mankind, assisted by the meer Light of his own Reason, may attain to understand the Existence of some superiour Power from whom all Things in this World proceed, and all the Motions which are observ'd in it', but 'from these Speculations alone, if no further light be added to them, Mankind cannot gather what Acknowledgment and Veneration God requires from him, nor in what Signs and Actions it ought to consist'.[24]

The punishment for the failure to acknowledge and worship God in the manner required by revelation, however, was eternal death. Natural religion, he emphasized in his *De officio hominis et civis*, had 'no effect on winning eternal salvation'.[25] It is important to take seriously Pufendorf's concern with the effects of religious ignorance or error, because he was convinced that the consequences for the individual were real and severe. Those divine commands that were derived from Christian revelation were just as binding as those grounded in natural law.[26] Religious orthodoxy thus remained a pressing concern, not an issue that could be set aside, let alone sacrificed to civil peace. The fact that natural law did not justify the repression of any religious views that met the minimal criteria of natural religion did not mean such repression could not be justified on other grounds.

[23] Dreitzel, 'Gewissensfreiheit und soziale Ordnung', p. 12.

[24] Samuel Pufendorf, *The divine feudal law: or, covenants with mankind, represented*, ed. Simone Zurbuchen (Indianapolis, 2002), §17, p. 61.

[25] Pufendorf, *On the duty of man and citizen*, I.4.8, p. 43.

[26] Christoph Link, 'Staat und Kirche bei Samuel Pufendorf', in B. Geyer and H. Goerlich, eds., *Samuel Pufendorf und seine Wirkungen bis auf die heutige Zeit* (Baden-Baden, 1996), pp. 208–22, at p. 214.

II

Pufendorf in the *De habitu* is, however, reacting to the Revocation of the Edict of Nantes, which he denounces in strong terms. The question, then, is to what extent he is putting forward a theory of religious toleration that is opposed to the actions of the French king. There is a theory of religious toleration in *De habitu*, but Pufendorf's critique of the Revocation and his ideas on toleration do not rely exclusively or even very heavily on natural religion, but on arguments about the nature of Christianity, which Pufendorf draws largely from Scripture, not from natural religion. Indeed, in the *De habitu* Pufendorf does not refer directly to the concept of toleration in connection with his discussion of natural religion at all. The significance of Pufendorf's discussion of natural religion in the *De habitu* for his theory of religious toleration is usually inferred, rather than being explicitly stated by Pufendorf himself. When he does mention toleration it is at the very end of *De habitu*, in paragraph 50, and then it is not as part of an argument from natural religion or natural law. There Pufendorf declares that the prince may 'with a safe conscience' tolerate dissenters from the established religion in his territories, for the following reason: 'For, it may so happen, that the number of the Dissenters is so great, as not to be expelled without great Prejudice to the State, and, not without danger to the Commonwealth, if they should settle under another Government.'[27] Here the question whether dissenters are to be tolerated is to be determined by very specific, pragmatic considerations, which are not theorized and are not derived from the moral and legal principles of natural religion or natural law.

In fact, most of the *De habitu*, from paragraph 8 onwards, is not even about natural religion, but is devoted to examining the proper religious authority of the Christian church, using scriptural evidence. Pufendorf demonstrates that the Christian church does not exercise coercive power, that it is impossible to compel individuals to be sincere Christians, and that no human being holds the power of the keys that according to the Roman Catholic church had been conferred on Peter and his successors. Christ did not come into the world as a temporal ruler; he never wielded any secular jurisdictional authority. Religious worship emerged first before any political community had been formed, and thus evidently did not depend on the coercive authority of the state. No church held secular power by its own right, nor was it entitled to use secular power to achieve its religious ends. Like the pope or any clergyman, a secular ruler could not compel his subjects to adopt particular religious beliefs. If he tried, 'by such Methods, perhaps the Commonwealth may be stock'd with Hypocrites, and dissembling Heretics, but few will be brought

[27] Pufendorf, *Nature and qualification of religion*, §50, p. 107.

over to the Christian faith'.[28] This, Pufendorf believes, is what happened after the Revocation of the Edict of Nantes: religious coercion led to false conversions. Pufendorf therefore *is* offering a defence of religious toleration, but it is based centrally on arguments from revelation, not from natural religion.

There are also passages in which Pufendorf advocates religious intolerance, or at least allows the prince to exercise it by, for example, expelling dissenters from his territories. There is the particularly curious incident, referred to earlier, when Pufendorf, in spite of criticizing the Revocation of the Edict of Nantes, defended the decision of the Lutheran king of Sweden to forbid French Huguenot refugees to enter his territories and settle in them. This may seem inconsistent or confused on Pufendorf's part, but it is possible to argue that his support for the Swedish king's actions did not necessarily contradict his particular tolerationist beliefs. The reason is that Pufendorf appears to distinguish between two notions that are normally conflated, at least in modern discussions of religious toleration. These two notions are religious coercion and religious intolerance. They overlap, in that religious coercion is also a form of intolerance, but they are not identical. Religious coercion is the attempt to compel another person to adopt particular religious beliefs. Such coercion, according to Pufendorf and many of his contemporaries, would only produce hypocrites and secret heretics, and was contrary to the genius of Christian religion, for

> Truth, by the help of the Christian Doctrine, and with the assistance of God's grace, does gently insinuate it self into the Hearts of Men, and the Rewards or Punishments, which those are to receive, that either accept or despise this Doctrine, are reserved for the Life to come.[29]

It has been suggested that Pufendorf's main objection to the measures of the French king is not that they are repressive, but that they are directed against Protestants, that is, adherents to orthodox Christianity.[30] This explanation does not, however, seem sufficient. It is, of course, true that Pufendorf regarded Roman Catholicism as a false religion, but even so he would not have advocated forced conversions of Roman Catholics to Protestantism, which were likely to be just as insincere as those brought about by the measures of Louis XIV.

Religious intolerance, however, was not always a variety of religious coercion, because intolerance could also take the form of expelling dissenters from a territory, or refusing them entry to it, as in the case of the Swedish

[28] Ibid., §35, p. 78.
[29] Ibid., §29, p. 57.
[30] Döring, 'Einleitung', in Pufendorf, *Jus feciale*, p. xxxvii, n. 155.
[31] Pufendorf, *Nature and qualification of religion*, §49, p. 107.

king and the Huguenot refugees. As Pufendorf said in *De habitu*, once a particular form of Christian worship had been received in a territory,

> a Prince may justly deny his Protection to all such as will not comply with it, unless he find it to be against the Common Interest of the Commonweal. If any one should undertake to contradict this Publick Form, especially in such Points as are the Heads of Christian Religion, he ought to be admonished to desist, his Reasons, if he has any, to be examined, and when convicted of his Error, to be silenced; if all this prove fruitless, *he may lawfully be banished* [emphasis added]... But we allow no other Punishment in such a case, except their Doctrine should amount to Blasphemy.[31]

This kind of intolerance was not accompanied by forced conversion. It therefore was not a case of religious coercion and thus could be legitimate.

Drawing a distinction between religious intolerance and religious coercion may seem rather unconvincing and, indeed, hypocritical, but it was not unusual in Pufendorf's own time. It was reflected for example in the so-called *ius* (or *beneficium*) *emigrandi* established in the Holy Roman Empire by the Peace of Augsburg in 1555. The *ius emigrandi* was the right of dissenters to leave their territory rather than being compelled to adopt the faith of their territory's dominant church. The measures of Louis XIV that preceded the Revocation, such as the forced billeting of troops, as well as the Revocation itself, however, were not intended to expel Huguenots from France, even if in the end they had that effect. The Edict of Fontainebleau itself prohibited Huguenots from leaving the country,[32] and the French king's measures were meant to convert the Huguenots to Catholicism by force (and, as Mark Goldie has shown, there were very serious and powerful arguments for the usefulness of force in bringing about a sincere religious conversion).[33] On Pufendorf's own terms, therefore, his argument against religious coercion was quite compatible with defending the expulsion or non-admittance of religious heretics on religious grounds, and the secular ruler did, in principle, have the right to enforce religious homogeneity within his territories, by removing all dissenters from them. The question then was, whether, and if so, under what circumstances, he should do so.

[32] Heinz Duchhardt, 'Die Konfessionspolitik Ludwigs XIV. und die Aufhebung des Edikts von Nantes', in Heinz Duchhardt, ed., *Der Exodus der Hugenotten: die Aufhebung des Edikts von Nantes 1685 als europäisches Ereignis* (Cologne and Vienna, 1985), pp. 29–52, at p. 40.

[33] M. Goldie, 'The Theory of Religious Intolerance in Restoration England', in Ole Peter Grell, Jonathan Israel, and Nicholas Tyacke, eds., *From persecution to toleration: the Glorious Revolution and religion in England* (Oxford, 1991), pp. 331–68. Not even all of the Huguenot refugees were advocates of religious toleration: see Mario Turchetti, 'Religious concord and political tolerance in sixteenth- and seventeenth-century France', *Sixteenth-Century Journal*, 22 (1991), pp. 15–25.

III

Pufendorf was convinced that religious uniformity in a state was highly desirable. By that he did not mean *any* religious uniformity, but one that was based on true, orthodox Christianity: as he put it in *De habitu*, 'it is to be wished, and ought to be endeavoured, to procure but one Faith and Religion in a State, and especially such a one as is absolutely agreeable to the Doctrine of Christ and his Apostles, contained in the Holy Scripture'.[34] Pufendorf was quite clear that the division of Christianity into a multitude of different churches did not allow setting aside the question of religious truth, or even of putting up with these divisions as an inevitable feature of European religious life.

Pufendorf's constant aim was to reunite Christianity, purge it of the corruption it had suffered since the rise of papalism in late antiquity, and thus restore it to its original purity. The Lutheran Reformation, he said, had made considerable progress towards this goal, but this progress had been frustrated by the rise of Calvinism, of which Pufendorf was often very critical. In a letter to Adam Rechenberg in August 1691 there is a long attack by Pufendorf on Calvinism, at a time when he was in the services of a Calvinist prince, the Elector of Brandenburg (though the Elector did not subscribe to the doctrine of predestination, the main reason for Pufendorf's objection to Calvinism). Without Calvinism, the Protestant Reformation would have been a united and more powerful force. '[C]lever papists', Pufendorf wrote, 'themselves acknowledge that if the Reformation had been continued the way it had been begun by Luther, it would have become universal.'[35] Already in the *De concordia* of 1673 he had argued that the Calvinist notion of predestination was not only theologically wrong, but a danger to secular morality, because it denied the freedom of the will.[36] Much of the *Jus feciale* was devoted to refuting the views of the Calvinist theologian Pierre Jurieu on predestination. Pufendorf also believed that, because of their peculiar form of church government and their struggles against despotic monarchical overlords, Calvinists were often characterized by a very unhealthy and extreme tendency towards democratic politics. Pufendorf blamed this for the 'disturbances, which have in recent years plagued England most miserably'.[37] Still, as Pufendorf stressed in the *Jus feciale*, he rated the chance of a reconciliation between Lutherans and

[34] Pufendorf, *Nature and qualification of religion*, §49, p. 106.

[35] 'Die klugen Papisten gestehen selbst, daß wenn die reformation auf die weise, wie sie Lutherus angefangen, were fort gesetzet worden, so were sie universal worden': Pufendorf, *Briefwechsel*, p. 320 (letter from Pufendorf to Adam Rechenberg, 29 August 1691).

[36] Pufendorf, 'De concordia', §16.

[37] '[T]urbas istas, quae superioribus annis Angliam miserrime exercuerunt' : ibid., §17.

Calvinists much more highly than that of resolving the differences with Roman Catholicism.

In theory, establishing orthodox faith was straightforward. The key beliefs of Christianity would be evident to an impartial reader of Scripture. Controversies over religious doctrines among the different confessions arose only from the passions and self-interest of their respective members. As Pufendorf wrote in the *Jus feciale*, once Scripture was examined without these distractions, its meaning on any contested point would become obvious.[38] All other differences of opinion that could not be resolved by recourse to Scripture concerned only a few particular articles that were not fundamental to faith. The study of revelation also had to be separated from philosophy. The truths of revelation were compatible with those of human reason, but at the same time far superior to them. Human reason was inadequate to understand the mysteries of faith and the philosophical investigation of revealed truths would only lead into error and further disagreement.[39]

To some extent the distorting influence of the passions on the interpretation of Scripture was a general problem of humanity, but Pufendorf believed that particular religious groups had a systematic tendency to pervert or even ignore revelation completely as a source of Christian belief. In Roman Catholicism religious truth was regularly subordinated to papal self-interest. But Pufendorf was also very critical of certain Christian sects, especially those that had come to light since the Reformation, such as the Anabaptists and the Socinians.[40] Although these were opposed to the papacy, Pufendorf believed that papalism and heresies such as Anabaptism and Socinianism had a significant characteristic in common, that is, a radical disregard, in different ways, for revelation. Papalists corrupted and distorted Christian revelation in order to use it to legitimate the clergy's pursuit of secular wealth and influence. Anabaptists abandoned scriptural orthodoxy in favour of an 'enthusiastic' belief in immediate divine inspiration as the foundation of faith. Socinians, on the other hand, believed, wrongly, that revealed doctrine could be reduced to rational truths, which were accessible to human understanding. Thus, according to Pufendorf, 'those, who adhere to the first [that is, Socinianism], do not consider the Christian doctrine other than a moral philosophy, and the latter [that is, the Anabaptists] scarce know what to believe themselves'.[41]

Given Pufendorf's belief that the duties of Christian religion were binding on its adherents, it is not surprising that he endorsed a view of the orthodox

[38] Pufendorf, *The divine feudal law*, §9.

[39] Ibid.

[40] Ibid., §14; see also Samuel Pufendorf, *An introduction to the history of Europe* (London, 1697), p. 442.

[41] Pufendorf, *An introduction*, pp. 442–3. See also Döring, 'Einleitung', in Pufendorf, *Jus feciale*, p. xlvi.

Christian prince as the 'foremost member of the church', *praecipuum membrum ecclesiae*, which is at least similar to that found in traditional Lutheranism.[42] According to this, the prince was under a particular obligation to take care of his territory's church, because of his pre-eminent position in that church. In *De habitu*, for example, Pufendorf concedes that the offices of the Christian prince and the teacher of Christian religion should not be united in one person, not, he adds, 'because of any natural repugnancy betwixt them', but because 'each of them is involved in such a multitude of Trouble and variety of Business, that it cannot rationally be supposed for one Man to be able to undergo such a Fatigue'.[43] A secular ruler by virtue of being Christian does, however, hold particular rights and obligations towards his territory's Christian church, which a pagan magistrate did not share. There are 'certain Obligations, which owe their off-spring to the union of that Duty, which is incumbent to every Christian, with that of the Royal Office'.[44] The sovereign's duty to act as 'defender of the Church' and protect his subjects from attacks on their Christian religion could perhaps be explained in terms of the secular purposes of the state. But Pufendorf also declared that it was the duty of 'Christian princes … to provide necessary Revenues for the exercise of the Christian religion', an obligation that can hardly be explained in terms of secular political theory. Moreover, princes 'ought not only to take care of Church-Buildings, but also to erect and maintain Schools', for, 'if the first Rudiments of Christianity be not implanted in the Schools, it cannot scarce be expected, that Men, when grown up, should receive much benefit by publick Sermons'.[45] Although the prince could not appoint ministers as he did civil magistrates, he had to constitute inspectors who had the power to reprove and if necessary punish clergymen, and who were accountable to a consistory constituted by the prince, or to the prince himself.[46] The ruler even enjoyed the power of 'making Ecclesiastical Statutes', though this had to be 'exercised with a great deal of caution', to avoid turning into compulsion.[47]

This duty to take care of his subjects' salvation, however, was not the only reason why the prince should encourage the establishment of orthodox Christianity in his territories. The prince also had a legitimate secular interest in Christianity. Pufendorf, it can be argued, was not really aiming 'to drive a wedge between the duties of the Christian and those of the citizen', as has

[42] On the notion of the prince as the *praecipuum membrum ecclesiae*, see Martin Heckel, *Staat und Kirche nach den Lehren der evangelischen Juristen in der ersten Hälfte des 17. Jahrhunderts* (Munich, 1968).

[43] Pufendorf, *Nature and qualification of religion*, §42, p. 94.

[44] Ibid., §43, p. 94.

[45] Ibid., p. 96.

[46] Ibid., §45, pp. 98–9.

[47] Ibid., §48, p. 102.

been suggested.[48] Rather, he was persuaded that true Christian belief reinforced secular morality in ways that human laws never could. Christianity therefore was of very real and immediate interest to the secular magistrate: 'The minds of the faithful are elevated with divine help, so that they shun vice and pursue honest deeds, even when there is no fear of human punishment.'[49] Human laws, as Pufendorf had already noted in his *De concordia*, were often ineffective. They only punished the most obvious crimes, and frequently failed to act over less serious ones:

> Civil laws are concerned with repressing vices in a crude fashion, and remove deceit to the extent that they can get hold of it; but they conceal a great part of human malice and leave it unpunished. They only ban the more serious evils by using punishment; they pass over the minor ones, as if they were not worthy of attention, because the Praetor is overworked in dealing with them. And yet these cause not a little irritation, and if they persist are a thorn in the flesh.[50]

This should not be interpreted to mean that the Christian religion could be instrumentalized and become a civil religion, which was subordinated to political calculations. '[N]o sane person would assert that the prince has the right to shape or interpolate [*interpolare*] Christian religion as he pleases, in any way that differs from the clear word of God.'[51] But the fact that Christianity and the true secular interest of rulers and subjects were in perfect harmony with each other provided additional confirmation of Christianity's truth as a religion.[52]

Pufendorf's emphasis on the close relationship between Christian faith and morality was characteristic of a more general trend within German Lutheranism (and in all of the Christian confessions in the seventeenth century) towards a belief that religious faith that was not accompanied by virtuous conduct (or 'holiness of life') could not be real or sincere. In the German states this trend was represented especially by the Pietist movement,

[48] Ian Hunter, *Rival enlightenments: civil and metaphysical philosophy in early modern Germany* (Cambridge, 2001), p. 149.

[49] 'Sane enim divino auxilio sublevantur fidelium animi, ut vitia refugiant, & honesta sectuntur, etiam ubi nullus humanae metus poenae urgere videtur' (Pufendorf, 'De concordia', §7, p. 436–7).

[50] Pufendorf, 'De concordia', §7, p. 437: '[L]eges civiles satis crasse circa reprimenda vitia versantur, & tollunt astutias, quatenus manu rem tenere possunt: magnam partem malitiae humanae dissimulant, & impunitam dimittunt. Graviores duntaxat injurias poenis prohibent: minutes fere praetereunt, quasi non dignas, quibus cognoscendis Praetor defatigetur. Quae tamen non parum molestiae afferunt, & continuatae inprimis sat acriter mordent.'

[51] Pufendorf, 'De concordia', §11, p. 449: '[N]emo sanus asseruerit, imperio civili fas esse pro lubitu Religionem formare aut interpolare, secus quam clarum Dei verbum tradit.'

[52] On this 'systemic consistency' between the aims of the secular state and those of religion, see Michael Seidler, 'Pufendorf and the politics of recognition', in Ian Hunter and David Saunders, eds., *Natural law and civil sovereignty: moral right and state authority in early modern political thought* (Basingstoke, 2002), pp. 235–51, at p. 242.

which was named after a devotional work, the *Pia desideria* (1675), by the Lutheran theologian Philipp Jakob Spener (1635–1705), and which emerged fully around 1690 in Leipzig, in a series of controversies between university theologians and students who had begun to hold private devotional meetings without the presence of a trained theologian.[53] Although Pufendorf was critical of certain aspects of Pietism, especially its perceived tendency towards religious 'enthusiasm', he maintained close and regular contacts with several leading Pietists, especially Spener, who eventually even delivered Pufendorf's funeral sermon.[54] Pufendorf was also keen to hear Spener's opinion on the draft of his *Jus feciale*.[55] Moreover, Pufendorf's writings echo spiritual and moral concerns that are very close to those of the Pietists, especially concerning the connection between sincere religious belief and true morality. Faith without holiness of life, Pufendorf wrote, for example, was a 'dead Tree without Fruit':[56] 'For the Profession of the Covenant in Christ requires another sort of Life and Manners than those of Heathens, and of them who follow the Inclination of the Flesh, or of the Corruption which proceeds from Original Sin.'[57] The 'holiness of life' in postlapsarian nature could never be as complete as it was before the Fall from Grace. The depravity of human nature was ineradicable and in itself would already merit eternal damnation by God.[58] Even the regenerate did not have the power to extinguish completely all evil inclinations of human nature, which followed from the Fall from Grace, 'tho' this is what they ought continually with all Diligence to endeavour'.[59] Humans did, however, enjoy at least the liberty of preventing their inherent sinfulness from issuing into outward action.[60] If they did this and grieved for their sinfulness, the 'Satisfaction of the Saviour', Jesus Christ, meant that the imperfections of postlapsarian human nature were 'as it were overlook'd, as are also the Faults committed without our Choice, and the evil Motions proceeding from the original Pollution'.[61]

[53] For a summary of the literature on the Pietist movement in Leipzig, see Thomas Ahnert, *Religion and the origins of the German Enlightenment: faith and the reform of learning in the thought of Christian Thomasius* (Rochester, NY, 2006), ch. 1.

[54] See Detlef Döring, 'Untersuchungen zur Entwicklung der theologischen und religionspolitischen Vorstellungen Samuel von Pufendorfs', in Dieter Breuer, ed., *Religion und Religiösität im Zeitalter des Barock*, vol. 2 (Wiesbaden, 1995), pp. 873–82, at p. 881; Martin Ohst, 'Gerard Wolter Molan und seine Stellung zum Projekt einer kirchlichen Reunion', in Duchhardt and May, eds., *Union—Conversion—Toleranz*, pp. 171–97, at p. 195.

[55] Döring, 'Einleitung', in Pufendorf, *Jus feciale*, p. xxvi.

[56] Pufendorf, *The divine feudal law*, §54, p. 117.

[57] Ibid., §50, p. 107.

[58] Ibid., §54, pp. 115–16.

[59] Ibid., p. 116.

[60] Ibid., §20, p. 65.

[61] Ibid., §54, pp. 115–16.

According to Pufendorf, natural law, together with natural religion, helped to maintain public peace to a certain extent, but it only ever represented a minimal, rather than a desirable, foundation for social life. The effect of natural law on human morality was superficial and limited. It could constrain human vice through fear of punishment, but it was 'an impossible thing that Humane Wit, without Divine Revelation, should frame a Religion that would purifie the Mind' and thus remove the cause of immorality itself.[62] For 'all those things which are deliver'd by the Philosophers for the Regulation of Manners' were 'plainly insipid and unsavoury', if compared with the precepts of Christian religion.[63] Therefore, while natural religion and natural law contributed nothing to attaining eternal salvation, Christian revelation was directly relevant to temporal morality: 'if ever there is to be a better Condition of Mankind, and a happier State of the World, it is not to be expected but from a serious and universal Practice of Christian Piety and Virtue'.[64]

Religious uniformity and orthodoxy thus were in the true interests of the prince, but they were not always practicable. If, for example, the majority of the population were dissenters, religious intolerance would result in the loss of a very large proportion of a territory's inhabitants, which would not be expedient. It is then that toleration becomes necessary. In the *Jus feciale* Pufendorf distinguishes between two main forms of toleration, political and ecclesiastical. Under the former, subjects are free to practise their own religion 'in Two manner of Ways; either in their own Right, or by the Concession and Favour of those who have Possession of the Government'. Subjects enjoy toleration by their own right if, for example, 'in any one Nation a great Part of the People depart from their ancient Rites of Religion, and the rest continue in them as formerly, or if any People Universally forsake their ancient Religion, but in forming the new One do differ from one another'. If these different parties then made an agreement to allow each other to continue in their respective religious beliefs, then 'both Parties in this Case must be judg'd to have a Right to their Liberty'. The multi-confessional system established by the Westphalian peace treaties of 1648 in the Holy Roman Empire was such a case.[65] Political toleration was either universal or limited, that is, the adherents of the tolerated religion either had equal liberty in the exercise of their religion or had this liberty on certain conditions. They might, for example, be obliged to keep their doors shut during religious services or to

[62] Ibid., §11, p. 32.
[63] Ibid., §56, p. 121.
[64] Ibid., §56, p. 122.
[65] Ibid., §4, pp. 16–17.

worship only in their private homes.[66] It was a different matter, if a ruling prince converted to another religion or succeeded to the government of a territory with a dominant confession different from his own. There the population continued to enjoy the right to practise their religion, because it was the ruling religion (though not necessarily the religion of the ruler). They did not require religious *toleration*, because toleration applied only to those 'who have their Liberty not in their own Right, but by the Concession of the Government'.[67]

Ecclesiastical toleration was the second main form of toleration, according to Pufendorf. It applied to those who differed on certain points of religion, but nevertheless considered themselves members of the same church.[68] Ecclesiastical toleration, he hoped, would be a means of reuniting Lutherans and Calvinists in a single church. While a complete reconciliation of all differences would always be preferable, at present no more than a mixture of reconciliation and ecclesiastical toleration was to be expected. A solution of this kind would first require

> an Agreement in a solid, sufficient, and adequate Foundation of Faith, or that those Articles of Faith should be clearly defin'd and agree upon which are so necessary to Salvation, as that they ought neither to be unknown to any Man, or deny'd by any one, nor wrested and drawn into a diverse Sense and Meaning.[69]

In those matters that were not part of these central articles of faith,

> and in which if a Man does err, his Errour would not so much as indirectly destroy the Foundation, in these a Toleration should be granted; and for the sake of them no Man should be cast out from the Communion of any Church, or withdraw and separate himself from it, nor should any form a distinct and separate Communion for the sake of them.[70]

Ecclesiastical toleration between Protestants and Roman Catholics, however, was impossible and indeed forbidden, 'since at least the far greater Part of the Protestants do believe the Papal Empire to be that Apocalyptical Beast, whose Tiranny by the great Favour of God they have thrown off', though Pufendorf admitted grudgingly that political toleration of papists was possible where it could not be removed, because of a 'Covenant or other

[66] Ibid., §5, p. 18. Some such conditions were imposed on members of the three confessions granted toleration by the Westphalian peace treaties. See Joachim Whaley, 'A tolerant society? Religious toleration in the Holy Roman Empire, 1648–1806', in Ole Peter Grell and Roy Porter, eds., *Toleration in Enlightenment Europe* (Cambridge, 2000), pp. 175–95.

[67] Pufendorf, *The divine feudal law*, §4, p. 18.

[68] Ibid., §6, p. 21.

[69] Ibid., §7, p. 23.

[70] Ibid.

weighty Considerations', as was the case in the Holy Roman Empire after 1648.[71]

Even then, however, Pufendorf implies that confessional unity within the state is the final aim, though it may lie in the distant future. As he puts it in the *Jus feciale*:

> And that Method [i.e., toleration] our Saviour himself seems to have recommended, while he forbad pulling up of the Tares, lest at the same time the good Wheat should be pluck'd up with them … by the time of Harvest it is not necessary that we must understand the End of the World; but it may perhaps mean that appointed Period which the Divine Providence has fix'd for every Sect. For manifest it is, that many Heresies are so perfectly vanish'd, that there is nothing remaining of them more than their Names in the History of the Church: Which if any Attempt had been unreasonably and violently made to have rooted them up, it might have given no small Trouble to the Orthodox.[72]

Orthodoxy is the eventual goal, but trying to bring this about by force may be counterproductive, and it is therefore sometimes better to leave the extermination of heresies to the mysterious workings of divine providence.

IV

'Toleration', Pufendorf wrote, 'is of the Nature of a Truce in War, which suspends the Effects of it, and the actual Hostilities, while the State and Cause of the War do remain.'[73] It is difficult to see Pufendorf as a principled defender of toleration, let alone of an idea of toleration based on natural law. He did not present a social and political order grounded in natural religion and natural law as a desirable alternative to an orthodox Christian commonwealth. Although it is clear, in retrospect, that the confessional divisions of Western Europe were permanent, they did not appear as such to Pufendorf. He was convinced that confessional disagreements could be resolved. Scripture provided an objective standard of Christian faith, which was clear on all matters that were essential to faith. The restoration of uniform religious orthodoxy might be a very long-term goal, given the vested interests and resistance of groups such as the papal clergy, the Anabaptists, or the Socinians. In the meantime, toleration might be justifiable in certain circumstances, but Pufendorf, it seems, did not consider it to be something that is good in itself. The fact that it was not always possible to rule over a religiously uniform population, and it was then necessary to fall back on natural law and natural

[71] Ibid., §13, p. 38.
[72] Ibid., §4, p. 16. Pufendorf is alluding to Matthew 13.24–30.
[73] Ibid., p. 15.

religion as a lowest common denominator in social and political life, did not imply that Pufendorf considered this situation to be preferable to a confessionally homogenous, orthodox Christian state.

Although Pufendorf believed that natural religion and natural law were adequate as a minimal basis for social life, rulers were not therefore obliged to restrict themselves to the inferior resources of their natural reason and to ignore the truths contained in scriptural revelation, which offered a system of morality that he believed was far superior to that of natural religion and natural law. As Kari Saastamoinen has put it, 'for Pufendorf natural religion is not a doctrine which should replace Lutheran Christianity as the publicly maintained religious practice. Natural religion is a purely theoretical model the purpose of which is to define those religious ideas and practices which are indispensable for human society.'[74]

Pufendorf was certainly no advocate of 'universal toleration', as the author of the Preface to the 1719 English edition of *De habitu* believed.[75] He was opposed to religious coercion in the form of forced conversions, because these were likely to result in religious hypocrisy, not sincere belief. But he was happy for the orthodox Christian prince to exercise religious intolerance by driving dissenters from his lands, though the use of this power had to be balanced against the impact that it would have on his territories' wealth and power relative to others, and had to be qualified by the particular positive laws and covenants the ruler was bound to observe. Thus, Pufendorf was willing to postpone the confessional state, but not to abandon it.

[74] Kari Saastamoinen, *The morality of the fallen man: Samuel Pufendorf on natural law* (Studia Historica, 50, Helsinki, 1995), p. 164.
[75] Pufendorf, 'Preface', in *Relation between church and state*, p. vii.

3

Natural Law, Nonconformity, and Toleration: Two Stages on Locke's Way

TIMOTHY STANTON*

In 1660 John Locke wrote in defence of the civil magistrate's authority to impose conformity in religious worship. By 1667 he had disembarrassed himself of this position. In 1685[1] he would argue that the civil magistrate *eo ipso* lacked the authority to enforce by law the use of any rites or ceremonies in the worship of God over the conscientious scruples of individual worshippers. The purpose of this chapter is to identify two significant stages in the development of Locke's mature position and to explain the connections between them.

The first stage occurred sometime after the writing of *Two tracts on government* in 1660–1—shortly before or during the writing of *Essays on the law of nature* in 1663–4—and the second stage in 1681–2 with the writing of the 'Defence of nonconformity'.[2] At each stage, Locke made a series of

*I wish to acknowledge the kind permission of the Keeper of Special Collections and Western Manuscripts at the Bodleian Library to quote Locke manuscripts, and the generous assistance of the Director and staff of the Beinecke Rare Books and Manuscripts Library during a period of archival research as Beinecke Fellow at Yale University in 2008. I am grateful to Dr Maria Rosa Antognazza, Professor John Dunn, Professor Knud Haakonssen, Professor Ian Hunter, Dr Jon Parkin, Dr Peter Schröder, Professor Michael J. Seidler, and Professor Simone Zurbuchen for comments made in discussion on 13 April 2007. For comments on the written version of this chapter I am indebted to Professor Dunn, Dr Ian Harris, Professor Susan Mendus, Dr Jakob de Roover, and Dr Parkin.

[1] For this dating of the *Epistola de tolerantia*, which leans heavily upon the recollections of Locke's friend Philipp van Limborch (to whom the *Epistola* was dedicated), see *Epistola de tolerantia / A letter on toleration*, ed. Raymond Klibansky, trans. J. W. Gough (Oxford, 1968), pp. ix–x.

[2] Bodleian Library, Oxford, MS. Locke c.34. 'Defence of nonconformity' was the title given to this manuscript by its first editor, Lord King. See Peter King, *The life of John Locke* (London, 1829), pp. 341–54. For some arguments in favour of retaining this title, and an account of the contents of the manuscript, see Timothy Stanton, 'The name and nature of Locke's "Defence of nonconformity"', *Locke Studies*, 6 (2006), pp. 143–72; for dating see idem, 'The context and composition of Locke's "Defence of nonconformity"' (*Locke Studies*, forthcoming). Work on the manuscript seems to have begun early in 1681 and continued intermittently into 1682: see *The correspondence of John Locke*, ed. Esmond S. de Beer (8 vols, Oxford, 1976–89), II, pp. 353–8, 360–5, 708–9, and compare MS. Locke c.34, p. 121, for the date '82' in the left margin.

Proceedings of the British Academy, **186**, 35–57.

conceptual moves whose effect, when combined, was to replace one understanding of the relations between church and state with another. As the position about toleration he set out in 1685 depended upon this second understanding, the significance of these two stages for that position will be immediately evident.

At the first stage, Locke dispensed with the view of conscience characteristic of the age in which he lived. On this view, conscience provided authoritative direction about God's wants because it embodied an authoritative law—the law of nature—which articulated His wants and which was known innately. The problem with this view was that whilst everyone was agreed that its direction ought to be followed, there was considerable disagreement about what in fact this involved. How was this disagreement to be explained?

Explanation typically included some reference to the deleterious consequences of the Fall of man for people's natural cognitive capacities. Those same consequences could be interpreted in a way that gave a central role to the church in instructing conscience and a supporting role to the state in manoeuvring into the church those whose consciences required instruction. In rejecting this view of conscience, Locke put question marks not only against the utility of claims to liberty of conscience advanced in its name, but also against the views of natural law, the Fall, and the relations of church and state with which such claims were associated.

At the second stage, Locke developed a positive view of the church freighted with none of these associations. On this view, churches were societies into which people entered voluntarily and for purposes quite distinct from those that underlay civil society. The choice of joining—or indeed of forming—a church could be made by people on the basis of their natural endowments. Upon their ability to make that choice or to act upon it the Fall had no direct bearing, for by an implication that was not the less obvious for its being silent they retained the capacity to choose for themselves. Neither could state coercion have any role to play in constituting churches, or in maintaining their union, if churches were voluntary associations. This set the relations of church and state in new terms. Not least it suggested that a plurality of churches would be likely to eventuate in a single kingdom. To a cast of mind that assumed that in a Christian kingdom the church and the commonwealth formed the one society, this suggestion would have appeared very remarkable.[3] Certainly it put Locke squarely at odds with the great bulk of contemporary opinion.

[3] See variously John Calvin, *Institutes of the Christian religion*, trans. F. L. Battles (2 vols., London, 1955), IV.xx.9, vol. II, pp. 657–8; Hugo Grotius, *De imperio summarum potestatum circa sacra* (Paris, 1647; 2nd edn, 1648), pp. 17–19; Thomas Hobbes, *Leviathan, or the matter, forme, & power of a common-wealth ecclesiasticall and civill* (London, 1651), III.xxxix.248; Richard Hooker, *Of the laws of ecclesiastical polity* in *The works of Mr. Richard Hooker*, ed. John Keble, rev. R. W. Church and F. Paget (3 vols., Oxford, 1888), VIII.i.2–5, vol. III, pp. 328–38.

If this second stage was significant for the space it opened between Locke and his contemporaries, it carried a further significance. The explanation of the state as a secular body that Locke would provide in *Two treatises of government* presumed the view of the church that the 'Defence of nonconformity' propounded. Having determined that churches were constituted by people's own consent for the ends of religion, and that religion had 'nothing at all to doe with secular affaires, or civil societyes',[4] Locke was able to explain what in 1667 he had merely premised, that the civil magistrate was authorized to secure those ends for which civil society was constituted as a means, but had no business whatever with the ends for the sake of which churches existed.[5] In this respect at least, the 'Defence of nonconformity' was the necessary propaedutic to *Two treatises*.

Neither Locke's account of civil society nor his account of churches could have been accommodated in the nexus of views he had implicitly rejected at the first stage. Having discounted those views, he substituted others that painted an alternative picture of the relations between churches and the state. It is well established that Locke's views on this topic underwrote the position about toleration for which, and famously, he argued in 1685.[6] It is less often acknowledged that his arguments make use of the conceptual apparatus that the 'Defence of nonconformity' had put in place, and which provided the resources to talk coherently about a multiplicity of voluntary churches with which the civil magistrate could not legitimately interfere. But whatever their immediate ancestry, Locke's arguments purposed to make a decisive shift in the terms of discussion about toleration—a shift, indeed, which exposed for what it was the purgatorial wrangling in which his contemporaries were immured.

It is abundantly clear from Locke's critical survey of their views in the 'Defence of nonconformity' that the contending parties of his day were deploying the same conceptual resources from different positions and

[4] MS. Locke c.34, pp. 76–7. But not entirely by their consent: a church includes some supernatural claims, *to* which people consent, but which they do not themselves *constitute*. See MS. Locke d.10, 'Ecclesia' (1682), pp. 43–4, at p. 43, where a church is said to be 'a supernatural societie, & a societie by consent'. Printed in *An essay concerning toleration and other writings on law and politics, 1667–1683*, ed. J. R. Milton and Philip Milton (Oxford, 2006), pp. 391–2, at p. 392.

[5] John Locke, 'An essay concerning toleration', in *An essay*, ed. Milton and Milton, pp. 269–302, at p. 270.

[6] See especially John Dunn, 'The claim to freedom of conscience: freedom of speech, freedom of thought, freedom of worship', in idem, *The history of political theory and other essays* (Cambridge, 1996), pp. 100–20; Ian Harris, *The mind of John Locke: a study of political theory in its intellectual setting* (Cambridge, 1994), pp. 160–191; idem, 'Tolérance, église et état chez Locke', in Yves Charles Zarka, Franck Lessay, and G. A. J. Rogers, eds., *Les fondements philosophiques de la tolérance* (3 vols., Paris, 2002), I, pp. 175–218.

endeavouring to establish the superiority of one position over another on the basis of those same resources—an impossible task, though one for which they evinced an unflagging enthusiasm. To see just why this task was impossible, it is necessary first of all to clarify the terms in which they developed their views. As Locke himself had written in these terms in 1660, he can act as our guide to their central components. As we shall see, these terms concealed a conceptual difficulty which his contemporaries, for all that they had strained against it, had been unable to resolve. If Locke eventually resolved this difficulty it was only by abstracting away from the terms in which it had originally arisen. In what did this difficulty consist, and how did it arise?

I

The difficulty that Locke inherited arose out of the conjunction of two distinct, if related, problems. The first problem concerned the existence of variation in normative opinions about God's wants between the magistrate and the individual worshipper or group of worshippers. The second problem concerned the extent of the magistrate's legitimate authority over things indifferent in religious worship. The first manifested itself in contrasting claims about liberty of conscience, the second in the refusal of some individuals and groups to defer to the magistrate's wishes in matters of religious belief and practice. In an institutional context in which the magistrate upheld a single national church, these problems were elided in the one practical problem of religious dissidence, or nonconformity. At the same time, they produced the one conceptual difficulty, which centred on the relation between religion and politics.

To be specific: Locke's position in 1660 implied that freedom in religious matters was compatible with obedience to the magistrate in politics. But because it offered no means of distinguishing what properly belonged to religion from what belonged to politics, in principle either category could be expanded until, at the limit, it exhausted the other. Locke was very much aware of this difficulty. His English tract took it as a cue to extend the authority of the civil magistrate over all things indifferent. Since there was 'no action so indifferent which a scrupulous conscience will not fetch in with some consequence from Scripture and make of spiritual concernment', it was manifestly imprudent to restrain the civil magistrate's authority to impose in the indifferent things of religious worship, for this was to invite a free-for-all in which any action, however lurid, might claim immunity from magisterial control. As Locke put it, 'Let the people … but once hear that the magistrate hath no authority to enjoin things indifferent in matters of religion [and] conscience and religion shall presently mingle itself with all their actions and be spread over their whole lives to protect them from the reach of the magistrate.'[7] Locke's response was that his reach had therefore to be extensive.

If this response seemed inescapable politically, it was obviously unsatisfactory conceptually, because it left unresolved the difficulty of establishing just what the respective limits of religion and politics were or ought to be. The problem was not simply that the limits could be drawn more or less advantageously for politics or for religion. It was rather that the two remained locked in a relation of mutual antagonism—something which the gimlet eye of Hobbes had seen rather more penetratingly than most of his contemporaries.[8] But then it was hard to understand how it ever could be otherwise if, as *Two tracts* assumed, the civil magistrate enjoyed unlimited jurisdiction in indifferent things—including the power to impose a uniform religious worship—and yet it was acknowledged that God would not find acceptable an external conformity to worship where conscience did not concur. If, as Locke supposed, 'God … abhor[red] the sacrifice of the hypocritical compliant', a Hobbesian response to the difficulty, which subsumed religion under politics, was effectively ruled out of court.[9]

A response of some description was imperative. Perhaps the difficulty would not have appeared so acute in a situation, however improbable, in which the magistrate's impositions were broadly acceptable to everyone, but the existence of nonconformity as a persistently intrusive feature of the political landscape after 1662 pressed it upon every serious thinker, not least upon Locke himself.

To resolve this difficulty, Locke needed to distance himself from the terms in which it had originally arisen. This entailed two connected moves, which addressed the two problems that together gave rise to the difficulty. The first move was made in relation to conscience, but it epitomized a second, more general move away from the Christian terms in which Locke's position of 1660 had been presented.

The following section of this chapter details the terms away from which Locke moved by repercussion. Its sequel identifies some of the effects of those moves and their implications for resolving the difficulty he had confronted. Thereafter, the chapter turns to examine the views Locke substituted into the place of those he had rejected, before addressing, finally, the bearing of these

[7] John Locke, *Two tracts on government*, ed. Philip Abrams (Cambridge, 1967), pp. 139, 140, 154.

[8] See e.g. Hobbes, *Leviathan*, III.xliii.321: 'The most frequent praetext of Sedition, and Civill Warre, in Christian Common-wealths hath a long time proceeded from a difficulty, not yet sufficiently resolved, of obeying at once, both God, and Man, then when their Commandements are one contrary to the other.' See also *Leviathan*, III.xli.271–2 for the logic which 'authorizeth all private men, to disobey their Princes, in maintenance of their Religion, true, or false'.

[9] Locke, *Two tracts*, p. 145. Cf. Hobbes, *Leviathan*, III.xliii.322.

views on his mature position about toleration and some of the more distinctive features of that position.

In the first place, then, it is a matter of conscience.

II

The traditional rubric of conscience involved two elements: a direct apprehension of the principles of natural law, and individual judgement which compared particular moral actions to those principles and acquitted or condemned them accordingly. These elements were known respectively as *synteresis* and *syneidesis*. The two were understood to present together the active faculty by which individuals deduced conclusions about what conduct was acceptable to God and what conduct was not. The relation that was assumed between these elements complemented the further, and widespread, assumption that all knowledge was ultimately resolvable into syllogistic form. *Synteresis* provided knowledge of the major premise of each syllogism, *syneidesis* of the minor premise, with conscience, as the whole course of reasoning, giving up the product of their interaction in its conclusions.[10] These conclusions dictated whether or not a particular action should be undertaken.

The ramifications of these assumptions for religious worship could hardly be more transparent. As Locke had conceded, an external conformity to imposed ecclesiastical practices would be acceptable to God only if conscience approved. It followed that those who objected to imposition could not conform to what was imposed without moving away from salvation by acting in ways that would convict them before God. This was not a cheerful prospect. But the character attributed to *synteresis* posed a more formidable problem still.On the logic of the given model of conscience, its conclusions, if securely deduced, were as authoritative as the premises from which they proceeded. With conscience, the premises supplied by *synteresis* were assumed to be principles of natural law, apprehensible innately, that is to say by the mind reflecting upon its own contents. Was not *all* imposition therefore arbitrary? For if it could require a form of external performance which the scrupulous had concluded was of dubious legality, what was to prevent that form being extended to include matters that were known to be false and abhorrent to God, if conscientious scruples were insufficient to justify the refusal of

[10] For conscience see Robert Sanderson, *De obligatione conscientiae praelectiones decem oxonii in schola theologica habitae Anno Domini M. DC. XLVII.*, ed. William Whewell (Cambridge, 1851), and for an inventory of earlier views, Timothy Potts, *Conscience in medieval philosophy* (Cambridge, 1980); for syllogistic logic, see e.g. Peter Ramus, *The logike of the moste excellent philosopher P. Ramus martyr* (London, 1574), pp. 80–93, and, at length, Robert Sanderson, *Logicae artis compendium* (Oxford, 1615).

communion in the imposed form? The presumption of the sanctity of conscience had at its root the presumption that one of its elements was a direct pipeline to God's requirements.

At first glance, this presumption would seem to render any and all imposition peremptory. Why, then, in the eyes of the advocates of imposition, did it not? A clue is provided by the first of the two problems whose conjunction produced our original difficulty, namely the existence of variation in normative opinions about God's wants. How can this be squared with the presumed accessibility to all of the authoritative articulation of those wants as principles of natural law? The answer is that although these principles were indeed assumed to be accessible to everyone, the consequences of the Fall of man could be construed to include a more or less severe diminution of people's capacity to grasp and follow the principles aright.

The degree to which people were supposed to have been diminished varied between thinkers,[11] but the assumption that damage had been done to them on account of the Fall was common to opponents and advocates of imposition alike. To Edward Bagshawe, the object of Locke's critical attention in the English tract, postlapsarian man's 'Reason at its best and utmost extent, is a Narrow, Shrunke, and limited thing, in Spiritual things altogether blind and perverse, in Naturall things either ignorant, or onely changing Ignorance to uncertainty'.[12] To Edward Stillingfleet, who advocated imposition, it was evident that 'man, as he came first out of God's hands, was the reflection of God himself … His knowledge then had been more intellectual than discursive'. Had Adam not sinned, men might yet have been able to know the principles of natural law inscribed within their souls by pure intellection; but they had now to occupy themselves 'in the operose deductions of reason (the pleasant toil of the rational faculties since the fall)' and in this fallen state they often reasoned fallaciously.[13] Indeed, Bagshawe and Stillingfleet concurred in thinking that it was only by the gift of grace that people could reason rightly: without grace, their reasoning was apt to lead them serially into error.[14] They

[11] For an elegant survey of a range of variations, see Ian Harris, 'The politics of Christianity', in G. A. J. Rogers, ed., *Locke's philosophy: content and context* (Oxford, 1994), pp. 197–215, at pp. 206–7.

[12] Edward Bagshawe [the younger], *A practicall discourse concerning God's decrees* (Oxford, 1659), p. 7.

[13] Edward Stillingfleet, *Irenicum: a weapon-salve for the churchs wounds* (London, 1660), pp. 11–12; Edward Stillingfleet, *Origines sacrae: or, A rational account of the grounds of natural and revealed religion* (2 vols., Oxford, 1836), I, p. 4.

[14] Hence Stillingfleet's sweeping diagnosis of 'why philosophy and idolatry did increase so much together as they did; for though right reason, fully improved, would have overthrown all those cursed and idolatrous practices among the heathens; yet reason, only discovering some general notions, without their particular application and improvement, did only dispose the most ordinary sort of people to a more ready entertainment of the most gross idolatry': idem, *Origines sacrae*, I, p. 10.

concurred, too, in thinking that grace flowed freely from Christ through the office of the Holy Spirit. But they differed over what reason indicated about the present locus of grace.

Bagshawe considered that natural reason was inadequate to the discovery of God's wants. He looked to Scripture, illuminated by the grace of the Spirit, to repair the shortcomings of reason and was passingly contemptuous of the idea that a church was needed to mediate that grace to individuals. Anyone 'that leanes upon a Church, of what denomination soever', he wrote, 'cannot be sure that he shall not be deceived'; whereas the man who leant only upon 'Scripture, *and the best, if not only interpreter of it*, Enlightned Reason', might 'infallibly be assured, that though in some things he may Erre, as a man, yet he shall never finally miscarry'.[15] Now whatever the role Bagshawe ostensibly conceded to reason, it was evidently the Spirit that carried the burden of responsibility for revealing God's wants to every individual. Bagshawe's conception was radically individualistic; ultimately, it deliquesced into enthusiasm.

In 1672 Stillingfleet too had wondered, rhetorically, whether natural reason alone might be insufficiently penetrative to locate the true church, which he conceived to be the repository of God's grace. 'Every one must use his own judgment and reason, in the choice of the *Church* he is to rely upon,' he wrote; 'is he certain in this or not? If he be uncertain, all that he receives on the *Authority* of that *Church*, must be uncertain too: if the use of reason be certain, then how comes the *Authority* of a *Church* to be a necessary means of certainty in matters of faith?' Happily, he concluded, 'every Christian, by the use of his reason, and common helps of Grace, may attain to so great a degree of certainty' in these matters, that 'on the same grounds, on which men doubt of the truth of them, they may as well doubt of the truth of those things which they judge to be most evident, to sense or reason'. We need hardly add that 'common helps of Grace' would be readily available because, or so Stillingfleet supposed, reason pointed to communion with the true church in its Anglican form.

The counterpart of this view, of course, was that those who failed to recognize its truth must, in some relevant respect, be deficient. Thus, Stillingfleet added, it could be 'nothing but wilful Ignorance, weakness of Judgement, strength of prejudice, or some sinful passion, *which makes any one forsake* … the Church of England', imputing these deficiencies in a different dimension

[15] Edward Bagshawe [the younger], *A brief enquiry into the grounds and reasons whereupon the infallibility of the pope and the church of Rome is said to be founded* (London, 1662), sig. C–C2; B3, 2; C2 (orthography original).

to Roman Catholics and to nonconformists as the danger posed by each waxed or waned over time.[16]

In taking this line, Stillingfleet was merely following in the footsteps of Robert Sanderson. It was a fundamental axiom of Sanderson's thinking that reason directed people to an assurance of the truth of Anglican claims. Throughout his life he had attempted to preserve the rational authority of the Church of England against the exaction of a pre-rational submission to papal authority on one side and the fissile excesses of enthusiasm on the other. In his view 'it were unreasonable for any man to think, that they either had, or did expect an immediate revelation from God every time … for the warranting of particular actions to their consciences', and less reasonable still to think that the Scriptures could direct individual conduct in every particular. 'Without all doubt', he affirmed, 'the *Law of nature*, and the *light of reason*, was the *rule* whereby they were guided … which the wisdom of God would never have left in them or us, as a *principal relique* of his decayed image in us, if he had not meant, that we should make use of it, for *the direction* of our lives and actions thereby.'[17]

Sanderson elaborated this idea by distinguishing these two items more exactly. The law of nature was defined as 'the common notions inscribed upon our hearts as the dictates of nature, preserved in the *synteresis*, a brand saved from the burning of the fall, and the remains of the image of God'. To this law was allied the light of reason, by which people made deductions from natural law and from revelation. The light of reason was 'a universal thing, and the subject matter to which it is to be applied is particular acts, hence it cannot but be that the kind of discursive reasoning is required which connects universals to particulars'.[18]

If this was the logic that underlay the relation of *synteresis* and *syneidesis* and the reasoning performed in the practical syllogisms of conscience, this was hardly coincidental. It provided, too, the model for the relation of the universal church to particular human beings, and therewith percolated into

[16] Edward Stillingfleet, *A discourse concerning the idolatry practised in the church of Rome* (London, 1672), pp. 470, 493, 496 (orthography original); for Stillingfleet's understanding of the church, see e.g. idem, *The mischief of separation* (London, 1680), pp. 9–10, 15–18, and, more expansively, idem, *Origines britannicae*, ed. Thomas P. Pantin (2 vols., Oxford, 1842).

[17] Robert Sanderson, *Reason and judgement, or special remarques of the life of the renowned Dr Sanderson* (Oxford, 1663), pp. 63–4 (orthography original).

[18] Sanderson, *De obligatione conscientiae*, lecture 1, §25, p. 28: 'communes sc. *Notiones* et ipsius Naturae dictamine cordibus humanis inscriptae, et in *Synteresi* conservatae, velut *titio ereptus* e communi incendio, et *reliquiae imaginis Dei* post lapsum'. Ibid., lecture 1, §.26, p. 29: '*Lumen* enim illud *quod applicandum est*, cum sit *Universale quid*, et id *ad quod applicandum est*, *Actus particulares* sive singulares; non potest fieri talis *applicatio*, nisi ejusmodi mediante *discursu*, qui universalia singularibus connectere valeat.'

Sanderson's argument in favour of the authority of that church in its Anglican guise. To his mind, conformity to its doctrines and practices provided an obtrusively material instance of the way in which reason could be employed to connect particulars to universals. Nonconformity, by contrast, instanced only obstinacy and the lack of judgement that those in want of grace were doomed to evidence in their conduct. Thus it was appropriate for the civil magistrate to induce nonconformists to submit to the authority of the church, for whatever conscientious scruples they possessed were self-evidently groundless.

Those who scrupled remained unconvinced. Bagshawe, for one, had indicated that reason, duly enlightened, would direct people away from, rather than towards, the Anglican Church. To barely insist on the rightness of its claims, as he was not slow to point out, was to resort to the posturing of papal infallibility; therefore

> to pretend to *Infallibility in determining*, or to practise *Tyranny in Imposing*, these are onely the wayes of Ambitious and self-seeking men, found out not so much to promote Truth (which stands not in need of such Arts) as to Augment a party; which makes all *Articles of Faith*, to be merely like the Civill Laws of a Land, where most Voices do carry the Cause.[19]

In the end, as Hobbes had understood, in practice everything came down to the persuasive power with which the respective claims of religion and politics were asserted and the ruthlessness with which they were manipulated.

Evidently, Locke was unwilling to accept this understanding for his own. He looked to draw limits between religion and politics that could not be massaged in either direction. The key to establishing these limits was to rethink the terms in which he had previously understood natural law and its relation to conscience.

III

Locke's *Two tracts* had understood both conscience and natural law in traditional terms. Conscience was 'that fundamental judgement of the practical intellect concerning any possible truth of a moral proposition about things to be done in life'. Its authority derived from the fact that 'God implanted the light of nature in our hearts and willed that there should be an inner legislator ... constantly present in us whose edicts it should not be lawful for us to transgress even a nail's breadth'.[20] It seems that Locke was already uncomfortable

[19] Bagshawe, *A brief enquiry*, p. 33.
[20] Locke, *Two tracts*, p. 196/225.

with these terms, for in the autumn of 1660 he had entered into a correspondence about them with Gabriel Towerson, a Fellow of All Souls. In one surviving letter, Towerson asked of Locke,

> I would willingly know of you whether you thinke the being of the law of nature can be evinc'd from the force of conscience in those men who have no other divine law to square their actions by. If you doe (as for my part I doe because I thinke it to be St. Pauls owne argument) I shall thinke it incumbent upon you, who have engaged in the same designe with your servant, to answer in short your owne objections.[21]

Locke's reply has not survived. In the disputations published as *Essays on the law of nature*, however, a definite response was offered. The argument invoked by Towerson was dismissed, and natural law discussed in new and distinctive terms.

Answering the objections of his earlier self, Locke now insisted that 'while we assert that the light of nature points to this law [sc. natural law], we should not wish this to be understood in the sense that some inward light is by nature implanted in man, which perpetually reminds him of his duty' and went on to reject right reason as the standard of law. Right reason, he suggested, was something that everyone attributed to himself and discounted from others.[22]

With this suggestion, Locke was rejecting a conception of law that was internal to man and the equation of reason and law that this conception embodied. He paused to underline the impropriety of speaking of natural law as the dictate of reason, 'since reason does not so much establish and pronounce this law of nature as search for it and discover it as a law enacted by a superior power'. 'Neither is reason so much the maker of that law as its interpreter', Locke continued, 'unless, violating the dignity of the supreme legislator, we wish to make reason responsible for that received law which it merely investigates; nor indeed can reason give us laws, since it is only a faculty of our mind.' Now, the traditional model of conscience had included the idea that reason prescribed laws in the notion of *synteresis*. For the polemical purposes of the English tract Locke had downplayed the significance of *synteresis* and elevated instead the role of *syneidesis*, the faculty in which he had taken 'the whole liberty of conscience' to reside. If his reticence then had been a rather desperate attempt to evade the implications of his own position, it was a small step now to do away with *synteresis* altogether.[23]

[21] Locke, *Correspondence*, I, p. 159. Compare Gabriel Towerson, *An explication of the decalogue or ten commandments* (London, 1676), pp. 1–7.

[22] John Locke, *Essays on the law of nature*, ed. Wolfgang von Leyden (Oxford, 1954), no. 2, p. 122, p. 133.

[23] Locke, *Essays*, no. 2, p. 122; no. 1, p. 110; idem, *Two tracts*, p. 207/238.

This was just what Locke did. He jettisoned from the idea of conscience any notion of law. In his subsequent writings conscience was understood as a mental capacity which pronounced judgement upon actions by acquitting or condemning but which did not itself legislate: 'Conscience is the judg not ye law', reads one marginal jotting in Locke's copy of Thomas Burnet's *Third remarks upon An essay concerning humane understanding*. Another announced what Bagshawe's claims had conspicuously indicated, that the supposition that conscience itself delivered moral rules was 'but laying down a foundation for Enthusiasme'.[24] From the *Essays* onwards, natural law with Locke was something inferred from without not discovered within.[25]

The view of natural law the *Essays* developed was of divinely ordained moral rules disclosed by sense data and reason. Reason could infer a singular and authoritative line of conduct from these rules, which established the purpose of civil society and, with it, its limits.

In arguing that in this matter reason was in principle univocal, Locke cast doubt upon Hobbes's explanation of the magistrate's authority. Like Locke after him, Hobbes had rejected the idea that right reason was an infallible faculty—indeed, it was his postulate that reason directed people to conduct that (in their view) conduced to their advantage that generated the conditions of contention which, in turn, made necessary the creation of a singular and authoritative sovereign. Emphasizing the singular character of reason, therefore, bore against Hobbes's design. So too did emphasizing its authoritative character, which Locke did by underscoring its certainty. This suggested that reason was an adequate guide to conduct, and that civil society might be upheld without a Hobbesian sovereign. Yet this emphasis also masked a silent manoeuvre of the highest significance on Locke's part, for it effectively severed the connection between grace and knowledge. Locke's *Essays* observed, in a deceptively casual aside, that the consequences of the Fall, whatever they were, were irrelevant to the subject being addressed.[26] As we have seen, others thought very differently.

[24] Yale University, Beinecke Rare Book and Manuscript Library, call number K8 L79 Zz 697 Pb: Thomas Burnet, *Third remarks upon An essay concerning humane understanding* (London, 1699), pp. 9 and 11. See also p. 10: 'Conscience is not ye law of Nature but judging by y^t^ wch is taken to be ye law.'

[25] Here, if anywhere, it may be worth adding that in coming to a view of conscience that did not involve the complementary relation of *syneidesis* and *synteresis*, Locke found little conceptual need, nor any immediate use, for the syllogistic model of reasoning that underwrote their relation. In *An essay concerning human understanding*, the syllogism was tolerated as a passable means of arranging known truths but debunked as a means of discovering new truths. See John Locke, *An essay concerning human understanding*, ed. Peter H. Nidditch (Oxford, 1975), IV.xvii.1–24, pp. 668–88.

[26] Locke, *Essays*, no. 3, p. 138.

If unassisted reason could direct people to knowledge of the conduct God required in relation to civil society, conscience could not rightly be adduced to ground alternative modes of conduct. Conscientious scruples could not very well justify conduct inimical to the order of society if God had disclosed that order definitively through natural law. The accent placed on natural law in regulating conscience suggested that liberty of conscience on the model Bagshawe favoured was delusory. On the other hand, it would be no easier to claim for the church a position of primacy in political life or to assign to it a unique mission in correcting conduct if its immediate assistance was not required for the successful administration of political life.

The suggestion that natural reason attained to certainty ramified into Locke's understanding of Scripture, whose revelations were not certain but probable. Consequently, they could not claim a greater authority than reason. Thus potentially eccentric Scriptural interpretations were trumped and those grounded in reason vindicated. At the same time, Scripture might yet be accorded the centrality it was due if revelation was needed to inform people about matters of faith that were above reason. These views would be refined and expanded in Locke's later writings, but they were present in a preliminary way in the *Essays*, as in the distinction insisted upon there between matters of faith and matters of knowledge.[27]

In sum, if conscience were informed by reason (or Scripture interpreted by reason) it could be supposed that in civil matters conscience would acquit only conduct that upheld civil society. This supposition allowed Locke to explain what was and was not properly a matter of conscience in relation to it. In this explanation natural law figured centrally. Natural law circumscribed human conduct in a way that was at once meticulous and general—it required actions of *this* sort, rather than any other.[28] This indicated that those who adduced conscience to license conduct of another sort, conduct that ran counter to civil order, were acting illegitimately and could be duly referred to the magistrate. In time, the assumption that conscience would be reasonable would be buttressed by an account of a Christian religion whose distinguishing feature was its reasonableness. For the moment, it supported the claim that the magistrate had no business whatever with conscientious beliefs and practice that did not concern civil affairs or threaten civil peace.[29]

This claim was a decisive index of Locke's movement away from the explicitly Christian terms of his *Two tracts*. The category of things indifferent,

[27] Ibid., no. 5, p. 176.
[28] Ibid., no. 4, pp. 156–8.
[29] These observations are amplified and turned to a wider purpose in Timothy Stanton, 'Freedom of conscience, political liberty, and the foundations of liberalism', in Martin van Gelderen and Quentin Skinner, eds., *Freedom and the construction of Europe* (2 vols., Cambridge, 2013), vol. I, pp. 134–54.

around which its arguments had revolved, had its roots in Christian doctrine: things indifferent constituted a class of matters about which God had issued no specific direction in the Scriptures, while the liberty enjoyed by individuals in these matters was understood to derive from Christ. As others before him, so Locke had discovered that this category was unequal to determining the respective limits of politics and religion. In discussing the conduct of political life primarily in terms of natural law, Locke conceptually abstracted the commonwealth away from Christianity.[30] But if doing so allowed him to draw the limits he required, it did not yet do much more than establish a basic structure. The content of this structure had still to be filled out.

Locke's discussion had implied the existence of two distinct spheres of activity, with the limits of each drawn both ways, so that the civil sphere did not entrench upon matters of faith and the ecclesiastical sphere, which was concerned with matters of faith, did not encroach upon civil society. This befitted Locke's sense that the civil magistrate *ex hypothesi* was no more certain about matters of faith than anyone else. Having arrived at a means of setting limits to civil and spiritual matters, he could now be confident that a genuinely religious conscience, which touched only the latter, could be reconciled with civil order. To the development of these means, Locke's moves in relation to conscience particularly and Christianity more generally were pivotal. They opened up the conceptual space for a different understanding of the relations of church and state, as part of a wider intellectual and institutional structure. When in time Locke came to fill out this structure, natural law once again was crucial.

[30] A point that seems to be lost on the procession of scholars influenced by Leo Strauss who have taken it as evidence of Locke's clandestine prejudice against Christianity. See e.g. Leo Strauss, *Natural right and history* (Chicago, 1953), pp. 202–51, and thereafter Steven Forde, 'Natural law, theology and morality in Locke', *American Journal of Political Science*, 45 (2001), pp. 396–409; Robert Horwitz, 'John Locke's *Questions concerning the law of nature*: a commentary', *Interpretation*, 19 (1992), pp. 251–306; Peter C. Myers, 'Locke on reasonable Christianity and reasonable politics', in Douglas Kries, ed., *Piety and humanity: essays on religion and early modern political philosophy* (Lanham, MD, 1997), pp. 145–80; idem, *Our only star and compass: Locke and the struggle for political rationality* (Lanham, MD, 1998); Michael Rabieh, 'The reasonableness of Locke, or the questionableness of Christianity', *Review of Politics*, 53 (1991), pp. 933–57; Michael P. Zuckert, *Natural rights and the new republicanism* (Princeton, 1994), pp. 187–246, and idem, *Launching liberalism: on Lockean political philosophy* (Lawrence, KS, 2002), pp. 147–200. For similar incomprehension on contrasting grounds, see Jeremy Waldron, *God, Locke, and equality: Christian foundations in Locke's political thought* (Cambridge, 2002), p. 216, and, for discussion, Timothy Stanton, 'Christian foundations; or some loose stones? Toleration and the philosophy of Locke's politics', *Critical Review of International Social and Political Philosophy*, 14 (2011), pp. 323–47, at pp. 340–2.

IV

Natural law did not only point to matters with an obviously secular reference, such as self-preservation and the preservation of society. In Locke's view it also disclosed with certainty that God should be worshipped publicly.[31] As a duty of natural law, worship might therefore be supposed relevant to civil government, especially if the latter was conceived, as it could be, as a body whose purpose was to uphold natural law.[32] Why was this duty irrelevant to civil government by Locke's account? The answer to this question is found at our second stage. It was given in the 'Defence of nonconformity'.

Locke had been working towards this answer during the 1670s along two fronts. In one direction he had produced a series of systematizations about the nature of the laws that patterned human existence, the domains of thought and activity that they regulated, and the conceptions by which these domains could be theorized. The domains were three: religion, politics, and morality. Within each domain different complex ideas of agency answered to the demands of the law that bounded it. These ideas in turn were related to other ideas of actions peculiar to each domain, so that not every action could be religious just as not every action could be political.[33] In another direction Locke had clarified the ends for which the institutions of politics and religion existed.

In 'Excommunication' (1673–4), the 'end of civil society' was identified as 'the preservation of the Society and every Member theereof in a free and peaceable enjoyment of all the good things of this life that belong to each of them'. This end was understood in parallel with that of religious society, or the church, which aimed at 'attaining happinesse after this life in another world'. Civil society 'beyond the concernments of this life … hath noething to doe at all', whereas the church was concerned *only* with those 'things tending to the attainement of future bliss'. But if the ends of civil and ecclesiastical society had been identified, it remained to explain exactly how the church stood in relation to the state—whether it should be understood, for example, as being firmly subordinated to the state, or whether it needed to be conceived as entirely separate from it organizationally speaking. 'Excommunication'

[31] Locke, *Essays*, no. 4, p. 156.

[32] As indeed it had been by Grotius and Hobbes, to name only two of the more important exponents of this view. Compare Hugo Grotius, *De jure belli et pacis libri tres, in quibus jus naturae et gentium, item juris publici praecipua explicantur* (Amsterdam, 1646), Prolegomena, p. xxii, and Hobbes, *Leviathan*, II.xxvi.137–40.

[33] See variously MS. Locke f.1, 'Obligation of penal laws' (1676), fos. 123–6; MS. Locke f.3, 'Law' (1678), fos. 111–12; MS. Locke f.3, 'Lex triplex' (1678), fo. 201. For the significance of these points in the context of Locke's philosophy and his view of toleration, see Stanton, 'Christian foundations', pp. 330–47.

omitted explanation in favour of the enumeration of contemporary instances from which a variety of acceptable arrangements were inferred.[34] The 'Defence of nonconformity' articulated a more definite view, one that incorporated an answer to the question raised by treating divine worship as a natural duty.

The answer, in part, was that this duty implied a matching right of every one to take care of their own souls, as well as an obligation to 'seek out the best way they could find to their salvation', which they could not rightly pass to another by any means.[35] As was the case elsewhere in Locke's writings, duty was matched by possession of the capacities needed to discharge that duty. So if people were not born into churches, they were able to enter them at their own volition: in his words, 'freely, & of their owne choice'.[36] More fundamentally, the duty to worship was irrelevant to civil society because churches existed on terms and for ends that differed from those of civil societies.

Churches were religious societies.[37] According to the 'Defence', religion was the name given to

> those opinions, & actions alone, which I entertaine, & performe, onely to please God, & such as have no concernement at all with my neighbour or ye interest, or affaires of this world, though many of these are outward & visible to others, are not within the Civill Magistrates inspection & care, whose proper province is onely civil society in order to mens well being in this world.

There being parts of religion that 'could not be performed in ye solitary recesses of a retired man', people were put under 'a necessity' of forming religious societies with one another so that they might engage in 'publick acts of devotion' to the God they served and to whom 'they payed the internal acts of veneration in their hearts'.[38] To these general requirements, Christianity had introduced additional specifications, such as an insistence upon the edification of believers and the propagation of its central truths, both of which specifications made the reading of Scripture a matter of central

[34] MS. Locke c.27, fos. 29a–29b. Compare Locke, 'An essay', pp. 327–34.

[35] For the right, see MS. Locke c.34, p. 49; for obligation, p. 131; for the responsibility to determine and pursue the best means of salvation, p. 107. Compare 'Ecclesia', p. 392, for 'the obligation man by the light of reason findes himself under to own & worship god publiquely in the world'.

[36] MS. Locke c.34, p. 49. For the obvious parallel, see John Locke, *Two treatises of government*, ed. Peter Laslett (Cambridge, 1988), II.vi.58, p. 306, where duties under natural law are matched by the freedom of will and liberty of acting necessary to discharging them.

[37] The two terms were treated as equivalents by Locke. See MS. Locke c.34, p. 78.

[38] MS. Locke c.34, pp. 76–7. It is difficult, in view of these words, to agree that Locke understood religion to be 'a private matter' or that he 'maintained a strong, normative preference for individual, interior religion'. See Jeffrey Collins, 'The early modern foundations of classic liberalism', in George Klosko, ed., *The Oxford handbook of the history of political philosophy* (Oxford, 2011), pp. 258–81, at 278–9.

importance to Christians. But what it had emphatically *not* introduced was any necessity, let alone any duty, for the civil magistrate to assist in the process of 'makeing or regulateing those societyes'.[39]

This was not only because, in Locke's words, 'force & ye sword & ye proper instruments of ye Magistrate' were 'altogether uncapeable to convince mens mindes, & bring them to ye beleife of ye truth of any Religion' (a familiar Lockean refrain),[40] or because, if a duty of assistance were postulated, true religion was as liable as the false to find itself on the receiving end of the magistrate's instruments in many parts of the world, but also because the key figures in its history had taken great pains to confine the Christian religion to appropriate limits: 'our Saviour & the Apostles in ye first institution, & propagation [of Christianity] took great care … to have nothing at all to doe with secular affaires, or civill societyes'.[41] In the light of these considerations, it was hard to see why the duty to worship the Christian God—or any other god for that matter—should be expressed through actions that touched directly upon secular affairs or civil society.

As if to emphasize these points, Locke discussed the forms of worship Christ was said to require. These focused on the disposition of the individual worshipper rather than on the peculiar ceremonies of his church. In general terms, the latter would have to be orderly and decent, but their purpose was only the edification of the individual believer, which Locke took to consist in 'right informing ye understanding & subdueing of ye will'. No particular ceremonial practice could be accounted necessary to salvation. 'God who onely can tell what is acceptable to him in his worship, has limitted his Church in these … things to decency order & Edification, & so every thing *in its self indifferent* is unlawfull in his worship unlesse it be expedient for those ends God has assigned.'[42] Nor could the worship God required be understood to presuppose or to issue in a specific set of institutional arrangements. Though Locke acknowledged that, as with any large association of individuals, so with churches there would have to be 'some order, & some distinction of offices amongst them, & some Laws to governe the Members of the society', this was something for every church to decide for itself, according to its own measures. Concomitantly, whatever each church decided applied only to 'those y^t are actuall members of that society, which if they will not submit to the utmost power they have is turne them out of ye society'.[43]

[39] MS. Locke c.34, p. 77.
[40] See e.g. Locke, 'An essay', p. 272. What matters is the way in which the 'Defence of nonconformity' incorporates this idea into its wider pattern of explanation.
[41] MS. Locke c.34, p. 77.
[42] Ibid., pp. 23 and 144 (orthography original).
[43] Ibid., p. 78.

The other side of this story was that the same freedom that people enjoyed to choose one church over another could be exercised at any subsequent point to leave it and to go over to another they judged better able to serve the ends for which they had entered that church to begin with. Just as the causal impetus for making or joining a church in the first place lay in the recognition by natural reason of an obligation to engage in public worship, together with the subsequent judgement that the mode of worship developed by this or that church—or even perhaps by no church yet constituted—was most closely in keeping with God's wants, so the impetus to leave a church was causally explicable in relation to a judgement made about its sufficiency to the same ends: 'when any one found either the doctrine or discipline of any such societie not serviceable to that end for which he was of it i.e. the salvation of his soule or lesse serviceable in his judgment then some other he was at liberty to quit that one & unite to the other'.[44] Indeed, it made sense to think of the freedom to join or to leave a church as a right, since with Locke rights were powers coordinated to ends. Thus he could write of people's 'natural & Evangelical right of takeing care of their owne salvation'.[45] But this was a right enjoyed only by those who espoused a religion and one that implied reciprocal duties only on the part of others who were similarly situated. It was not in any straightforward sense a civil right, for it had no connection to the ends of civil society and it was not borne by the individual qua political subject.[46]

[44] Ibid., p. 86.

[45] Ibid., p. 102. In this way, Locke translated liberty of conscience into his own terms. Having first reduced conscience to judgement, the liberty to judge for themselves to which religious society they should adhere was now attributed to all individuals qua men as a natural right. It may be worth adding that this point rather got lost in William Popple's famous translation of Locke's later *Epistola de tolerantia*, which, in writing lavishly of 'Liberty of Conscience' as 'every mans natural Right', departed from Locke's Latin—as it did elsewhere harmlessly—with grossly misleading results. Compare John Locke, *A Letter concerning toleration*, trans. William Popple (London, 1689), p. 48 and idem, *Epistola*, p. 134. It follows that claims to the effect that Locke espoused a 'right of conscience' or relied on conscience as the basis of his theory of toleration must be treated with some caution. See e.g. Gary Remer, *Humanism and the rhetoric of toleration* (University Park, PA, 1996), pp. 236 and 241.

[46] See John Locke, *A third letter for toleration, to the author of the Third letter concerning toleration* (London, 1692), pp. 60–1: 'The End of a Commonwealth constituted can be supposed no other, than what Men in the Constitution of, and entring into it propos'd; and that could be nothing but Protection from such Injuries from other Men, which they desiring to avoid, nothing but Force could prevent or remedy: all things but this being as well attainable by Men living in Neighbourhood without the Bonds of a Commonwealth, they could propose to themselves no other thing but this in quitting their Natural Liberty, and putting themselves under the Umpirage of a Civil Soveraign, who therefore had the Force of all the Members of the Commonwealth put into his Hands, to make his Decrees to this end be obeyed. Now since no Man, or Society of Men can by their Opinions in Religion, or Ways of Worship, do any Man who differed from them any Injury, which he could not avoid or redress, if he desired it, without the help of Force; the punishing any

The character Locke attributed to churches in the 'Defence' set them in a very particular relation to civil society. Churches, no less than civil societies, were understood by him to be productions of natural reason and natural will, the two faculties of mind God had given to people in order to know and pursue His purposes for them.[47] This understanding was now deployed to establish a crucial point. The point was that churches and states were categorically distinct associations, instituted by people for different ends.[48]

One immediate implication of this point was to make irrelevant to civil government claims to embody supernatural truth made by churches. These claims were central to the view that civil government should underwrite Christian doctrine and uphold the ecclesiastical order of the true church, and to the assumption that a single national church would issue from this arrangement. We saw this assumption in action in Sanderson's and Stillingfleet's writings in defence of conformity on Anglican terms, but it is present no less powerfully in the panoply of writings of innumerable nonconformists, who disagreed with their opponents only about the legitimacy of the national church which, to their deep regret, had for the present emerged from the arrangement.[49] Excluding questions of supernatural truth from consideration at one stroke undermined the plausibility of that assumption.

To treat a church as being in the relevant respects a natural body meant that supernatural truth could not be predicated of it in the manner the arrangement required. The supernatural attributes of churches were narrowed to the word of God: 'our Saviour accounts those onely Members of himself, & his Church, who beleive his doctrine & by good lives conforme to his precepts (the true conformity of ye Gospel)'. This indicated that the supernatural aspect of a church would be predicable of churches in general, not of specific churches. This lack of specificity obviated the need for the institutional support of a particular church—whatever its historic claims—by the

Opinion in Religion, or Ways of Worship by the Force given the Magistrate, could not be intended by those who constituted, or entred into the Commonwealth, and so could be no End of it, but quite the contrary.' Worship, then, falls outside the jurisdiction of the commonwealth, is not one of its ends, and its end cannot be served by the means at the magistrate's disposal. On these points see at length Ian Harris, Chapter 4, this volume.

[47] MS. Locke c.34, pp. 85–6. For intellect and will in relation to natural law, see *Essays*, no. 3, p. 136 in the light of Harris, Chapter 4, this volume.

[48] See MS. Locke c.34, p. 86.

[49] See e.g. John Barrett, *The rector of Sutton committed with the dean of St. Paul's* (London, 1680), p. 21; John Humfrey, *An answer to Dr. Stillingfleet's sermon, by some nonconformists, being the peaceable design renewed* (London, 1680), p. 30; Thomas Wall, *More work for the dean* (London, 1681), p. 20: 'As there is but … one God and Father of all, one Lord over all, and one Spirit, so there is but … one Truth, one Faith, one Salvation, one Church, called in one Hope, joined in one Profession, guided by one … Rule.' For a fuller discussion, see Stanton, 'The name and nature of Locke's "Defence of nonconformity"', pp. 165–8.

state.[50] At the least, it indicated that none could very easily lay exclusive claim to state support.

If the church and the state were, properly speaking, independent and parallel bodies, it was obvious to Locke that bending one to the ends of the other was bound to damage both impartially. Confining the business of the church to spiritual purposes limited its attention to questions of moral duty and salvation, to which, as a religious society, it was suited. Conversely, when 'ye temporall authority came to be mixt with Ecc^{t}ecall jurisdiction, & force was made use of contrary to ye nature of ye thing to make men Christians, or of this or y^{t} Church whether they would or no, Religion became a businesse of State', and its proper function was perverted.[51] The state was one body, the church quite another. Membership of the one did not in any way imply membership of the other.

The 'Defence', therefore, gave unambiguous expression to the view that the church should not impinge on civil life or vice versa. But its novelty lay in explaining how church and state could be conceptually and organizationally sundered from one another. This explanation turned on Locke's conceiving the church as a body to which members adhered voluntarily, a conception he would carry forward into the *Epistola de tolerantia* as a foundation for its claims about toleration between different churches.

V

The 'Defence of nonconformity' developed views that were crucial to Locke's mature position about toleration. In particular, it developed the view that churches were brought into being by the will of their members to unite with one another for the purpose of worshipping God as they saw fit. This view reflected assumptions about the irrelevance of the Fall to the adequacy (or otherwise) of human beings to self-direction in line with God's purposes that infused Locke's writings from *Essays on the law of nature* onwards. The 'Defence' explained that churches should be understood as products of a natural adequacy, as rational constructions constituted by the will and subsequent agreement of human beings to associate for particular, spiritual purposes; and that civil societies were constituted in a similar fashion, but for

[50] MS. Locke c.34, p. 144; see also p. 106 for the obvious problem, that 'a national Church tends to ye support of the national Religion, but with this scarey addition; *whether true or false*' ('scarey' in this context meaning terrifying, frightful: see *Oxford English Dictionary*, scary, *a*. 1).

[51] MS. Locke c.34, p. 102.

different, secular purposes.[52] In its way, it heralded both *Two treatises of government* and the *Epistola*.

The views Locke expounded at this second stage depended upon exclusions he had made at the first stage. These exclusions were more extensive, and the views that he put in the place of those he had rejected more radical, than is sometimes supposed. Locke had inherited a difficulty that implied in its aspects other views about conscience and natural law. These views could be associated with others again—about the Fall of man and the bearing of its consequences on the relations that were assumed to obtain between church and state – to throw the issue of nonconformity sharply into relief. In resolving this difficulty Locke at once dismantled the problematical conception of conscience he had inherited and cut his own view of it free of the associations that attended the view he had disavowed.

This ground-clearing exercise was followed by another, more constructive enterprise, which built upon the ground Locke had cleared. At both stages, natural law featured integrally. Locke's use of natural law enabled him to abstract away from the terms in which his original difficulty had arisen. In effect, this meant abstracting the commonwealth away from Christianity. Even when discussing churches in the 'Defence of nonconformity' he had continued this pattern of activity, treating them as religious societies whose denominational identity was less important than the natural causal history that accounted for their existence. In the unfolding of this pattern, the *Epistola* was a culminating statement. The position about toleration that it developed was made possible only by the series of moves Locke had made at earlier stages.

Now it may be thought unduly delicate, if not simply an irritating affectation, to have written again and again of Locke's position *about* toleration. Surely it is as safe as any historical claim we might possibly wish to make could be to write that Locke argued in favour of toleration. Yet if we attend to Locke's position in the *Epistola* it is evident that a degree of delicacy *is* necessary. For the three 'considerations' that Locke adduced towards the beginning of the *Epistola*—considerations that are conventionally regarded as arguments *for* toleration—are in fact arguments about why toleration is none of the civil magistrate's business.[53] These considerations preface an

[52] Locke, *Essays*, no. 3, p. 138. Hence, perhaps, the deafening silence about the Fall in the manuscript; *idem*, 'An essay', p. 270, cf. p. 275. For secular purposes, pre-eminently 'ye preservation of mankind in this world', see MS. Locke c.34, p. 76. It should be noted that Locke premises only the purposes of the state as a foundation in the earlier essay: the terms on which it subsists are left open. See 'An essay', pp. 269–70.

[53] Locke, *Epistola*, pp. 67–71. For a selection of conventional interpretations, see e.g. Sam Black, 'Locke and the skeptical argument for toleration', *History of Philosophy Quarterly*, 24 (2007), pp. 355–75; Paul Bou-Habib, 'Locke, sincerity and the rationality of persecution', *Political Studies*, 51 (2003), pp. 611–26; David McCabe, 'John Locke and the argument against strict separation',

account of churches and the ends for which they are constituted—an account that borrows liberally from the 'Defence'—and thence of toleration as a reciprocal duty between persons who differ from one another in religion, and between 'particular churches which stand in the same kind of relation to one another as private persons'.[54]

The correlated rights to join or to leave particular churches and the rights of particular churches to eject members who obstinately offend against their laws lie along a juridical axis which does not, at any point, intersect with the juridical axis of politics. This implies at least two considerations. The first consideration is that the rights that find their home along one axis cannot be passed along the other. Thus 'the civil government can give no new right to a church, nor a church to the civil government'. The second, and potentially more alarming, consideration is that when the attempted exercise of rights secured along one axis comes into conflict with the exercise of rights secured along the other axis, there is no judge on earth capable of mediating the claims of each.[55] Again, this juridical arrangement suggests that if there are reciprocal duties between religious believers and rights held one against another in the same capacity, religious believers possess no civil right to toleration at the hands of the civil magistrate, nor does the magistrate qua magistrate have the duty to tolerate those who differ from him in religion: *ceteris paribus*, he has the duty to refrain from interfering with all religious societies, his own as much as every other.[56] So while it is certainly true that Locke's position accommodates toleration—though not of course for those who espouse no religion—and liberty of conscience, it does so in terms quite unlike those in which Locke's closest contemporaries squabbled their way across the seventeenth century.

Review of Politics, 59 (1997), pp. 233–58; Susan Mendus, 'Locke: toleration, morality and rationality', in John Horton and Susan Mendus, eds., *John Locke: a letter concerning toleration in focus* (London, 1991), pp. 147–62; J. Judd Owen, 'Locke's case for religious toleration: its neglected foundation in *An essay concerning human understanding*', *Journal of Politics*, 69 (2007), pp. 156–68; Micah Schwartzman, 'The relevance of Locke's religious arguments for toleration', *Political Theory*, 33 (2005), pp. 678–705; John W. Tate, 'Locke and toleration: defending Locke's liberal credentials', *Philosophy & Social Criticism*, 35 (2009), pp. 761–91; Jeremy Waldron, 'Locke: toleration and the rationality of persecution', in Susan Mendus, ed., *Justifying Toleration* (Cambridge, 1988), pp. 61–86. For a fuller treatment of Waldron's claims, see Timothy Stanton, 'Locke and the politics and theology of toleration', *Political Studies*, 54 (2006), pp. 84–102.

[54] Locke, *Epistola*, pp. 71–81, at p. 81.

[55] Locke, *Epistola*, pp. 81 and 129. See at length Dunn, 'Freedom of conscience'.

[56] Locke, *Epistola*, p. 100. Compare MS. Locke c.34, pp. 74–5: 'as the civill magistrate hath noe power to determin of what Church or religious societie I shall be of & soe obleige me to the observance of any of those . . . things which are requird in that communion & made a part of it soe neither can he by the power he has . . . as civill magistrate enjoyne me any thing . . . as a part of my religious worship whether I am or am not of the state religion i.e. of that church communion where of he himself is'.

None of this is by any means to suggest that the association that posterity has made between Locke and toleration ought to be unmade. It is merely to say that it is not simple. The types of argument about toleration used at the time by nonconformists in self-defence, and by Anglicans to attack them, are polar opposites on a trajectory different from, and perhaps at the perpendicular to, the one on which Locke was travelling. If Locke's starting point was in some respects the same as theirs, his final destination was not. Consequently there is little to be gleaned about his speed or direction of travel from plotting his course along theirs. Indeed, the results of any attempt to do so are liable to be not merely uninformative but ineluctably unreliable, since they rely upon the silent elimination of a gamut of alternative possibilities. Whether this is done by identifying toleration as an expression of nonconformist opinions or Anglican attitudes in terms of which Locke's position about it should be understood, or by an assimilation to context which locates his position in the interstices of others' lines of thinking, the effect is the same.[57] Either way, the distinctiveness of Locke's thinking is obscured in the blur and fog of denominational self-consolation, tactical manoeuvring, and Anglican reciprocation, behind which toleration dissolves into a shapeless blob. By considering in some detail two stages in Locke's movement towards his mature position, a new Locke comes into view: it becomes possible to see the determinate and substantive content that he imparted to his own conclusions about toleration and how he reached them. In the process, something of the special character of Locke's thinking is revealed and with it, perhaps, the need for further reflection both upon the particular form that toleration received at his hands, and upon its deeper intellectual foundations.[58]

[57] For toleration as an expression of nonconformist opinion, see e.g. Geoffrey F. Nuttall and Owen Chadwick, eds., *From uniformity to unity 1662–1962* (London, 1962), *passim*; for Anglican attitudes, see e.g. H. R. McAdoo, *The spirit of Anglicanism* (London, 1965), pp. 156–239; for Locke's position as intersticial to those of others, see e.g. John Coffey, *Persecution and toleration in Protestant England 1558–1689* (Harlow, 2000), pp. 47–77; John Marshall, *John Locke: resistance, religion and responsibility* (Cambridge, 1994), p. 99; and in a wider European context idem, *John Locke, toleration and early Enlightenment culture* (Cambridge, 2006), *passim*; Jonathan Israel, *Radical Enlightenment: philosophy and the making of modernity, 1650–1750* (Oxford, 2001), pp. 265–8. It may not be out of place to observe at this point that the decisive steps Locke took between 1673 and 1678 towards developing his mature position about toleration came during a period in which the pamphlet literature on the topic on all sides was almost entirely in abeyance.

[58] See Harris, Chapter 4, this volume, for a pioneering step towards meeting this need.

4

John Locke and Natural Law: Free Worship and Toleration

IAN HARRIS*

LOCKE'S *EPISTOLA DE TOLERANTIA* seems an unpromising candidate for discussion in relation to natural law, because the latter is not deployed explicitly there. Where appearance is not encouraging, reality may be more welcoming. Here it turns paradox into plain statement. Natural law plays a fundamental role in *Epistola*, not alone, it is true, but in combination with a broader natural theology and with a matching conception of jurisdiction. The explicit arguments in the text depend upon positions supposed there but argued or used explicitly elsewhere in Locke's writings, positions which, therefore, a reading of *Epistola* alone cannot disclose. We shall see that natural theology was a fundamental feature of Locke's thinking about duty, worship, freedom, and toleration.

I

First, by way of preface, it will be as well to give a preliminary statement of the thesis of this chapter, and of its effects. Here we should start with natural theology in its bearing on questions of religious liberty, specifically freedom of worship and toleration.

* The writer acknowledges the kind permission of the Keeper of Special Collections and Western Manuscripts at the Bodleian Library to quote Locke manuscripts, and thanks the Head of the Department of Literary and Historical Manuscripts at the Pierpont Morgan Library, New York for helpful advice about the status of a manuscript in his care (MA 998). He is grateful to Professor Maria Rosa Antognazza, Professor John Dunn, Professor Knud Haakonssen, Professor Ian Hunter, Professor Thomas Pink, Professor Michael J. Seidler, Dr Timothy Stanton, and Professor Simone Zurbuchen for comments made in discussion on 13 April 2007. For comments on the present version the writer is indebted to Professor Dunn, Professor Haakonssen, Professor Geraint Parry, Professor Pink, Dr Brian Roots, Professor Graham Shipley, and Dr Stanton. He is also obliged to Professor G. A. J. Rogers and Dr Stanton for providing him with copies of essays.

Proceedings of the British Academy, **186**, 59–105.

A function of mankind in Locke's natural theology was to follow God, not least by obeying His laws. Thus, to take an example that is most important for our purpose, Locke identified a natural duty to worship God. That is not all: if human conduct and thought found their proper end in God's glory, then it is reasonable to suppose that the same applies to the origin and end of human institutions, and this teleological supposition is fundamental to Locke's account of freedom of worship. The natural duty to worship God, in fact, implied *ecclesia*, religious society, just as the rational way to secure some other ends of natural law required *respublica*, commonwealth or civil society. Questions arose about the definition of these two purposive subdivisions of the great community of mankind, and their mutual relations. For the fact that there is a natural duty to worship God, and, as we shall see, also a corresponding natural liberty, is obviously insufficient to establish that worship remains free within a commonwealth. That a commonwealth had no jurisdiction over the end of worship Locke established by a train of arguments in natural theology, the one contained in *Two treatises*—and in *Epistola* he drove that train home to its implication for free worship. The destination of this argument was that worship, not being subject to civil jurisdiction in certain respects, was free rather than tolerated. Indeed, worship on this understanding, far from being an evil, which is the proper object of toleration, was a duty—the first of duties, looking directly to God's glory.

What then of toleration, and intolerance? The same framework enabled Locke both to establish that there was no institutional duty of intolerance for a commonwealth towards worship and to generate a duty of mutual toleration about worship amongst religious societies; to define the positions that a commonwealth *should* have in relation to worship; and to identify the *in*tolerance that natural law required in some matters under civil jurisdiction. For to argue in terms of natural theology both required intolerance and widened the scope of toleration. Locke did not advocate toleration universally; rather, in civil and ecclesiastical cases alike he identified grounds on which natural law required coercion of those who broke it or undermined civil jurisdiction. Where mutual toleration of worship was required, Locke located its terms and boundaries in respect of theism rather than more narrowly, in respect of Christianity. Thus the arguments of Locke's *Epistola* presume much beyond that text.[1]

[1] The essay that comprises this chapter necessarily proceeds from the starting-points provided by this author's earlier writings about Locke, and sometimes refers to these in the course of developing its arguments: but the content and reach of the latter are substantially new. Compare, in order of composition, 'Locke on justice', *Oxford studies in the history of philosophy,* III: *English philosophy in the age of Locke*, ed. M. A. Stewart (Oxford, 2000), pp. 46–85; *The mind of John Locke* (Cambridge, 1994, 1998), esp. chs. 2–4, 6–7; 'Tolérance, église et état chez Locke', in Yves-Charles Zarka, Franck Lessay, and G. A. J. Rogers, eds., *Les fondements philosophiques de la*

This thesis is a historical one, devoted to identifying some of the key assumptions Locke made in writing *Epistola*, how he developed them there to reach his conclusions about free worship and toleration, and his grounds for proceeding in terms of these assumptions.[2] It makes claims fundamental to understanding how Locke wrote about worship, jurisdiction, and toleration: especially it shows that natural theology, including natural law, is implied in the generation of Locke's account of free worship and toleration. It has a number of effects on our understanding of Lockean thought.

First, it changes the scope of our thinking about Locke and natural law. Attention has focused most fully in that connection on a natural duty towards other people, namely to preserve them, and somewhat less on a coordinated duty to oneself, namely self-preservation.[3] Virtually nothing has been said about the natural duty of worship, so that its position and bearings in Locke's thinking have not been made evident.[4] If, therefore, it may surprise the reader of the scholarly literature that Locke stated that 'God hath given rules to ye actions of men both as a homage due to himself & for ye preservation of ye whole race of men',[5] yet once the natural duty of worship is brought into focus, the continuity of assumption and comprehensiveness of scope in *Epistola* can be brought into relief. Secondly, Locke's leading arguments there concern worship and its relationship to jurisdiction under natural law, the upshot being a delimitation of jurisdiction according to end. Thirdly, Locke's arguments establish the scope of religious liberty according to his conceptions. They proceed from premises and lead to conclusions that are applicable to worship, and not only to Christian worship. They start from natural duty, and produce both the freedom that worship enjoys from civil jurisdiction and a duty of mutual toleration amongst worshippers that embraces all theists. The obverse of this latter duty lays bare the ground of conclusions that have

tolerance (3 vols., Paris, 2002), I, pp. 175–214; 'Sex, power and consent in *Two treatises of government*', paper presented at the British Society for the History of Philosophy Locke Tricentenary Conference, St Anne's College, Oxford on 3 April 2004; 'The legacy of *Two treatises*', *Eighteenth-Century Thought*, 3 (2007), pp. 143–67. Compare '"And the least sceptical": knowledge, natural theology, and liberty of conscience in Bayle's *Commentaire Philosophique*', *Politics and Religion* (forthcoming).

[2] For some other aspects of Locke's situation, see Gordon J. Schochet, 'John Locke and religious toleration', in Lois J. Schwoerer, ed., *The revolution of 1688–1689* (Cambridge, 1992), ch. 9.

[3] For self-preservation as a fundamental duty in Lockean natural law, and its role in generating the duty to preserve others, see Harris, 'Locke on justice', esp. s.2, and idem, *Mind*, pp. 218–24.

[4] Harris, *Mind*, p. 39, and 'Tolérance', p. 182, excuse the present writer, but this chapter attests a felt need to explore the topic. Alex Tuckness, *Locke and the legislative point of view* (Princeton, 2002), p. 186, adopts the point, whilst Roger Woolhouse, *Locke* (Cambridge, 2007), p. 270, quotes the letter cited in n. 8 below. Neither makes anything of this duty. Nor did the scholar who was the first to identify it, John W. Yolton, 'Locke on the law of nature', *Philosophical Review*, 67 (1958), pp. 477–98, at p. 487.

[5] Pierpont Morgan Library, MA 998, *Draft C* [of *An essay concerning human understanding*], II.xxxi.16.

been thought exceptionable, namely the coercion of Roman Catholics and atheists: these conclusions were in a basic sense natural to Locke, for the commonwealth was a body that implied the truth of theism because it required natural law, and Locke took atheists and Roman Catholics, in their different ways, to subvert that law and the commonwealth, atheists undermining both and Roman Catholics the latter. The commonwealth, indeed, had a duty under natural law to enforce other aspects of morality, besides exercising this coercion, so that coercion and toleration alike flow from natural duty. So, fourthly, the arguments in *Epistola* are not just practical ones: they are not free-standing reasons or recommendations about action. Rather they both rest on claims to universal truth and make claims of the most general scope about worship and toleration.

It must be added that the scholarly literature about Locke's *Epistola* is less helpful than one would wish. This literature overlooks natural law, and so fails to treat Lockean freedom of worship and toleration in a proper way. Some of it overlooks them almost by declared policy; much of it fails to take them as seriously as it should, for by overlooking the natural duty of worship, it treats Locke as if his only focus of attention in *Epistola* was toleration, rather than also—and importantly—jurisdiction and freedom of worship. Hence this literature fails to take into proper account much of the text, and, it must be said, uses the freedom that follows from this neglect to depart from Locke, not least in ways that make him look like Mill or Rawls. It focuses wholly upon the individual, rather than upon religious and civil societies, and develops a number of views bearing this impress. It ends with a vague acknowledgement of Christianity that treats the latter as a supplement to contemporary liberalism. The exceptions to this condition are few, and they are partial, having been entered summarily or in passing, and are far from being a sustained treatment of *Epistola*.[6] Much in Locke's thinking, then, has been omitted or misunderstood: a new account is required.

This chapter, then, provides a new set of terms for reading *Epistola*: it changes both the scope and content of our understanding of that work. By the same measure, it displaces the terms that have been central to much previous writing. Here one pattern of ideas is substituted for another.

This chapter begins by setting out Locke's natural duty to worship, some of his natural theology, and the bearing of these upon liberty and jurisdiction. It indicates next how natural law made mankind one community, situating both civil and religious societies as functions of that law's teleological requirements. Locke's manner of defining these societies according to those ends separated their respective jurisdictions and made each free of the other.

[6] These are identified at appropriate points as this chapter advances. The prevalent trend in the scholarly literature is addressed at the end.

If Lockean natural theology is thus an antecedent of conceiving worship as free, it also generates a duty of mutual toleration amongst worshippers. Conversely, this natural law thinking condemns atheism, the Roman Catholic's extra-jurisdictional loyalty to the Pope, and other offences against the commonwealth: for in these terms *respublica*, as much as *ecclesia*, presumes the truth of theism and, of course, the validity of natural law, because both are subordinate to God's natural jurisdiction, and to no other. These points change our understanding of Locke on religious liberty. The view that he was a critic of natural law is as mistaken as the view that he was a Millian or Rawlsian figure. He is, rather, better understood in *Epistola* as an exponent of natural theology and natural law, and as one who developed their consequences in terms of jurisdiction.[7]

II

It is best to confront doubt at the outset. If natural law is not mentioned in the *Epistola*, does it play any part in it? An intelligent friend of Locke's concluded that it did, describing it as a work that demonstrated its case by *ius naturae*.[8] This claim provides sufficient grounds for exploring the question. The answer begins with Locke's account of natural law. For his answers to the question of religious liberty presupposed an account of natural law. Locke's fullest account of this is found in the lectures that he wrote in 1663–4.[9]

If *Epistola* supposes *ius naturae*, that implies one or both of duty and right, as *ius* can embrace both ideas. Locke's thinking about free worship and toleration, as we shall see, supposes a natural duty and a natural liberty to worship. The duty claims our attention first.[10] The duty is classified as natural, in part because its content can be known by anyone. That is to say, this content is accessible to our intellectual faculties and rests upon data available to all people at all places and times. The duty is disclosed by a comparison between ourselves and the world: this comparison suggests a God who is omnipotent, wise, and purposeful, and who applies His attributes to create, sustain, and guide us. This discovery both indicates that we, as the beneficiaries of His actions, should be grateful to and suggests that reflection on the fact stimulates sentiments of gratitude and reverence in us.[11] Our duty finds an inward

[7] Locke is, of course, more than this. I shall explore the philosophical and theological reference of his arguments elsewhere, and also say more about his natural theology in particular.

[8] Philipp van Limborch to Locke, 26 April 1689, in *The correspondence of John Locke*, ed. E. S. de Beer (8 vols., Oxford, 1976–89), III, p. 608.

[9] John Locke, *Essays on the law of nature*, ed. Wolfgang von Leyden (Oxford, 1954).

[10] Some questions about right will be treated in another publication.

[11] Locke, *Essays*, no. 4, esp. p. 156.

expression as love of God, and an outward expression in worship of Him.[12] So there is a natural duty to worship God, which goes along with inward love of Him, and the duty is one apprehensible by all.

The character of worship reflects God's purpose in creating the world: as He is perfect, all things reflect His glory, and worship glorifies Him as witness in the presence of others.[13] As Locke pointed out, the 'great businesse of Religion is to glorifye God', but 'the actions of a private solitary life cannot reach to all the instances & purposes of religion', and these included 'the publick worship of God'.[14] The 'solitary recesses of a retired man' were insufficient because people recognized that 'their duty to honour, & worship the God they served' implied 'publick acts of devotion': that is to say, they understood the need for 'owneing to ye world thereby that Diety by solemne acts of worship to whom they payed the internal acts of veneration in their hearts'.[15] Again, Locke referred, without argument, to 'the obligation man by the light of reason findes himself under to own & worship god publiquely in the world'.[16] He stated, in *Epistola* itself, that 'all know and recognize that God is to be worshipped in public'.[17]

[12] Ibid., no. 7, p. 198.

[13] This does not imply that solitary worship is not part of religion. For a succinct summary of such devotions in the early church, see R. M. Grant, *Augustus to Constantine* (London, 1971), ch. 21, §.vi.

[14] Bodleian Library, Oxford, MS. Locke c.34, pp. 19, 23. I am indebted to Dr Timothy Stanton for sight of his excellent transcript of this document.

[15] Ibid., pp. 76–7. Compare Locke's earlier explanation in terms of people having both souls and bodies: 'deus … utriusque postulat obsequium, et exigit ab utroque quod solvi potest tributum, cumque honorem sibi in terris et nomen quaerit, non tacito illo et quasi furtivo solummodo cultu contentus est, cultores suos nomen palam profiteri voluit quorum exemplis edocti reliqui mortales ad cultum et reverentiam divini numinis incitarentur'. John Locke, *Two tracts on government*, ed. Philip Abrams (Cambridge, 1967), p. 188.

[16] MS. Locke d.10, 'Ecclesia' (1682), p. 43, printed in John Locke, *An essay concerning toleration and other writings on law and politics, 1667–1683*, ed. J. R. Milton and Philip Milton (Oxford, 2006), pp. 391–2, at p. 391.

[17] John Locke, *Epistola de tolerantia / A letter on toleration*, ed. Raymond Klibansky, trans. J. W. Gough (Oxford, 1968), p. 100. Locke implied that the purpose of worship is the glory of God (p. 60). Because the deficiencies of this edition will be mentioned from time to time, it should be said now that it remains the best, combining a Latin text, facing page translation, and lengthy introduction. Also noteworthy is the translation of *Epistola* by Michael Silverthorne in Richard Vernon, ed., *Locke on toleration* (Cambridge, 2010), pp. 3–46. See also Patrick Romanell, ed., *A letter concerning toleration* (2nd edn, Indianapolis, 1955); Mario Montuori, ed., *A letter concerning toleration* (The Hague, 1963) and idem, ed., *John Locke on toleration and the unity of God* (Amsterdam, 1983); James Tully, ed., *A letter concerning toleration* (Indianapolis, 1983); John Horton and Susan Mendus, eds., *John Locke, A letter concerning toleration in focus* (London, 1991); Mark Goldie, ed., *A letter concerning toleration and other writings* (Indianapolis, 2010). These reprint William Popple's translation, as printed originally as *A letter concerning toleration* (London,1689). For an example of the radical interpretative hazards of using Popple's rendering, see n.128 below. Comments on Popple, Gough, and Silverthorne are made where relevant below. All translations from Latin are my own.

Locke identified two presuppositions of natural law. He required both God and the immortality of souls, *et Deus et animarum immortalitas*.[18] The soul had been treated as equivalent to life,[19] and therefore its immortality implied eternal life and the possibility of eternal happiness. These had come to be understood as the destiny of mankind.[20] All human beings, then, had a welfare that comprised more than the solely secular. This welfare, the welfare of their souls, was a high priority: indeed Locke reckoned that because every mortal had an immortal soul, and its welfare depended upon what was prescribed by God, to follow those prescriptions was an obligatory requirement to be observed before all others, for nothing belonging to a mortal condition was to be counted equal to the soul.[21] Eternal happiness, assuming Locke's understanding of God, would be secured by obedience to Him.

The destiny of mankind was thus bound up with obedience to God. This has the effect of raising the question of what is proper to mankind. The word *proper* denotes the distinctive function of a human being, what Aristotle had called its ἔργον. This was what both differentiated one type of being from another and denoted what it alone did or did better than anything else.[22] Aristotle had found the human function in the active exercise of the soul's faculties according to reason, and Locke assumed this claim was valid, describing this work as *proprium opus*, the proper task.[23] Function is relative to an end. What end was mankind to pursue by this action of the soul according to reason? The answer, according to Locke, was that God made all things for His glory—*non videntur ab eo ad alium destinari finem quam ad sui ipsius gloriae ad quem omnia referri debent*—and that obedience to natural law was one way for people to glorify Him.[24]

We now see why glorifying God is a proper activity for mankind and a proper end for it: it was a feature of God's plans and mankind's destiny. Here worship had a high place: indeed, Locke emphasized that '*God is to be worshipped*' was 'as great a Truth as any can enter into the mind of Man', and that it 'deserves the first place amongst all practical Principles'.[25]

[18] Locke, *Essays*, no. 5, p. 172.

[19] See e.g. Cicero, *Pro Murena* xvi, 34, *tantum in unius anima posuit ut … non ante quam illum vita expulit bellum confectum iudicarit*. Matthew 20.28 = Mark 10.45, ὁ υἱὸς τοῦ ἀνθρώπου … ἦλθεν … δοῦναι τὴν ψυχὴν αὐτοῦ λύτρον ἀντὶ πολλῶν.

[20] e.g. I Peter 1.9, τὸ τέλος τῆς πίστεως σωτηρίαν ψυχῶν

[21] Locke, *Epistola*, pp. 122, 124, cf. p. 130.

[22] Compare Plato, *Republic*, I, 352 e–353 b; *Theaetetus*, 174 b 1–3.

[23] Aristotle, *Nicomachean ethics*, I.vii.14, 1098 a 7; Locke, *Essays*, no. 1, p. 112. Von Leyden, who cites Aristotle from the version by Harris Rackham, silently changes his 'soul' into 'mind'. The latter is not obviously the best way to render ψυχή where the sense requires that which originates action, i.e. that which includes will, desires, and affections.

[24] Locke, *Essays*, no. 4, p. 156.

[25] John Locke, *An essay concerning human understanding*, ed. P. H. Nidditch (Oxford, 1975), I.iv.7, p. 87.

But worship was not the only way of glorifying Him. All our actions should reflect God's purpose for the world. The ends that characterize the present life in particular complement the end of our love of God. We exist and act not only in relation to God but also in relation to human beings, ourselves as well as others. Thus, not only to love God but also to love one's fellow human beings as oneself,[26] and *eo ipso* to cultivate one's own well-being, were sorts of duty. Duties to others included obedience to superiors, fidelity to promises, speaking truth, respect for parents, feeding the hungry, and love of neighbours.[27] Such duties answer to the end of glorifying God, for all are duties to Him, though in some cases others besides God or the agent benefit from them.

What do we know about God? Information about Him becomes known to us by natural means, and, being known to us in this way, He is a natural rather than a revealed object of worship. One can call Locke's God natural in the sense that His existence and those of His attributes which He uses to act in the world can be identified by human reason and senses, though He is supernatural in the sense that He possesses a superabundance of these and other attributes, infinitely above the degree we find in terrestrial beings. So, for instance, He is omnipotent and omniscient rather than merely powerful and wise.[28] This natural character is to be emphasized, because this understanding of God, as it is in natural theology, is *limited* to what can be inferred from our own senses and reason. Historical claims about God are not available by this route: they are to be inferred only via the testimony of witnesses and other sacred historians given in the Bible.

The facts about God and worship of disclosed by our natural faculties implied that we should exercise the latter, since thought was requisite to apprehend these truths.[29] Natural theology, then, took truth about God as its object and thought as its means. The thought was limited to the information accessible to anyone's natural faculties. In short, as Locke put it, 'religion being the homage and obedience which man pays immediately to God, it supposes that man is capeable of knowing that there is a god, and what is required by and will be acceptable to him thereby to avoid his anger and procure his favour'.[30] Truth, in natural theology, was to be pursued by our natural faculties of mind

[26] For this, see below pp. 84–6.

[27] Locke, *Essays*, no. 4, p. 158; no. 2, p. 128; no. 7, p. 194.

[28] For reason and senses, see especially Locke, *Essays*, no. 4.

[29] Compare MS. Locke f.3, 'lex naa', 15 July 1678, pp. 201–2: 'God having given man *above other creatures of the habitable part of the universe* a knowledge of himself w[ch] the beasts have not, he is thereby under obligations w[ch] the beasts have not, for knowing god to be a wise agent' (emphasis original).

[30] MS. Locke f.5, Locke's journal entry, 3 April 1681, p. 33, printed in Richard I. Aaron and Jocelyn Gibb, eds., *An early draft of Locke's Essay, together with excerpts from his journals* (Oxford, 1936), p. 114.

and will. Locke thought both adequate to understand and follow natural law, for 'God having given Man an Understanding to direct his Actions, has allowed him a freedom of Will … as properly belonging thereunto.'[31]

Natural theology, then, comprised that amount of truth about divine reality and its implications for us which can be known by the human understanding here and now. But this truth was not the whole truth about God. Much about Him and His will for mankind remained unknown by any means. The means He *had* chosen to use included direct disclosure at particular places and times to those whom He had chosen as exponents of His will for this purpose, ranging from Moses and the Hebrew prophets to Jesus Christ and His Apostles, and these disclosures included truths of vital importance in the economy of salvation. Such revelations were complementary to natural theology, both in that they added further content to our information about divine reality, and in that revelation and natural theology were mutually consistent.

The mutual consistency of natural and revealed theology is not the same as equal utility in all arguments. Revelation, the inferences made from it by theologians, and the practical consequences drawn from these had generated a diversity of ways for Christian worship. Here the problem was not so much an excess of information from the authoritative source, but a scarcity. God had provided a sufficient revelation of His will to save mankind, and the conditions of belief for that purpose, through Jesus Christ. Yet, when we turn to worship, the only information from revelation is Christ's institution of the Lord's Prayer and the Lord's Supper, and His use of Baptism. About the rest—everything else that belongs to liturgy in the broadest sense—there is no information from God, though more can be inferred about the practices of the very earliest congregations from Acts and the Epistles.[32] This ignorance about how to proceed definitively in worship had a sequel in the proliferation of Christian denominations and civil conflict about ecclesiastical questions. Yet the need to proceed was unavoidable. For any reader of the Old Testament—of which Locke made such full use in *Two treatises*[33]—understood that the human condition after Adam was such that natural religion alone could not bring souls to their proper destiny: and the remedy received by Locke, amongst many other thinkers, was the work of Christ and belief in

[31] John Locke, *Two treatises of government*, ed. Peter Laslett (2nd edn, Cambridge, 1967), II.vi.58, p. 324.

[32] C. F. D. Moule, *Worship in the New Testament* (London, 1961) summarizes the evidence.

[33] Harris, 'Locke on justice', s.1; idem, *Mind*, chs 1, 4, 7; idem, 'Legacy', ss. 3, 5; cf. Fania Oz-Salzberger, 'The political thought of John Locke and the significance of political Hebraism', *Hebraic Political Studies*, 1 (2006), pp. 568–92, and Andrew Rehfeld, 'Jephthah, the Hebrew Bible, and John Locke's *Second treatise of government*', *Hebraic Political Studies*, 3 (2008), pp. 60–93.

it.[34] Here, then, is a dilemma. On the one hand, we see that the God of truth has disclosed little about His requirements for worship; on the other hand, duty and destiny require worship. This dilemma is exquisite, for it is accompanied by the assumption that God regarded only *one* style of worship as acceptable, so that there is *one* way to please Him and so find one's way to Heaven, which is, of course, just as much an objective for worshippers as it is a desire of God's.[35] The problem of ignorance, diversity, and conflict about the authoritative requirements for worship was not to be escaped easily within Christian assumptions. One solution was to postulate an infallible judge, but Locke, not being a Roman Catholic, had rejected that.[36] He approached the question via another way of discussing worship and its implications.

A need to proceed in this way is evident from an example. *Epistola* opens with an extended contrast between true religion, which Locke described as the religion of love, piety, and virtue, on the one hand, and, on the other, the use of coercion, which he represented as a tool of worldly dominion.[37] This contrast provides a rhetorically obvious way of connecting love and worship with toleration (of which more will be said later in respect of a more important connection, namely duty) and contrasting them all with government and force, but it emphasizes a significant point: that intelligent Christians had been known to treat their religion as continuous with political action. For instance, Bossuet described the Edict of Fontainebleau as a '*grand ouvrage de la religion*', and had inferred this opinion from the New Testament.[38] Thinking in terms of Scripture had not established a case about religious liberty unequivocally. *Epistola*, instead, is conducted through the information of natural theology: revelation figures only in ways that reinforced or complemented its content.[39]

Thus *Epistola* opens by saying that the religion of love, piety, and virtue is Christianity; yet this is a Christianity described in a way that does not comprise anything that Locke could not assign also to natural religion. People, he stated, had 'agreed in the duties of natural religion, and we find them … owning that piety and virtue, clean hands and a pure heart, not polluted with

[34] John Locke, *The reasonableness of Christianity, as delivered in the Scriptures*, ed. John Higgins-Biddle (Oxford, 1999)

[35] Compare *Epistola*, pp. 90, 92, 96.

[36] John [Higgins-] Biddle, ed., 'John Locke's essay on infallibility', *Journal of Church and State*, 19 (1977), pp. 301–28.

[37] Locke, *Epistola*, pp. 58–64.

[38] Jacques-Bénigne Bossuet, 'Oraison funèbre de Le Tellier', ed. Franck Lessay, in Zarka et al., eds., *Les fondements*, II, pp. 290–7, at 297 (emphasis original); one text was Ephesians 4.4–6 (see p. 293 n. 1), but Bossuet made liberal use of the New Testament throughout.

[39] See, for an example of Locke searching Scripture for support, MS. Locke c.33, fo. 24v, 'Tolerantia pro' (1688), which lists biblical texts supporting toleration.

the breaches of the law of nature, was the best worship of the gods'; and he added, more precisely, that 'Reason discovered to them that a good life was the most acceptable thing to the Deity.'[40] It is 'a good life' of piety and virtue that Locke used to describe Christianity at the outset of *Epistola*. Further than that he did not need to go.

This limitation of attention has an important effect: it reduces the number of elements involved in thinking about freedom of worship. By doing so, it alters the terms of discussion in a way that facilitates Locke's view of that freedom. It reduces the elements to God, natural duty to worship and love Him, our ability to understand and will, the contents of our duty—and it omits many other potential objects of reference. The contents of duty in this instance are a disposition to love God and actions that are taken to express that attitude. Absent from this list of constituents are the inferences from revelation that generations of Christian theologians and church historians had made, with the result that questions not only about liturgy but also about ecclesiastical order, ecclesiastical historiography, revealed theology, and the Christian character of magistracy, were not amongst the terms Locke used to formulate his position. Even the sacraments appeared only by the way in *Epistola*.[41]

Mark the difference: suppose that in addition to our natural duty, you introduce a duty inferred from revelation, specifically from the First Commandment. Sins forbidden in the First Commandment, according to the larger *Westminster catechism*, include 'heresy'.[42] If this implies that any Christian has a duty to avoid heresy, it suggests also that Christian authorities, whether ecclesiastical or civil, might also have a duty to suppress it: in other words, to act against some ways of thought and worship. This is by no means an exhaustive account of the results of treating questions concerning worship in terms of Scripture: but it is enough to remind us that when, just after the Restoration of Charles II in 1660, Locke had thought in the terms that included those of revealed theology, he had encountered complications. In particular, his position that the magistrate was entitled to impose his will in worship generated a conflict in the conscience of believers who differed from the magistrate's views about it.[43] But Locke, by thinking in terms of natural theology, relieved himself of this embarrassment, for worship, if a natural duty, need not involve the magistrate.

[40] John Locke, 'A third letter for toleration', in *The works of John Locke* (10 vols., London, 1823), VI, p. 156.

[41] Locke, *Epistola*, pp. 78, 106, 110, cf. 120 (refers obliquely to Holy Communion) and 106 (refers to Baptism).

[42] *The Westminster larger catechism* (1648), q.105, in Thomas F. Torrance, ed., *The school of faith. The catechisms of the reformed Church* (London, 1959), p. 208.

[43] Harris, *Mind*, ch. 2.

Natural duty and natural theology, then, were postulates of the position about freedom of worship that Locke reached, because they not only contributed content to it, but also provided an alternative to the way of thinking that had introduced difficulties. That Locke thought it important to obviate those difficulties is evident from what he 'premisd' in 1667, namely that the business of government lay solely with the relations amongst people, and did not touch 'Divine worship' at all.[44]

The position that Locke had reached by 1667 via natural theology was summarized neatly in his later 'Defence of nonconformity':

> The light of nature discovering to man that he is under the Gove[rn]m[e]nt & disposal of an invisible & supreme being, teaches him also that … Religion being … those opinions, & actions alone which I entertaine, & performe, onely to please God, & such as have no concernement at all with my neighbour or y[e] interest, or affaires of this world, though many of these are outward & visible to others: are not within the civill Magistrates inspection & care,

but how adequate was that position?[45] Locke postulated a natural liberty to worship according to one's own judgement about which manner of worship to adopt, 'my liberty … as a man', [46] which makes perfect sense as a natural law doctrine: for Locke reckoned that God had not only given man the understanding and will to obey natural law, but also 'has allowed him a … liberty of Acting, … within the bounds of that Law he is under'.[47] That is not all He gave. We know from natural law thinking that every human being, at least everyone constituted without defect, has faculties adequate to understanding and obeying natural law. But 'liberty as … a man' in worship implies more. It implies an equality of faculties by nature, because that in its turn implies no one has a jurisdiction by natural endowment to direct others, and therefore implies an equality of status. This is what Locke articulated in writing of a '*State* … of *Equality*, wherein all the Power and Jurisdiction is reciprocal, no one having more than another: there being nothing more evident, than that Creatures of the same species and rank … born to all the same advantages of Nature, and the use of the same faculties, should also be equal one amongst

[44] 'This being premisd that the magistrate ought to doe or medle with noething but barely in order to secureing the civill peace & proprietys of his subjects': Locke, 'An essay concerning toleration', in Milton and Milton, eds., *An essay*, p. 270–1.

[45] MS. Locke c.34, pp. 75–6.

[46] See MS. Locke c.34, p. 74: 'my liberty as a christian & as a man to choose of what church or religious societie I will be of as most conduceing to the salvation of my soule of w[ch] I alone am judg & over w[ch] the magistrate hath noe power at all'. For the character of this document, see Timothy Stanton, 'The name and nature of Locke's "Defence of nonconformity"', *Locke Studies*, 6 (2006), pp. 143–72.

[47] Locke, *Two treatises*, II.vi.58, p. 324.

another without Subordination or Subjection'.[48] Such an equality by nature does not imply equal attainments in all people, or tell us precisely the limits that 'the same faculties' could reach, but Locke did suppose that God had 'put within the reach of their Discovery the comfortable Provision for this Life and the Way that leads to a better'.[49] Locke implied that people possessed *cura suae aeternae salutis*.[50] That point reminds us that to this combination of understanding, freedom of will, equality, and duty, we need to add the destiny of eternal happiness implied in the immortality of souls in order to see that worship is a duty that is free in that it answers to an end that is not secular, that is to say, to a destiny that terminates beyond terrestrial life. But worship takes place in this world. Our combination does not demonstrate a duty on the part of others, whether civil magistrate or churchman, to permit worship in a manner other than their own within the locus of their jurisdictions. The restriction of liberty which this absence of demonstration might facilitate was important to worshippers. For the liberty to worship according to one's judgement is the liberty by which worshippers hope to depart from this world and return to God. The importance of natural liberty is emphasized again by Locke's coupling to it 'my liberty as a christian'; that is to say, the liberty from the Jewish ceremonial law enjoyed by Christians, so much emphasized by St Paul in Galatians 5.[51] To Christians, Hebrew regulations would be a needless obstacle on their way to Heaven, for they could scarcely think them necessary for their eternal welfare, and could not subscribe to them: and so with any other unacceptable restrictions. So there was a need to show that there really was a liberty, unaffected by the claims of civil or ecclesiastical jurisdiction, to pursue a chosen route towards Heaven.

Natural law and natural liberty are not sufficient to establish this by themselves. Their proponents included Suarez, Hooker, and Hobbes. None of these thought natural law inconsistent with the control of worship by a single authority, whether, according to their different prepossessions, ecclesiastical

[48] Ibid., II.ii.4, pp .4 and 287. This state of equality is, of course, 'the State all Men are naturally in'; for its relation to civil society, see below, s. III, esp. pp. 73–8.

[49] Locke, *An essay*, I.i.5, p. 45.

[50] Locke's claim that 'non ab hominibus magisratui potest ejusmodi tribui potestas, quia nemo potest ita salutis suae aeternae curam abjicere' (*Epistola*, p. 66) implies that *homo* possesses 'cura salutis suae aeternae' in the first place. At p. 124, with reference to the formation of the commonwealth, Locke was more precise: 'relicta … uniquique salutis suae aeternae cura'. The notion of an 'egalitarian background' to Locke's account supposed by Vernon, 'Introduction', in idem, ed., *Locke on toleration*, p. xxviii, is therefore inadequate, and though his 'basic importance'(p. xxix) is better, it fails to reach the point that natural equality is one amongst a connected range of features.

[51] Especially v.1. Compare Locke, *Epistola*, p. 108 (cf. 154) for evangelical liberty. For 'my liberty as a christian', see MS. Locke c.34, p. 74.

or civil or both.[52] Locke, then, if he was to sustain worship as free in relation to institutions needed to show something about the character of jurisdiction and those bodies that had it.

If, in particular, Locke had 'premisd' that the jurisdiction of government did not comprise 'Divine worship', this is not the same as saying that he had been able to validate his claim in 1667. He showed no signs of doing so then: he had 'premisd' about the scope of government without proof, claiming only to 'cleare the way'.[53] Neither had he identified the scope of ecclesiastical jurisdiction. In short, if Locke himself had reached a position, he had not obviously provided a thoroughly laid route to it. He had much to demonstrate, and his way of demonstrating had implications for his arguments in *Epistola*.

III

Locke needed to make good the claims he had 'premisd' in 1667. One way to do so was to explore the implications of natural law thinking, especially the inferences that could be drawn from it for two institutions, namely *ecclesia* and *respublica*. It was necessary to pursue this way. These institutions, plainly, are relevant to worship, the one performing it and the other regulating the conduct of people who also worship. To understand worship as natural duty and to complement it with natural liberty, as Locke did, gives a clear view of the end of *ecclesia*, but does not show otherwise how worship relates to *respublica*, and this silence is noticeable enough: for the juxtaposition of worship and institutions brings jurisdiction into view. On the character of the relation in view turns the answer to the question of freedom of worship in a commonwealth. This relation, as Locke developed it, continued natural freedom of worship.

This outcome is connected with his teleological thinking, and that in two ways. Firstly, Locke understood these institutions as aspects of an end-directed scheme implied in natural law and in goals coordinated with it, and in these terms he explained civil jurisdiction in a way that put worship in important respects beyond its bounds. Thus we shall see that Locke's account of the civil society or commonwealth, *respublica*, in *Two treatises* was fundamental in

[52] Francisco Suarez, *Tractatus de legibus, ac Deo legislatore* (London, 1679), III.vi, pp. 123–7 [recte 5]; Richard Hooker, *The laws of ecclesiastical polity*, VIII.iv–viii, in his *Works*, ed. John Keble, rev. R. W. Church, and F. Paget (3 vols., Oxford, 1888), III, pp. 368–444; Thomas Hobbes, *Leviathan, or the matter, forme, & power of a common-wealth ecclesiasticall and civil* (London, 1651), II.xxxi, III.xxxix, xlii, pp. 192, 248, 299.

[53] Locke, 'An essay', pp. 270, 269.

delineating the origin and scope of civil jurisdiction, and therefore its relation to worship; and we shall see also that this was not all. For, secondly, a result of natural law and jurisdiction considered in Lockean terms is freedom of worship, or, to state the matter more broadly, the freedom of *ecclesia* and commonwealth from each other, indeed of one *ecclesia* from another and one state from another.

Natural law makes mankind all members of one community, community implying their being under one law. Locke observed that '*Mankind are one Community*' by 'the *Law of Nature*',[54] and he was not alone in defining community in connection with law.[55] We have seen that the laws of this natural community include the love and worship of God, and all readers of Locke know of a natural duty to preserve others—and should know of one to preserve oneself. An obvious question arises: how best to produce the ends in view—to worship God and to secure terrestrial survival? The answer is that the rational means include institutions such as, for instance, religious society and civil society. The latter institution is a means to an end, as Locke claimed 'the greatest meanes of y[e] preservation of mankind in this world',[56] but a religious society is integral to the very act of worship. For worship in public is necessary, as we have seen, because worshippers are required to bear witness to God, and witness implies more than one human being. Religious society, then, is an implicit requirement of natural law, whereas a commonwealth is an instrument of natural law: but both answer to the ends of that law.

If there are such subdivisions within the great community of mankind, two interconnected questions arise concerning their character and relations. Locke had written about association in his lectures on natural law in a very general way, using the term *conjunctio*, which means nothing more precise than 'combination' or even 'joint occurrence'.[57] In *Epistola* he chose terms that have a more distinctive bearing. He understood both religious and civil society in terms of *res* and *societas*, that is to say, in purposive terms. *Res* denotes something that can be conceived as a separate entity.[58] Locke understood such *res* to be purposive, so, for instance, *vera religio* was *res . . . ad vitam recte pieque instituendam natae*, naturally suited to forming a life rightly

[54] Locke, *Two treatises*, II.ix.128, p. 370 (orthography original). Compare *Epistola*, p. 78.

[55] Compare Ian Harris, 'La communauté chez Hobbes et Kant', in Luc Foisneau and Denis Thouard, eds., *Kant et Hobbes: De la violence à la politique* (Paris, 2005), pp. 143–62.

[56] MS. Locke c.34, p. 76.

[57] For the latter, Cicero, *De oratore*, II.xlix.200: 'et populi ... cuius ius etiam cum seditionis coniunctione defenderam', with the note in A. S. Wilkins' edition (3 vols., Oxford, 1879–92), II, p. 296.

[58] e.g. Lucretius, *De rerum natura*, V.1087–1090: 'ergo si varii sensus animalia cogunt, / muta tamen cum sint, varias emittere voces, / quanto mortalis magis aequumst tum potuisse / dissimilis alia atque alia res voce notare'.

and piously.[59] *Societas* suited the same pattern of thought, for it is a condition of being associated for a common purpose,[60] and by metonymy a body of people associated for such a purpose.[61] Locke defined both *respublica* (civil society or commonwealth) and *ecclesia* (religious society) as *societates*. So our first question about them concerns their respective purposes.

This is a decisive question, because the answer identifies the end and therefore the character proper to each. The ends in view for each of these *societates* are prescribed by natural law, since they are its vehicles.[62] The term *res* implies that we can at least conceive *res civitatis et religionis* as distinct.[63] Locke defined *ecclesia* in terms of a *societas* of people combining in order that they may worship God publicly in the way they believe will be acceptable to the Spirit for the welfare of their souls.[64] *Respublica* was *societas* of people constituted for the end of conserving and promoting civil goods.[65] Locke framed both definitions, then, in terms of an end, and each *societas* concerned an end wholly different in content from the other. For salvation and civil goods obviously and markedly differ markedly in content.

Why did Locke think himself entitled to define in these ways? The question is significant, for there is a notable omission from one of his definitions. *Ecclesia* is defined, but in a way that comprises neither *ecclesia verae religionis* nor *ecclesia Christiana*, and the difference is readily apparent because these had appeared a few pages earlier in *Epistola*.[66] *Ecclesia* is defined without reference to truth generally or Christianity particularly, but instead refers to the opinion about salvation held by its members.[67]

[59] Locke, *Epistola*, p. 58.

[60] e.g. Cicero, *De lege agraria*, II.5.11: 'arbitrabar … esse aliquam oportere inter nos rei publicae bene administrandae societatem'.

[61] e.g. Tacitus, *Annales*, XIII.50.3: 'plerasque vectigalium societates a consulibus et tribunis plebei constitutas'.

[62] This account of *societas* is very different from that in Michael Oakeshott, *On human conduct* (Oxford, 1975), pp. 199–203, 206–13. Oakeshott's account, though mentioning natural law once (p. 202), is not sensitive to its consequences.

[63] Compare Tacitus, *Agricola*, III.i: 'res olim dissociabiles miscuerit, principatum ac libertatem'. For *res civitatis et religionis*, *Epistola*, p. 64.

[64] Locke, *Epistola*, p. 70: 'societas … hominum …coeuntium, ut Deum publice colant eo modo quem credunt numini acceptum fore ad salutem animarum'.

[65] Ibid., p. 64: 'Respublica mihi videtur societas …ad bona civilia conservanda promovendaque constituta.'

[66] Ibid., p. 62.

[67] For which reason the term *ecclesia* is here either left in Latin or rendered as 'religious society', rather than being translated as 'church'. Often a Christian church is the object of discussion: sometimes it is specified as such (e.g. Locke, *Epistola*, pp. 62, 74, 144) or implied by the setting (e.g. pp. 82, 86, 94), but other references are unspecific (e.g. pp. 120, 140). The word *ecclesia* is used with reference to non-Christian worship (at p. 134, where the example given for *ecclesia* is of *Mahumedanus religione*, and at p.116 *ecclesia* must be Jewish, cf. p. 118, referring to *religio Mosaica et veri Dei cultus* in Israel). Some examples of worship are far from Christian, as at pp.

This choice of definition is very noticeable. Anyone in Locke's time could see that the natural duty to worship had been worked out according to specifically Christian thinking in various ways through different intellectual developments, and in response to different practical needs, so that it had come to be connected with a range of institutional characteristics. There was also a wide range of non-Christian theistic opinions, whether in Europe or in the wider world. That there were many religions and versions of religions could not be ignored. But if that fact informed Locke's thinking, it did not determine his definition.

His definition is an inference from natural law. Natural law implies the abilities to understand it and to will it, as Locke recognized. We can infer that these abilities reach recognition of means to the ends of natural law and voluntary adherence to those means; otherwise the requirements of the law would be beyond those directed by it. In fact, Locke's definition of *ecclesia* states that people combine *sua sponte* to worship, as they suppose for their salvation: an exercise of will is implied in the definition, and declared in the ensuing paragraph where *ecclesia* is termed *societas … voluntaria*.[68] This difference of end that marks religious and civil societies, however, contrasts with a similarity of origin in respect of membership. For if we have seen the teleological function in their definitions, we now need to add something about membership in terms of efficient causation.[69] Just as the cause that begins membership of the commonwealth is, of course, the consent of people—that is to say, consent first to incorporate into one society under one government—in order to secure terrestrial ends, including the better performance of natural duties, what begins membership of *ecclesia* is joining a *societas* to satisfy one's end of performing a natural duty in the particular way one supposes beneficial to one's soul. *Ecclesia*, like *respublica*, is, in an important sense, an organization that is voluntary: will is exercised according to understanding in joining it. Hence, in those terms, Locke's definition of *ecclesia*, as *societas* of people in which they combine by their initiative according to what they suppose promotes the end of their salvation, is transparent.

If *respublica* and *ecclesia* are different in respect of function and end, despite their sharing the same sort of origin in that their members became

108, 110, on sacrificing a calf *in cultu divino*, whilst *religio* is applied more widely than Christianity, as at p. 112, which refers implicitly to the religion of the Indies (cf. p. 114 in the same way for pagan and Islamic religions), and p. 148, where *Turci et Christiani* are said to be *diversae … religionis*. God Himself is acknowledged as the legislator in the Jewish commonwealth (p. 116). Popple, Gough, and Silverthorne render *ecclesia* as 'church' throughout. Locke used the phrase *societas ecclesiastica* at p.100, where he also stated that *has societates religiosas ecclesias voco*.

[68] Locke, *Epistola*, p. 70.

[69] For the importance of efficient causality in understanding *Two treatises*, see Harris, 'Legacy', esp. ss. 1–2, 4.

such because they required means to the ends prescribed by natural law and co-ordinated with them, then in natural law thinking they have different jurisdictions. Central to this thinking is the right to legislate for and superintend those within one's domain.[70] Such thinking maps into a conception of government that treats the latter as a giver, executor, and judge of laws. To treat government in terms of jurisdiction is also to treat it in terms of the ends to which laws, whether natural or civil, answer. The same applies to any other institution with legislative authority: it has a jurisdiction, and its laws are such that they conform to its purpose and promote its ends. *Ecclesia* has jurisdiction within its own domain, so a question arises about the relation of ecclesiastical jurisdiction to civil jurisdiction. The answer depends on the character one attributes to the commonwealth.

The natural duty of worship required a specific kind of commonwealth if it was to be exercised freely. That much Locke adumbrated in 1667. He supplied further arguments that established what he had 'premisd' then.[71] Did Locke establish that the function and end purpose of government imply jurisdiction over religious society, or the opposite? His definition of commonwealth attributes to it an end which is so different from that of *ecclesia* that it implies no overlap of jurisdiction in respect of that end. For if human faculties are sufficient for religious membership to be voluntary in the sense of proceeding from the faculties of one's own soul, there is also a question about whether people have a freedom of action about worship which makes such membership voluntary in a further sense: as liberty of external action in respect of worship. To put the matter another way, definition is one thing and demonstration is another. Locke's demonstration is in *Two treatises of government*.

Two treatises specified two natural duties which established the character of government as an institution of strictly *civil* scope. The duties under natural

[70] Locke coupled *jus* and *imperium*: *Epistola*, p. 66.

[71] Compare my earlier treatments of this point in *Mind*, p. 191, 'Tolérance', pp. 199–208, and 'Legacy', s. 5. The point, in its earlier forms, has been adopted by others: Selina Chen, 'Locke's political arguments for toleration', *History of Political Thought*, 19 (1998), pp. 167–85, esp. at pp. 170–2, 176–8; Mark Michael, 'Locke, religious toleration, and the limits of social contract theory', *History of Philosophy Quarterly*, 20 (2003), pp. 21–40, at p. 21; Timothy Stanton, 'Locke and the politics and theology of toleration', *Political Studies*, 54 (2006), pp. 84–102, at pp. 90–2; Vernon, 'Introduction', pp. xxvii–xxix. The view that 'it [is] impossible to understand the argument of …*Letter* [i.e. *Epistola*] without connecting it to the rest of his [Locke's] political thought' is found further afield: Martha C. Nussbaum, 'Radical evil in liberal democracies: the neglect of the political emotions', in Thomas Banchoff, ed., *Democracy and the new religious pluralism* (Oxford, 2007), pp. 171–202, at p. 173. The phrase 'the rest of his political thought' covers at once too much and too little: on the one hand, it is hard to see that the argument of *Epistola* cannot be understood without e.g. Locke's views about private property in land, whilst on the other hand, his opinions about such matters as natural law, natural theology more widely, and philosophy require attention.

law to preserve oneself and to preserve others generate rights to punish and restrain those who endanger oneself and others, and people make a commonwealth the better to achieve the end of living in accordance with their duties under natural law, and so to secure their interests. There arise from natural law rights to act coercively, and these concern the relations of one human to another.[72] It follows that a government authorized in terms of these latter rights to act coercively has jurisdiction over such actions, but not over matters beyond their scope.

This may sound a strange conclusion, for apparently obvious reasons, as that worship, like other activities, takes place spatially within the commonwealth. Again, Locke defined worship in a way that implied its exponents were groups and that the groups' actions were overt. This *looks* like an activity subject to civil jurisdiction. The deceptiveness of appearance becomes evident only when we consider the role of purpose and end in Locke's natural theology. Locke placed worship beyond civil jurisdiction in that the law that prescribed worship had an end that had no intrinsic connection with the end that governed civil jurisdiction, and *ecclesia* was an institution the purpose of which was to answer to the end entertained by its members. This end, which belonged to a conception of destiny understood as the welfare of the soul, was not within the scope of civil jurisdiction.

In this frame of mind the fundamental question is, what is the purpose God intends for an entity or activity? It makes sense, also, to ask this about human inventions, such as civil government, which exist in order that we may further God's requirements of us. The purpose in view here is the one implied in our natural duty of worship. The purpose of civil government is to coerce those who undermine our natural duties of self-preservation and the preservation of others. These purposes share no content. So, as soon as we consider worship in respect of its purpose and end, the absence of connection between it and civil government becomes clear. One can see that if government is concerned only with civil relations, and worship as such has no relation to these concerns, then the two are unconnected: so, as Locke put it, 'in truth the whole jurisdiction of the magistrate looks only to … civil goods, all civil right and command both achieves its end in the care and promotion of these only and is confined [to them]'.[73] The end implied in the presence of jurisdiction limits the scope of the latter, and the purpose of civil government was to procure the end of civil benefit, not homage to God. Indeed, Locke emphasized

[72] Locke, *Two treatises*, esp. II.ii.ix, pp. 287–96, 368–71.

[73] 'vero ad bona … civilia unice spectat tota magistratus jurisdictio, et in iis solis curandis promovendisque terminatur et circumscribitur omne civilis potestatis jus et imperium': Locke, *Epistola*, p. 66.

as forcibly as the Latin language allowed that this was the only purpose for government, *solummodo*.[74]

This was true in more senses than one. We have seen that the efficient cause of civil government is consent, and emphasis needs to fall now on another point, that this consent is action with an end in view, here the securing of civil benefits. That is to say, the causal origin of government realizes the end implied in that institution. *Two treatises* specified the 'great end of Mens entring into Society' as 'the enjoyment of their Properties in Peace and Safety',[75] and *Epistola* stated that the end was a secure possession of the private goods useful for living.[76] Though these formulations about ends differ in some particulars, they both refer to civil goods only. Hence Locke's *solummodo*.

Ecclesia and *respublica* differ not only in their respective ends but also in the means proper to those ends. The function of civil government is to provide protection for the members of the commonwealth, produce civil laws, and to punish those who invade the rights accompanying natural law. To achieve this end implies that it by some way acquires the right to coerce and the ability to apply force. It gains these because people gave up to its use their right to do whatever promotes self-preservation and the preservation of others, and so engages their 'natural force' to punish offenders.[77] The result is that this force belongs entirely to civil government within the commonwealth, as Locke indicated in *Epistola*,[78] so that *magistratus proprium est edictis jubere, gladio cogere*, the distinctive attribute of the magistrate is to command by edict and to constrain by the sword.[79] This function and its equipment, like the end for which the commonwealth exists, contain nothing that refers to worship. So there is nothing in the commonwealth's remit that bears upon free worship. Locke concentrated the expectations about coercion to which natural law obviously gives rise into a particular place and directed them towards a particular end.

Thus far, *Epistola* relies principally upon arguments from *Two treatises* in order to develop natural law thinking in a way that made the proper scope of worship free of civil jurisdiction. Civil government was an institution with a secular end, not one of worship.[80] That is to say, there are requirements that

[74] Ibid., p. 64.

[75] Locke, *Two treatises*, II.xi.134, p. 373.

[76] 'ad vitam utilium sua cuique privata et secura sit possessio': *Epistola*, p. 124.

[77] Locke, *Two treatises*, II.ix.128–30, pp. 370–1, at p. 371.

[78] Locke, *Epistola*, p. 76. Locke added that no private person has the right of coercion (p. 78).

[79] Ibid., p. 68. *Proprium* might be rendered equally well as special feature or exclusive property.

[80] Thomas Fowler, *Locke* (London, 1883), p. 162, picked out as the 'main thesis' of *Epistola* and its successors the point that 'the jurisdiction of the civil magistrate does not extend to the regulation of religious worship'. This salutary emphasis upon jurisdiction is explored here, though in considering a book that develops interconnected arguments it may not be profitable to

God laid on mankind which implied ends that terminated in the present life. It was in sustaining the achievement of *these* ends that civil government had its purpose, and it was for these ends that it came into existence.

We can see how closely *Epistola* depends on claims in *Two treatises* if we look once more at natural liberty to worship. One might imagine that this freedom would be given up when people entered a commonwealth, in the same way as the rights to enforce natural law. But there is a difference. Since the end of civil society is the promotion of secular ends, so secular means are required for achieving this, specifically the protection that comes from government. People give up the use of relevant rights to the extent that this act provides for protection. There is no sign that this allocation includes their natural liberty to worship. That lies beyond the scope of the end in view and comprises nothing of use in achieving it. Civil government is constituted in a way that does not promote the welfare of the soul, since combination and force do not assist the latter. Locke added that a commonwealth, conversely, is not affected by the fate of someone's soul. Thus in *Epistola*, when he outlined the formation of the commonwealth, he made it clear that *relicta … unicuique salutis suae aeternae cura*, the care of the eternal welfare of the soul is left to each one).[81] On the one hand, the commonwealth is constituted only for the sake of matters specific to the present life, so it follows that *ex altera parte privatis restat in rebus ad futuram vitam spectantibus libertas*; on the other hand, people retain a liberty in those things that are concerned with future life.[82] In short, the account of a commonwealth in *Two treatises* leaves to people in the civil state their natural liberty to worship in the manner they judge best for themselves.

But suppose someone asked, why cannot the jurisdiction of civil government be *extended* to include worship?[83] This was a question Locke could not overlook. For his own suppositions about the origin of government implied that its end lay with civil benefit, so that if this end were taken to comprise worship then some such extension would be necessary, and since worship was a duty in natural law, it might seem to be the government's business to require

single out a main thesis, still less to address it alone. For an emphasis on free worship without that claim, see John Dunn, 'The claim to freedom of conscience: freedom of speech, freedom of thought, freedom of worship' (1991), in idem, *The history of political theory and other essays* (Cambridge, 1996), ch. 6, pp. 100–20, at pp. 102–3.

[81] Locke, *Epistola*, p. 124.

[82] Ibid., p. 126. The use of *privatus* for a human being in this passage is in contrast with the jurisdiction of the *magistratus*, i.e. *potestas reipublicae*, mentioned earlier on page 126. For the significance of these terms, see pp. 89–91 below.

[83] J. F. Stephen, 'Locke on toleration', *Horae sabbaticae*, 2nd series (London, 1892), pp. 157–73, at p. 161, implies that jurisdiction was Locke's subject at this point in *Epistola*. Other commentators mistakenly think this part of *Epistola* is an account of why the state should tolerate, see n. 183 below.

that it be performed. Locke had to explain why such an extension was impossible. In *Epistola* he addressed at once why civil jurisdiction was not, nor could be cast in terms of, the end of worship, and its lack of purposive connection with the means available to civil government. He argued that there was no factual evidence for such a jurisdiction; that the means at the disposal of civil government were not appropriate for the end in view, namely a worship giving outward expression to the inward disposition of the soul; and, even if such means did somehow produce it, they did nothing to promote the soul's welfare. These claims imply important points about jurisdiction, and therefore we should follow Locke's sequence of arguments in a little more detail.

For Locke had to go beyond the claims of *Two treatises*, but the conclusions of that book were assumptions of his argumentation. Locke developed his general proposition that civil government and *ecclesia*, serving different ends, have incompatible means in ways which bear the impress of his arguments in *Two treatises*. First, he argued that a 'care of souls is not committed' to government by either God or man.[84] This claim requires a story that is comprehensive but inconsistent with government receiving that *cura*. *Two treatises*, by telling how government came to be established in terms that do not include it, provides just such a story. Locke's second argument required that as a matter of fact the powers of the civil magistrate consisted entirely in coercion. *Two treatises* showed that; in *Epistola* Locke added that it was not coercion, but evidence that determined belief.

These were leading claims in his first two arguments about the scope of governmental authority, but Locke had to follow them up in order to reach his further destination. If neither God nor people *had* given civil government any jurisdiction over worship, there remained the possibility that the latter *might* do so because they could do so. Locke excluded this possibility, indicating that human beings did not have the means to do this, by stating three connected claims: that truth was required for salvation, that a soul had to be persuaded of truth for its belief to count towards its salvation, and that no one can believe at another's dictation—and so no one can leave *cura animae* to another.[85] Mankind, in short, did not have the means to surrender that *cura* to the magistrate (or anyone else), because God's requirements and the way He had constituted the soul made this impossible.

This set of arguments had the effect of establishing freedom of worship rather than toleration of worship. First, the concept of toleration implies that its object is something that is considered evil: but no one can rationally conceive worship as such in that way on Locke's showing, for it is a duty under

[84] Locke, *Epistola*, p. 66.
[85] Ibid., pp. 70, 68, 66.

natural law.[86] If worship is not an object of toleration from anyone, properly speaking, neither is its end within the scope of civil jurisdiction. The latter, as we have seen, has for its end secular benefits and has for its means coercion. Neither civil jurisdiction nor coercion is applicable to the end of worship, so that we cannot speak properly of government tolerating worship insofar as the latter is understood in respect of its end. That is simply beyond civil jurisdiction, so that there is no civil superior to which this religious goal is subject. The absence of such a superior means that in this respect in relation to government worship is free.

So far, then, *Epistola* has established not toleration, but worship free of civil jurisdiction. Locke's order in stating his definitions and developing their consequences recognized this. His definition of *ecclesia* appeared only after the jurisdiction of *respublica* had been delimited. *Ecclesia*, therefore, could be defined there as *libera*, that is, without a terrestrial superior,[87] because it is not subject to civil jurisdiction in respect of its purpose and end.

What of the jurisdiction of a religious society? If this society was *libera* in relation to other institutions, it had to be self-subsistent in relation to them, and that implied jurisdiction over its own activities. This was juridically permissible, in that religious society was defined as free of civil jurisdiction, but that state of being does not establish either that it had its own jurisdiction or the scope of the latter. Jurisdiction was necessary because natural law thinking supposed that law was constitutive of *societas*. Jurisdiction supposes an origin. People combined *sua sponte* in order to worship God, so that *ecclesia* was, in the absence of a civil superior, *societas libera et voluntaria*.[88] That it was willed by its members implied acceptance by them of what was necessary to *ecclesia*, and so there arose jurisdiction over them.

This voluntary origin of jurisdiction, conversely, restricted the jurisdiction of a religious society to its own members. This implied that no *ecclesia* has jurisdiction over another *ecclesia* and that no *ecclesia* has jurisdiction over *respublica* or in it.[89] Each *respublica* and each *ecclesia* had jurisdiction over their own members only; that is to say, over them in relation to the ends for which people joined these *societates*. From this follows the freedom of each body from the jurisdiction of the other. For instance, there were prohibitions on ecclesiastical action in strictly civil matters on religious grounds, such as that *ecclesia* had no business to interfere with civil rights on account of

[86] The notion that toleration is of evil is an old one, e.g. Quintilian, *Institutio*, V.x.33, 'malorum evitationem, liberationem, imminutionem, tolerantiam'.

[87] Locke, *Epistola*, p. 70.

[88] Locke, *Epistola*, p. 70.

[89] Ibid., p. 142, cf. pp. 86 and 148. For Locke's rejection of ecclesiastical rule over civil society, see ibid., p. 132.

worship, and neither could any officer of *ecclesia*,[90] or any private member of it:[91] in short, *ecclesiae* had no jurisdiction in *res terrestres*.[92] Neither could ecclesiastical authority be extended over civil affairs, because the boundaries of the two had been distinguished, Locke thought.[93]

Just as no *ecclesia* had jurisdiction over another, or over a commonwealth, because each was constituted independently of the other, so no *respublica* had jurisdiction over another commonwealth. People joined both sorts of *societas* the better to achieve their ends. It is worth emphasizing that they acted for themselves only, and this was how a commonwealth came into existence.[94] This implied that one commonwealth is separate from another, and has no jurisdiction over any other: they are all alike independent. Hence Locke by '*Common-wealth*' meant '*any Independent Community*', and this was to be distinguished from a usage of community which admitted 'Subordinate Communities'.[95] In short, just as *ecclesia* and commonwealth had no jurisdiction over one another, so one *ecclesia* had no jurisdiction over any other, and one commonwealth no jurisdiction over any other. Those who claimed otherwise had practical beliefs that were inconsistent with the commonwealth, as we shall see.

What, then, of toleration?

IV

So far we have discussed free worship and its relation to civil and ecclesiastical jurisdiction. Toleration is a different idea, and it is best to pause a moment in order to examine it. *Tolerantia* is how Latin renders two words of the Greek New Testament, ὑπομονή and μακροθυμία.[96] Both denote endurance of an evil, that is to say the persistent courage or patience which is directed to producing an end. In particular, the former denotes perseverance,[97] the latter the quality of long-suffering and therefore self-restraint,[98] productive of forbearance, ἀνοχή.[99] So to a Christian mind, *tolerantia* involves endurance of an

[90] Ibid., pp. 84 and 86.

[91] Ibid., p. 78. Compare p. 84 for a blanket denial of any right for people, churches, and commonwealths to interfere in civil matters on religious grounds.

[92] Ibid., p. 82.

[93] Ibid., p. 84.

[94] For the setting of his view, Harris, *Mind*, pp. 232–40, esp. pp. 239–40.

[95] Locke, *Two treatises*, II.x.133, p. 373.

[96] For instance the Vulgate renders ὑπομονή of II Corinthians 1.6 as *tolerantia*. Colossians 1.11 uses *patientia* for it, and renders μακροθυμία as *longanimitas*.

[97] e.g. Luke 8.15.

[98] e.g. Colossians 1.11.

[99] Romans 2.4; 3.26.

evil, whether in respect of suffering from it or in restraining oneself from exercising one's wrath against it; endurance that is purposeful and has a goal. An obvious question about toleration, then, is, what end does this endurance promote? The soteriological end is life eternal, as in Romans 2. The same passage suggests that an absence of ὑπομονή towards other people will produce affliction and anguish.[100] What of natural theology?

These terms, and their reference to an implied end, remind us that religious liberty is not, so to speak, free-standing. It is a portion of a scheme of thought, and figures in the terms of the latter.[101] This is true of Locke for reasons that we have explored. Central to these are natural law, and the institutional inferences Locke drew from it. The former establishes and the latter preserve freedom of worship, amongst other freedoms. The same scheme, as we shall see, requires a duty of toleration, but conversely, and perhaps surprisingly, we will find that *in*tolerance is required by the same scheme. Locke's natural theology generates both toleration and intolerance. For natural law, as we have seen, prescribes ends, and this raises questions about what promotes an end and what is evil in relation to that end. Evil raises the question of toleration: we need to decide whether we are to tolerate it, or be intolerant of it. It would be odd if Locke were tolerant of all things, ready to endure all evils, unless he wished to promote all ends. In fact, it is hard to think that anyone would wish to do that. Locke has figured as the promoter of the ends of natural law, which law, according to his mind, implied free worship. We shall see, next, how natural law made him also a proponent of both toleration and intolerance.

Intolerance, strange though it may sound to contemporary ears, may be a duty. There may be sins that should not be endured, and false religion had seemed to some to be one of these. Whilst Locke did not suppose that, he did write in a way that relieved others from a duty of intolerance in relation to the worship of other religious societies. This was a consequence of his account of jurisdiction.

Jurisdiction is the right to make, judge, and enforce laws. Locke's account of civil jurisdiction placed the purpose and end of worship beyond its scope; his account of ecclesiastical jurisdiction put all civil affairs and all questions of worship outside the *ecclesia* to which it pertained beyond its scope. Since no civil authority has jurisdiction over a religious society's purpose and end, and no other *ecclesia* has any jurisdiction over another, it follows that no jurisdiction implies a duty to be intolerant of its worship.

In fact the opposite was true. The natural duty of worship, as Locke had situated it, implied a duty of mutual toleration amongst religious societies.

[100] Romans 2.7–10.
[101] Compare Harris, '"And the least sceptical"'.

Why should one group of worshippers thus bear another's choices in worship? We have seen already that ecclesiastical jurisdiction bears only on the members of a given society and not on any other *ecclesia*, but this establishes only that one religious society has no jurisdiction over another, and so burkes a duty of intolerance. This generates no right for *ecclesia* A to be tolerated by *ecclesia* B, and does not do so because B has no jurisdiction over A. Toleration, then, had to be found amongst religious societies as a duty.

Tolerantia is a product of love. For St Paul, ἡ ἀγάπη μακροθυμεῖ. Though Locke did not quote I Corinthians 13, that chapter plainly warrants his characterization of Christianity as a religion that works through love, not force.[102] He did quote another Pauline text, Galatians 5, where faith operating through love of God is a constituent of righteousness, a text that is a few lines from the verse where the fruit of the Spirit includes not only love but also, following from it, μακροθυμία.[103] Thus Christianity is a religion of love and love produces *tolerantia* as self-restraint. So Locke's claim that *tolerantia* is a criterion of a true church, otherwise so puzzling, becomes transparent: *tolerantia* is a requirement of love. [104] Other matters, however, remain unclear. St Paul suggests that love of God produces tolerance, but this does not specify how the former functions. The answer is that the duty to love others was specified in the Bible as the complement of the duty to love God, whence it obtained wider currency and, eventually, this duty to love others acquired the special name of the golden rule. Yet it may seem that the Christian character of *tolerantia* raises a problem for Locke: it might suggest a dependence on revelation alone, which might imply the inadequacy of natural theology to his subject matter, and so raise questions about his conclusions in *Epistola*. It did not: for though love is certainly emphasized in the New Testament, it was also to Locke's mind a requirement of natural law.

Our duty of worship is one manner of exercising our love of God, a love that is both a sentiment and a natural duty. One's sentiments towards one's fellow humans may vary, but natural law required people not only to love God but also to love their fellows. This duty of love towards other people appeared in *Two treatises* as a natural duty, and there Locke used it to generate from a duty of self-preservation a duty to preserve all.[105] This was to put the duty of love towards other people in a positive way. It could be put

[102] I Corinthians 13.4; *Epistola*, p. 58.

[103] Galatians 5.6 and 22. Compare I Thessalonians 5.14 and especially Ephesians 4.2, and contrast Proverbs 14.17. For this reading of Gal. 5.22, J. B. Lightfoot, *St. Paul's epistle to the Galatians* (London, 1890), p. 212. Verse 22 is next to verses that Locke cited at *Epistola*, p. 62, namely vv.19–21.

[104] Locke, *Epistola*, p. 58.

[105] Locke, *Essays*, no.7, p. 194; Locke, *Two treatises*, II.ii.5, p. 288 (using Hooker, *The laws*). For the generation of the duty to preserve others, see Harris, 'Locke on justice', s. 2.

negatively also: to do nothing to another that one would not have done to oneself.[106] Both versions generate Lockean duties of toleration.

The negative version fits the situation of worshippers, for each *ecclesia* has its conception of how to fill out the natural duty of worship, a belief that this is the proper way to glorify God, and a corresponding need to be unhindered in worshipping Him in that way. That need was secure in relation to jurisdiction, whether civil or ecclesiastical, which made worship free. Such natural liberty, however, is not the same as the duty that would make it free of hindrance from other sorts of worshipper. Rather, a negative statement of the golden rule—that is to say, the duty not to do to others what one would not wish to have done to oneself —generates amongst worshippers precisely the duty required for an unhindered exercise of one's own ways of worship. For all worshippers, without exception, wish to glorify God as they think proper, and so there is implied a wish for an absence of obstruction to that end. Hence a duty to do nothing to another that one would not do to oneself generates a duty to leave others unhindered in their liberty of worship—a duty to take care that they in no way injure those from whom they have suffered no injury.[107] This duty is reciprocal, precisely because the desire is common to worshippers, and so it makes sense of the phrase *mutua tolerantia inter Christianos* and—as we shall see—amongst other worshippers too.[108]

The positive version of the golden rule is also implied in *Epistola*. Natural duties which are also Christian duties should be promulgated from the pulpit. Hence there was a positive duty to promote toleration by religious societies, for instance the clergy were supposed to preach it.[109] Love, being a criterion of a true church, implies an institutional duty to propagate (as well as follow) the golden rule, and the golden rule implies toleration amongst religious societies. We can add that it becomes clear why Locke had begun by saying that toleration fitted obviously with both reason and the Gospel, for he found the golden rule in both,[110] and why he should exhort Christians to *charitas*, for charity means love.[111]

We may conclude that Gibbon was right when he wrote that 'when we listen to the voice … of Locke, and of genuine reason, in favour of religious

[106] The positive version has a stronger biblical warrant—Deuteronomy 6.5; Leviticus 19.18; Matthew 7.12 and 22, 37–9; Mark 12.30–1; Luke 6.31 and 10.27—but for the negative version, cf. Luke 6.37.

[107] Locke, *Epistola*, pp. 86, 88: 'cavere maxime ne illos quoquo modo laedant a quibus nulla in re fuerint laesi'. Locke adduced at the same time the Christian duty of Matthew 18.22.

[108] Locke, *Epistola*, p. 58.

[109] Ibid., p. 86.

[110] Ibid., p. 64.

[111] Ibid., pp. 78, 86, cf. p. 58. That charity denotes love can be seen from I Timothy 1.5 and 6.11, as translated in the Authorized Version. Both passages use ἀγάπη, which is rendered in the first passage as charity and in the second as love.

toleration, we shall easily perceive that our most forcible appeal is made to our mutual feelings'.[112] But more needs to be added. For while the golden rule generates from the desire of worshippers a duty of mutual toleration, it also develops Locke's argument in a way that suits his preceding claims. Locke understood the duty of worship to require external acts. His arguments about action were cast in terms of supposition rather than revealed truth. They did not affirm that acts in worship of God were justifiable because they were acceptable to Him in fact, but because worshippers *supposed* them to be so. Hence what a worshipper had in view was prominent in Locke's discussion of mutual toleration.[113] It is not a duty of love alone that generates a duty of toleration towards other worshippers, but rather a duty of love which omits truth claims about the specific varieties of worship and requires the generic natural duty of worship.

Arguments from purpose hold in a parallel way in excluding the commonwealth from questions of truth in worship. Locke's argument implied that whatever was offered to God in worship was justifiable for one reason only, that a worshipper believed it conscientiously to be acceptable to Him. Locke made it clear that the magistrate had no business to interfere with such beliefs. Religious opinions were analogous to speculative truths because they related only to worship, and so did not bear on civil relations.[114] Hence, as the purpose of a commonwealth, according to Locke's version of natural law thinking, was terrestrial security and safety, its laws were not concerned with the truth of speculative opinions—*de opinionum veritate non cavent leges*.[115]

This conception of the commonwealth went along with a negative view of its position in relation to worship. Locke began his discussion not with *officia* for the magistrate, but *partes*,[116] that is to say, roles, and each and every role was one of inaction or self-restraint, because government lacked the means to

[112] Edward Gibbon, 'A vindication', in *Decline and fall of the Roman Empire*, ed. David Womersley (3 vols., London, 1994), III, pp. 1157–8.

[113] Locke, *Epistola*, pp. 102, 106, 108.

[114] Ibid., pp. 120 and 122.

[115] Ibid., cf. p. 128; and compare p. 134 for the toleration of practical beliefs advanced in church which are erroneous but no danger to the commonwealth.

[116] Ibid., p. 90. Gough's rendering of *partes* as 'duties' obscures this point, and Popple's 'duty' adds inaccuracy to imprecision . *Officium* indicates the fulfilment of duty towards someone by a helpful or beneficial act or acts, e.g. *officium benivoli animi finem non habet* (Publilius Syrus, *Sententiae*, 484), whereas *partes* suggests the function one has in an undertaking, which may require one to refrain from action, e.g. *iustitiae partes sunt non uiolere homines, uerecundiae non offendere; in quo maxime vis perspicitur decori* (Cicero, *De officiis*, I.xxviii.99). Locke had used *officium* for an active duty on the magistrate's part, had referred to *officia cujusque circa tolerantiam*, and had discussed *officium tolerantiae* (Locke, *Epistola*, pp. 66, 78, 84). Silverthorne renders *partes* as role (*Locke on toleration*, p.17), but also inserts a cross-heading into the text 'Duties of rulers with regard to mutual toleration'.

promote the end implied in worship. The same, obviously enough, applied to the relations of *ecclesiae*: because none had jurisdiction over another, there was no directive or coercive relationship amongst them. Toleration from institutions was thus taken to be established.

This is not the same as toleration within institutions. *Ecclesia* was constituted by its *leges*, as we would expect in the model of thinking that flows from natural law. Those of its members who breached those laws thus undermined its existence and therefore its fitness for the common purpose it served. Every *ecclesia*, therefore, had a disciplinary power over its members. This might be exercised as admonition or, if admonition failed, as excommunication.[117] No doubt the excommunicate would find their way to more congenial *ecclesiae* or establish their own. They would have to do so, given that worship is an activity that implies membership of a group.

It should be added at this point that it is necessary to distinguish in thinking about the individual in respect of worship. Natural theology does not imply the same conceptions as modern individualism. This theology postulated God, the soul, and a natural duty. That duty was *eo ipso* universal: incumbent and obligatory upon every human being. What applies to everyone by way of duty applies to each. In that sense, we can say that Locke thought about the individual—what applies to all applies to one. Yet we should beware of supposing that metaphysical individuation and care for one's soul are the same in character as the individualism of modern thought. Any thinking about 'individual' implies an entity that is single, and some thinking about 'individual' implies that this entity is separable, independent, and incapable of being divided into parts to which its name will apply. Thus an individual can be distinguished in some connections from a concept and/or group. Modern individualism is distinctive in that it attributes to each person a destiny in self-development of a scope that belongs to this life, and which is understood as making it appropriate, possibly mandatory, to understanding one's destiny by contrast with the norms basic to human groups and by contrast with the destiny common to all.[118] The individual who is implied in these terms, like Locke's, thinks on his or her own behalf. But his or her thinking is not situated in the terms of the overriding calls of natural theology, which are those of universal duty and care for the soul, and he or she is considered without reference to such requirements. In short, there is a contrast between natural theology, which requires the same duties of all, and the individualism which stands in contrast with duties of that sort.[119]

[117] *Epistola*, pp. 76 and 78.

[118] For a subtle commentary, see Peter Strawson, 'Social morality and the individual ideal', *Philosophy*, 36 (1961), pp. 1–17.

[119] Interestingly, Steven Lukes, *Individualism* (Oxford, 1973), does not discuss Locke on free worship and toleration.

Hence this modern understanding of 'the individual', in terms of secular self-development, is not the subject of Locke's *Epistola*. His explicit argument focused there upon *societates*, jurisdictions, and their relations. This follows from Locke's assuming a natural duty of worship, for worship required a group. A contrast between a group or some other whole and an individual was not one on which Locke needed to dwell in discussing how *societates* and their jurisdictions were connected to worship, these entities being vehicles for performing the duty of worship. For this duty, being a natural one, was not a duty with exceptions for individuals as such. The duty, like the proper destiny of the soul, was the same for all.

The character of the soul called for attention to the manner of exercising their duty and achieving their eternal destiny: it was in connection with these activities that Locke emphasized *singulus* in contrast with the group. All people have *cura* for their souls: in discussing *how* they are to understand and pursue it effectively, Locke emphasized that *cura* lay with each individual. No one can pass *cura animae* to another according to Locke, this being an effect of his thinking about God, the character of the soul, belief, and human destiny: for the soul is persuaded by evidence, not by external dictation, in its search for eternal welfare. Conversely, Locke's understanding of jurisdiction and its bearings preserves this exercise to *singulus.* His placing of worship implies that no mortal other than the worshipper can suffer injury from his or her *cura animae*, and therefore no one else has the final word in judging what is appropriate for him or her.[120] Again, this *cura* remains with one alone rather than with a commonwealth, this being an effect of *that* group's inability to assist or retard salvation and its not being liable to suffer any consequences if salvation is missed.[121] In short, it was questions about the manner of exercising one's natural duty that required attention to *singulus*.

So when Locke discussed *singulus*, he did not suppose a destiny that contrasted with the duty to worship that was incumbent on all and the care of the soul with which it was connected. He emphasized, instead, the features that promoted worship which could be supposed effective: for instance that worship cannot be performed satisfactorily by one alone, that the duty of worship justifies worship in *ecclesia*, and that how to exercise that duty belonged to *singulus*, caring for his or her soul, rather than to groups.[122]

[120] Locke, *Epistola*, p. 124.

[121] Locke, *Epistola*, p. 124, with reference to the formation of the commonwealth: 'relicta interim uniquique salutis suae aeternae cura; cum illius acquisitio nec alterius juvari poterit industria, nec amissio alterius cedere in damnum, nec spes ulla vi abripi'. Stephen, 'Locke', p. 161, observed that 'the social contract' did not commit the care of souls to the magistrate. This point is different from the one in this chapter, but is sufficiently close to merit acknowledgement.

[122] Locke's references to *singulus* in *Epistola* can be assigned to various classes. (1) Where the object is civil goods: *Epistola*, pp. 66 and 126. At p. 126 it is a correlate of Locke's earlier claim, on p. 66, that civil magistracy should protect the goods of every and each citizen, *omni universim*

One correlate of 'the individual' in a modern sense is 'the private'; that is to say, the notion that there contrasts with 'the public', as the realm of law and government, a realm in which the individual is sovereign, and free from the norms of groups to which people must belong, free to pursue self-development as of right. This distinction is sometimes attributed to Locke.[123] But it does not sit well with natural law, a normative code which is superior to every human being and human government alike, and which contains duties that regulate aspects of life including those beyond the scope of the latter's jurisdiction. So Locke, thinking in terms of natural law, did not use this distinction in respect of worship or toleration.[124] He did suppose that the goal implied in worship, like worship itself, lay beyond civil jurisdiction, but we shall see that he did think that the magistrate had jurisdiction over *some* religious opinions and actions: religion *as a whole* was not 'private' in the specific sense required, beyond the concern of government and law. Indeed, worship was not an option in self-development, but a duty in natural law. God, of course, required natural duty of mankind not only for His glory but also as a key to achieving its proper destiny, a destiny that was in principle the same for all and constituted not by them but by Him. The way to that destiny included worship.

Locke used a different distinction. He used the word *privatus* and connected terms in drawing a contrast between those who did not and those

populo et singulis pravitim. (2) Where the object is worship: here emphasis rests on the fact that in important instances worship cannot be performed satisfactorily by one alone, see *Epistola*, p. 100 (cited in the next paragraph of this chapter), and on worship in religious society being legitimated by the duty incumbent upon men taken individually because the duty of worship implies *ecclesia*, see *Epistola*, p. 100: 'a populo ita in coetus collecto non aliud agitur, quam quod singulis hominibus seorisim integrum est et licitum, scilicet de salute animarum'. (3) Where the object is the manner of Christian worship, i.e. finding the right way to Heaven, as an activity that is to be pursued by oneself and so (a) not reserved for one sort of person only, see ibid., pp. 92 and 94, and (b) to be conducted in accordance with Christ's teaching of the faith and morals by which eternal life should be obtained by individuals, as contrasted with the fact that He instituted no civil group, that is to say, no commonwealth, see *ibid.*, p.116, and (c) because error in one's manner of worship does not trench on others' concerns, so *ad singulos solum salutis suae curam pertinere*, see *ibid.*, p. 124 (and cf. n.121 above). (4) Where the object is to contrast the particular with the general, in respect of Locke's lack of interest in the rights of magistrates in particular countries, contrasting with his remarks of general applicability in the same passage, see *ibid.* p.130. 'Man' does appear, e.g. at pp. 68, 100, 124, but the word is *homo*, i.e. a collective noun for the human species, not 'an individual'. Gough renders *unicus* and related terms in a number of passages, e.g. *ibid.*, pp. 66, 70, 72, 78, 82, 90, 92, 96, 126, as 'only one', 'one only', or 'sole', but at p. 125 renders 'unicuique saltutis suae aeternae cura' as 'the care of his salvation is left to each individual' (Silverthorne, *Locke on toleration*, p. 32, also translates as 'each individual'), rather than 'to each one' or 'each one alone'. It is not clear why he made this departure.

[123] For a subtle rendering of the distinction, Jean Bethke Elshtain, *Public man, private woman* (Princeton, 1981), pp. 116–27.

[124] Or, elsewhere, with reference to the family. See Harris, 'Legacy', p. 157, with references.

who did have a special duty in *respublica*, and therefore between what did or did not relate to the status and authority of the latter. So *privatus* was understood in contrast with an office-holder, or with civil authority.[125] Correspondingly, in 1667 Locke had contrasted 'my private interest in an other world' with the magistrate's 'authority': the contrast did not relate to self-development or freedom from natural law, but rather indicated that my salvation was not part of the magistrate's concern, 'the good of the publique'. *Privatus* and magistrate alike know that they 'are ... both equally subjects' of God.[126] Again, the institution of civil society for the sake of protection is contrasted with the material goods, *privata*, which remain in the citizen's hands.[127]

The notion of 'the private', indeed, was at odds with more than the theological requirement of witness and the consequent group character of worship.[128] For Locke understood that there was a duty to admonish and persuade others to the faith one took to be true, and identified this as a high duty for Christians, such a concern for the souls of others being an obvious implication of the golden rule, and he gave a prominent place to the missionary work of the Apostles.[129] Neither, of course, is worship itself an optional activity, it being a natural duty. From these considerations, it follows that the liberty people had to choose their religious society found its proper destination in the necessary task of joining one: for

> we have people free from another's authority in the matter of worship. Now what will they do? All both know and recognize that God must be worshipped publicly; why otherwise are we bound to corporate groups? Therefore people situated in this liberty must enter an ecclesiastical society, in order that they worship as a group, not only for mutual edification, but also in order that they witness in the public presence that they are worshippers of God, and to offer that worship, which does not shame them, which they do not think either inappropriate or unwelcome to God; in order, by purity of teaching, holiness of life and rites of becoming decency, that they may instil in others love of religion

[125] *Privatus* is contrasted with an office-holder at Locke, *Epistola*, pp. 78, 80, 86, 126.

[126] Locke, 'An essay', pp. 272–3, cf. MS. Locke d.1, 'Toleratio' (1679), p. 125: 'Noe man has power to prescribe to an other what he should beleive or doe in order to the saveing of his own soule, because it is only his owne private interest & concerns not another man', printed in Locke, *An essay*, ed. Milton and Milton, pp. 388–9.

[127] Locke, *Epistola*, p. 124.

[128] Ingrid Creppell, 'Locke on toleration: the transformation of constraint', *Political Theory*, 24 (1996), pp. 200–40, at p. 225, builds a public/private interpretation on a passage from Popple's translation of *Epistola* (*A letter concerning toleration*, ed. Tully, p. 34). But Popple's 'private' is not in Locke's original, *Epistola*, p. 88.

[129] Locke, *Epistola*, p. 90 (*cura* for the magistrate, though not qua magistrate), 124 (a Christian's greatest duty), 64 (Apostles).

> and truth and may present those other things which cannot be done by an individual privately[130]

In short, liberty here was liberty in the manner of worshipping—as Locke put it, the end of liberty of religion is to please God[131]—that is to say, liberty to perform in one way or another a duty that implied collective and public activity. It is significant that the passage just cited about *singulus* indicates how individual activity did not meet these requirements of worship.

The end of toleration, therefore, considered as an external condition, was the uncoerced conduct of worship or, to put it another way, a condition in which jurisdiction and duty were consistent with people worshipping in a way that they supposed would secure the salvation of their souls. The end of mutual toleration, considered with respect to the souls of those exercising self-restraint, was obedience to the ends and duties required by God.

Yet Locke required the magistrate to tolerate—*tolerare debet*—religious societies.[132] This seems an odd stipulation, especially as it appears in *Epistola after* the arguments showing that a commonwealth has no jurisdiction over *ecclesia*. Its appearance makes better sense if we remember that *tolerantia* includes self-restraint and that the self in view here was at that date likely to be the patron or head of *ecclesia aulica*, as Locke in fact presumed.[133] The relation between sovereign and this *ecclesia* might be supposed to imply a special duty towards it, or to suggest a temptation in relation to other *ecclesiae*. Locke emphasized, with regard to duty, what his account of jurisdiction implied, that rulers stood in the same relation to all religious societies, their own amongst others, and had no jurisdiction even in the ones of which they were members.[134] As to temptation, he recognized the obvious possibility that governors would lend the sword to an *ecclesia*,[135] or use their coercive power against those who did not adhere to their preferred religious society, and he implied his recognition of the strength of this temptation in urging prudential arguments against indulging it.[136] Their duty lay elsewhere, of course.

[130] Ibid., p. 100: 'homines habemus in rebus religionis ab alieno dominio liberos. Quid jam facient? Deum publice colendum et sciunt et agnoscunt omnes; quorsum alias ad coetus publicos cogimur? Hominibus itaque in ea libertate constitutis ineunda est societas ecclesiastica, ut coetus celebrent, non solum ad mutuam aedificationem, sed etiam ut se coram populo testentur cultores esse Dei, eumque se divino numini cultum offerre, cujus ipsos non pudet, nec Deo credunt aut indignum aut ingratum; ut doctrinae puritate, vitae sanctimonia et rituum modesto decore, alios ad religionis veritatisque amorem pelliceant aliaque praestent quae a singulis privatim fieri non possunt.'

[131] Ibid., p. 102.

[132] Ibid., p. 100.

[133] Ibid., p. 100.

[134] Locke, *Epistola*, pp. 100 and 102.

[135] Ibid., p. 82.

[136] e.g. ibid., pp. 134–40.

That toleration and the duties required by God should dovetail is important for Locke's concern for both souls and the safety of the commonwealth. For both have at their core duties to God—the duty of worship and the magistrate's duty to uphold the commonwealth in his charge. The question of how these bear upon one another was one, therefore, that Locke needed to answer as a high priority. He gave considerable space to the question of the duty of worship and the magistrate's role in relation to it.[137] The magistrate, true, had no jurisdiction over the purpose and end of worship—but his business was to address whatever did or could threaten the commonwealth. That threat, insofar as it came *from* religious societies, was not *de iure*, since in Locke's eyes these societies had no jurisdiction in civil matters, and therefore they had no business to advance religious claims that undermined civil authority;[138] but that did not deal with what occurred within religious societies. Locke, accordingly, analysed duty towards God there into acts of worship and beliefs. The former lay beyond magisterial concern in general because to regulate worship by civil coercion would contradict the very end of worshipping freely, namely to worship God as seemed best to the members of each *ecclesia*, and would be contradictory in particular because the sole concern of the church was the salvation of souls, a concern which in no way trenched on civil concerns.[139] By the same token, beliefs about worship were no business of the magistrate. This emphasis cohered with Locke's placing of such beliefs and concerns with speculative opinions, and his conclusion that such opinions were not the concern of civil laws. What of practical opinions, those affecting conduct, not least behaviour towards others? Locke thought that religious dogma about conduct did fall under civil jurisdiction, and dogmas that were inconsistent with human society or tended to undermine civil government were not to be tolerated, a point about the scope of jurisdiction made in a different way when he gathered together those practical opinions which did not disturb the commonwealth as objects of toleration from the magistrate.[140]

Locke inferred from the end of government its duty to coerce belief and behaviour that either threatened people's lives and related concerns, or compromised its own continuance. So it was entitled to be *in*tolerant in some ecclesiastical questions relating to some beliefs and action. Activities in church that undermined civil government were not to be tolerated by the magistrate, and neither were other breaches of natural law there. Such activities, precisely

[137] Ibid., pp. 100–48 are concerned with this theme in one way or another, a point obscured by the way in which Klibansky and Gough attempted to summarize the argument (pp. 53–5).

[138] Ibid., pp. 130–4.

[139] Ibid., pp. 102, 106, 114.

[140] Ibid., pp. 130 and 134.

because they are not consonant with natural law, plainly have no role in securing the ends God prescribes. So, for instance, ritual infanticide and sacred orgies were forbidden, even in church, these being obvious breaches of such duties as the preservation of life and marriage. [141] Coercion of breaches of natural law in secular matters flowed from this way of thinking. The magistrate's duty to prevent harm to the commonwealth required action for public welfare, and defined its extent.[142] For example, support of virtue was required to the extent that it sustained the commonwealth and in precisely those respects in which it did so. As Locke had put it in 1667, 'the countenanceing vertue is soe necessary a prop to a state, & the allowance of some vices brings soe certaine a disturbance & ruin to society, that it was never found that any magistrate did; nor can be suspected, that he ever will, establish vice by a law, or prohibit the practise of virtue'.[143] He evidently stuck to this position, for later he wrote that a range of anti-social figures, 'spreaders of sedition, murderers, assassins, thieves, adulterers, highwaymen, libellers, calumniators and so forth … should be denounced and punished', and this was true regardless of their ecclesiastical loyalty.[144] This firm attitude towards breaches of natural law should not be supposed an enforcement of morals as such, but it is an enforcement of morals required to prevent injury to *respublica* and one's neighbour.[145]

The result is that Locke stood for coercing some beliefs and regulating some morals. He judged beliefs and practices that he considered anti-social to be fit objects of coercion. Their exponents were to be coerced, however, not because they committed sins, but because their sins undermined society. So government should not coerce sin because it was sinful, but coerce only such sins as thwarted the ends of the commonwealth.[146]

The criterion for the toleration of actions, then, was whether or not they endangered the ends of the commonwealth and its own continuance. The same applied to beliefs. We should not suppose that because Locke argued for the toleration of different ways of worshipping God he thought practical opinion was to be unregulated by government. For it is one thing to leave unhindered different ways of performing a natural duty, another to tolerate what may militate against that duty or other natural duties or the institutions these imply. Thus, beliefs about conduct that were inconsistent with the end of the commonwealth were subject to prohibition. That is precisely the role in which Locke cast one position he had attributed to Roman Catholics (though

[141] Ibid., p. 108.
[142] Ibid., pp. 102 and 110.
[143] Locke, 'An essay', pp. 280–1.
[144] *Epistola*, p. 142.
[145] Ibid., p. 114.
[146] Ibid., p. 114.

he did not name them in *Epistola*), leading him to place its exponents beyond the scope of toleration. This was not because of such distinctively Roman Catholic tenets as transubstantiation,[147] but because Locke objected to beliefs that, by requiring obedience to the Pope, would make Roman Catholics answerable to the dictates of a power beyond and, as it claimed, above the commonwealth. In the same way, Locke explicitly objected to a Muslim under civil jurisdiction who gave implicit obedience to the Mufti of Constantinople and therefore to the Ottoman emperor.[148] Such extraterritorial allegiance was inconsistent with Locke's conception of a commonwealth as an independent body. If belief or action, however holy its inspiration, was contrary to the being of the commonwealth, and therefore natural law thinking, it should be coerced.[149] The same applied to beliefs with unholy inspiration. Locke stated, famously, that an atheist is not to be tolerated.[150] Because an atheist has no belief in a god, he or she cannot adhere to God's law—which includes natural law. So it followed from Locke's tenets that atheism should not be tolerated by the civil government, the function of which was to enforce the rights implied by natural law or coordinated with it. In fact, Locke was adamant that not only civil sanctions but social disapproval too should be brought to bear against exponents of atheism. If 'only some profligate Wretches own it too barefacedly now', he reflected, 'yet, perhaps, we should hear, more than we do, of it, from others, did not the Magistrate's Sword or their Neighbour's Censure, tie up Peoples Tongues'. The 'Apprehensions of Punishment, or Shame', then, were evidently proper means in coercing this opinion about religion.[151] Opinion, whether pro-religion or against it, was within the province of the civil magistrate if it was inconsistent with the being of the commonwealth.

It follows from Locke's thinking that his treatment of coercion is not about the irrationality of coercing religious tenets as such.[152] Some religious positions *were* proper objects of coercion according to Locke, because they contradicted the ends which the commonwealth existed to serve. Freedom

[147] Locke, *Epistola,* p. 120. The reader must judge whether this fact squares with the claim that *Epistola* 'rake[s] up the most basic antipopery prejudices and fears' of the day: Richard Ashcraft, *Revolutionary politics & Locke's Two treatises of government* (Princeton, 1986), p. 498.

[148] Locke, *Epistola*, pp. 132 and 134; compare Locke, 'An essay', pp. 290–3. The stated example in the former is the Muslim, but Locke continued: 'apertius … renuntiaret ille inter Christianos Turca, si eundem agnosceret esse ecclesiae suae qui et imperii caput'.

[149] Locke, *Epistola*, pp. 130–4.

[150] Locke, *Epistola*, p. 134.

[151] Locke, *An essay*, I.iv.8, p. 88.

[152] As is claimed by Jeremy Waldron, 'Locke: toleration and the rationality of persecution', in Susan Mendus, ed., *Justifying toleration* (Cambridge, 1988), pp. 61–86, repeated in idem, *God, Locke and equality: Christian foundations in Locke's political thought* (Cambridge, 2002), pp. 209–10, and followed by others (see n. 183 below).

from coercion was reserved for beliefs that were consistent with those ends and therefore did not contradict any part of natural law. Just as natural law implied free worship, and Lockean conceptions of *respublica* and *ecclesia* carried it into a commonwealth, so natural law required toleration amongst theists: but those whose practical beliefs were inconsistent with these conceptions, whether theists or not, did not benefit from the arrangements generated from Lockean natural theology.

It is true that there is one great exception to Locke's manner of arguing by saying little about revelation beyond the scope of natural theology. This is his treatment of the sacred history given by the Bible: but this is brief, for there Locke argued negatively, insisting that Christians were not bound by the Mosaic law and that the Jewish commonwealth was very different from all others. For in that commonwealth alone God had ruled directly, and under theocracy there was no distinction between *ecclesia* and *res publica*. The birth of Christ implied a distinction between these two, for He instituted no commonwealth, so that there was absolutely no Christian commonwealth *sub Evangelio*, under the gospel.[153]

Toleration, then, arose from natural law, like freedom of worship. Unlike free worship, however, it implied the golden rule. It was a duty incumbent on all theists, and figures in Locke's pages especially amongst *ecclesiae* and between the magistrate and *ecclesiae*. Yet natural law did not require toleration across the board: practical beliefs and actions towards other people, whether religious or otherwise, were intolerable if they contradicted the being and the ends of the commonwealth, and the magistrate should coerce them. What follows from establishing freedom of worship and toleration in these terms?

V

A result is that the location of freedom of worship and the limits of enforcement change. It was no longer Christian worship as such, despite Locke's

[153] *Epistola*, pp. 114 and 116. The interesting treatment in Eric Nelson, *The Hebrew republic: Jewish sources and the transformation of European political thought* (Cambridge, MA, 2010), pp. 135–7, omits that Locke thought the Jewish commonwealth was very different from all others. There was also an Old Testament critique which both cohered with some Lockean prohibitions and militated against treating other practices in the Jewish commonwealth as an unqualified precedent: for which compare Genesis 38.21; I Kings 14.24 (prostitution, possibly sacred prostitution) and Judges 11.30–9; II Kings 16.3, 23.10; Micah 6.7 (child sacrifice), with the prohibitions of Deuteronomy 18.10 and 23.17 and with Locke's own condemnation of the ritual infanticide and orgies alleged amongst the early Christians (*Epistola*, p.108). Locke's sense that the sacrifice of a calf in *ecclesia* (*Epistola*, p. 108) is not subject to civil jurisdiction would apply also to the sacrifice of the paschal lamb in the Temple at Jerusalem during the period of Roman rule.

opening reference to *mutua tolerantia inter Christianos*, which was to enjoy freedom in the commonwealth, rather it was the broader class of which it is part, namely theistic worship; and it is no longer Christian truth that marked the boundary of coercion, but theism.

Lockean natural theology identified the boundaries of jurisdiction, generated a duty of toleration, and defined its proper scope. It follows that the types of worship to be practised freely are defined by the boundary of natural theology, as becomes clear in considering its content. For if the duty to worship and how others are to respond to it depend on arguments from natural theology, then theism rather than Christianity alone is the object of attention.

These arguments tend to establish free worship for theists. For it is a *natural* duty to worship that helped to generate Locke's account of jurisdiction and toleration, and it is the purpose and end of theistic worship, rather than any specific type of it, that placed it outside civil jurisdiction. The arguments therefore establish that worship *as such* is to be free. Hence any theist is free to worship on these terms, not just a Christian. Locke's examples of worshippers included not only Remonstrants, Contra-Remonstrants, Lutherans, Anabaptists, and Socinians but also Jews, Muslims, Amerindians amongst other pagans, and heathens generally.[154] Likewise, this freedom is not to be hindered by worshippers of persuasions other than those characteristic of a given group of theists, for the proponents of natural law owe a mutual duty of toleration, as the golden rule states a natural duty. In short, religions that worshipped at least one god should be free, and should be tolerated by worshippers of other hues. So Locke's limits of free worship and toleration were set by theism, other things being equal.

These limits were thus set beyond the specifics that distinguish any *revealed* religion, and though by the same token they permit these, *ceteris paribus*, they do not identify these specifics as qualifications for toleration. This has the interesting consequence that the duty to tolerate does not relate to any one revealed religion as such, but rather regards such religions as specific ways of working out a natural duty. Conversely, the limits of mutual toleration amongst worshippers, with Locke also marked the beginning of the enforcement of religion. Natural theology was needed by the commonwealth because belief in a god, Locke thought, was fundamental to it.

Whence this insistence on theism? The question, perhaps, is otiose in addressing natural law thinking: for instance, Grotius, Hobbes, and Pufendorf

[154] Locke, *Epistola*, pp. 142 (Remonstrants, etc.), 120, 122, 144 (Jews), 112, 114 (Amerindians), 78, 114 (pagans in general), 114, 144, cf. 148 (Muslims), 122 (heathens). At p. 114 Locke implied that the worship by the Amerindians was idolatrous.

explicitly rejected its opposite, atheism.[155] Yet here it is worthwhile to explore Locke's reasons for condemning atheism because these bring into relief the role of theism in his thinking about *societas*. The atheist was intolerable in a Lockean commonwealth because his denial or lack of thought implied the absence of many ideas and things that Locke took to be valuable. An atheist is someone who lacks an idea.[156] The lack of that idea is a serious deficiency according to Locke's way of thinking. For instance, some society, analogous to that of animals, would be conceivable without theism, but a great deal of human potentiality would be lacking there.[157] Without God there would be no natural law, and neither civil nor ecclesiastical society. The very notion of these societies implies natural law, and therefore God as Locke understood Him. The atheist, by denying God, makes natural law inconceivable, for 'without a Notion of a Law-maker, it is impossible to have a Notion of a Law'.[158] The consequence of the atheist's mental vacancy is that there is simply no idea of such societies in an atheist's mind: so atheism was said to dissolve the agreements, oaths, and promises that constituted the terms on which they existed.[159] Thus much of Locke's thought was impossible for the atheist. What underlies Lockean distance from atheism, besides this cognitive fact?

This need of theism and the matching rejection of atheism are not only intelligible in the terms in which Locke thought: they were also urgent, for example because his commitments in *Two treatises* made his commonwealth depend on agreements. There is also a fact about behaviour. As civil society, according to Locke, depends upon an agreement, specifically on consent,

[155] Hugo Grotius, *De iure belli ac pacis*, ed. William Whewell (3 vols., Cambridge, 1853), II.xx.45.3, vol. II, pp. 320–1; Thomas Hobbes, *De cive*, ed. Howard Warrender (Oxford, 1983), xiv.19, pp. 214–5, *Leviathan*, II.xxxi, pp. 186–7; Samuel Pufendorf, *De officio hominis et civis juxta legem naturalem libri duo* (Lund, 1673), I.iv.2. Grotius argued from Scripture, but added 'haud dubie etiam petitis ex verum natura argumentiis demonstrari potest'.

[156] Locke, *An essay*, IV.x.7, p. 622, on 'that *Idea* of GOD' contrasting with the fact that 'some Men have none'.

[157] Compare ibid., I.iv.9, p. 89: 'the influence, that the discovery of such a Being [as God] must necessarily have on the Minds of all, that have but once heard of it, is so great, and carries such a weight of Thought and Communication with it, that it seem stranger to me, that a whole Nation of Men should be any where found so brutish, as to want the Notion of a God; than that they should be without any Notion of Numbers, or Fire'.

[158] Ibid., I.iv.8, p. 87. The observation is close to Locke, *Essays*, no. 4, p. 150: 'ut se lege teneri quisquam cognoscat, scire prius oportet esse legislatorem'.

[159] Locke, *Epistola*, p. 134: 'For an atheist neither faith nor agreement nor oath, which are the bonds of human society, can be at all stable and sacred; so entirely do all these collapse when God is removed even in supposition' / 'Athei enim nec fides nec pactum nec jusjurandum aliquod stabile et sanctum esse potest, quae sunt societatis humanae vincula; adeo ut Deo vel ipsa opinione sublato haec omnia corruant.' For a similar observation, emphasizing the role of natural law, Locke, *Essays*, no. 6, p. 188, and again no. 7, p. 200.

including explicit consent, if an atheist paid no regard to such considerations, because he did not recognize that his word before God bound him conscientiously, he would not be a reliable citizen. Neither could he be relied upon to be reliable, for Locke supposed that 'the solemn Appeal to Heaven by an Oath' was a 'great Bond of Society'.[160] Nor would he be a reasonable figure at all: since the duty to worship God was a natural one, one known by all, the atheist's denial of it was inexcusable. Besides this irrationality—'madness' as Locke called it—atheism, because it was a breach of natural law, was 'a crime'.[161] It was also, by that token, a denial which would disrupt Locke's arguments about religious society and toleration in *Epistola*; an atheist had no duty to tolerate others' worship, of whatever style, since he or she did not recognize duties to worship and to join an *ecclesia*, just as he or she neither recognized nor observed the duties involved in civil membership. There was a certain piquancy, then, in Locke's conclusion that no one could use atheism to claim toleration on *religious* grounds.[162]

In short, as Locke's natural theology is fundamental to his case for free and tolerated worship, the prohibition on atheism is integral to that case. It is the obverse of the arguments that explain why worship is free of civil jurisdiction and mutual toleration is proper amongst theists.

VI

That central arguments of Locke's *Epistola* relied upon natural theology does not mean that it opposed Christianity. It supported Christian belief in that it required toleration of Christian worship, amongst other types of theistic *cultus*. Rather, the conclusion should be that Locke's friend, Philipp van Limborch, was correct: *Epistola* is a work of *ius naturae*, and, in important ways, more precisely *lex naturae*. It proceeds from a natural duty to worship, and the natural theology that accompanies that view. Limborch, it is true, could not see its connections with *Two treatises*, since at the time of writing

[160] For *pacta*, see Locke, *Epistola*, p. 126; for oaths, John Locke, 'Some considerations of the consequences of the lowering of interest and raising the value of money', in Patrick H. Kelly, ed., *Locke on money* (2 vols., Oxford, 1991), I, p. 213. The dependence of society on pacts, and therefore on natural law, is examined at Locke, *Essays*, no. 1, p. 118.

[161] For the duty being known (and recognized) by all, Locke, *Epistola*, p. 100 (quoted at pp. 90–1 above); for the consequent character of the atheist, compare 'atheism being a crime, which, for its madness as well as guilt, ought to shut a man out of all sober and civil society': John Locke, *A vindication of the reasonableness of Christianity*, in *Works*, VII, p. 161.

[162] *Epistola*, p. 134: 'nullum sibi religionis nomine vendicare potest tolerantiae privilegium, qui omnem funditus tollit per atheismum religionem'.

he had no sense of the authorship of the latter. But he could evidently see enough in Locke's treatment of commonwealth, religious society, and their character in order to distinguish the genre of thought to which *Epistola* belonged.

Why, then, has Lockean natural theology, and natural law in particular, not received due recognition in connection with free worship and toleration? Several sorts of reason could be given, but one in particular calls for attention here: the direction of some subsequent thinking. Some later developments in thinking about natural law and about toleration have not brought the combination of natural theology, natural law, and freedom of worship, and their relation to jurisdiction and toleration into notice: indeed, they have tended to obscure the connections Locke made. Intellectual streams from quite different sources of scholarship have driven against appropriate recognition of his arguments. The mighty flow of German liberal historiography and the submerged currents of Straussianism alike bear the reader away from the natural duty of worship. Gierke treated natural law principally in relation to civil groups, wrote little about churches in the period 1500 to 1800, and from that little omitted natural law.[163] Troeltsch implied a natural duty to worship when he remarked on identifications of the Decalogue with natural law, but did not explore the implication: instead he supposed that Christian thought gave way to *das profane Naturrecht* and silently assumed the same about natural theology.[164] Neither did one for whom the waters of liberalism were pollution find in Lockean natural law a duty to worship. Leo Strauss had a conception of religion in which ritual was central, so that he would not have found such a duty congenial—even had he not thought that Locke's references to natural law concealed an anti-religious ambition.[165] From such copious sources have come, respectively, a liberal textbook that carried nothing of the natural duty

[163] Otto von Gierke, *Natural law and the theory of society 1500 to 1800*, ed. and trans. Ernest Barker (2 vols., Cambridge, 1934), ss. 14.III, 18.III, pp. 44–50, 162–5 (continuously paginated). There is slightly more in Gierke, *Associations and law: the classical and early Christian stages*, ed. and trans. George Heiman (Toronto, 1977), pp. 156 n.34, 159, which concerns Christian thinking about the state.

[164] Most clearly in Ernst Troeltsch, 'Das stoisch-christliche Naturrecht und das profane Naturrecht', in *Gesammelte Schriften* (4 vols., Tübingen, 1922), IV, pp. 166–91, but see in particular his *The social teachings of the Christian churches*, trans. Olive Wyon (London, 1931), pp. 261, 613–4, 674 (continuously paginated).

[165] Leo Strauss, *Natural right and history* (Chicago, 1953), pp. 202–51. The publication of *Essays* the next year, which made this view untenable, had no effect on its proponent: see Strauss, 'Locke's doctrine of natural law', in his *What is political philosophy? and other studies* (Glencoe, IL, 1959), pp. 197–220. On Strauss's account of Locke, see Yolton, 'Locke on the law of nature'.

to worship,[166] and Straussian studies that bring to the surface such corks as that *Epistola* was fundamentally prudential, calculated to ignore Christianity, perhaps to replace it with 'rational' religion, and to suggest that civil society is unconcerned with truth.[167]

Locke's accounts of free worship and toleration do not sink into the watery grave prepared by Straussianism. His natural theology yields a natural duty to worship God, which is developed by believers into Christian forms, amongst others, and which, according to Locke's account of *societates*, provides for free worship and mutual toleration amongst theists. Natural theology therefore has the effect of legitimating Christian worship, along with the worship in other varieties of theism, according to natural law rather than ignoring or replacing that law. Worse still for the Straussian type of argument, what is present inexplicitly in the text of *Epistola*, because assumed there, is not an anti-theistic allegiance but the very natural theology that yields free worship and mutual toleration; and not anti-Christian theism, but instead allusion to I Corinthians 13 and Galatians 5.

This is not all. The liberal current running against the natural duty to worship has raised a mist, within which there appears an obscure figure who is called John Locke but who looks much more like John Stuart Mill. For, when we are wrapped in this mist, it seems that *Epistola* 'has the sense and tone of J. S. Mill's definition of individual sovereignty', and that Locke 'is one of the founders of modern individuality'.[168] Seen through this medium, *Epistola* figures as a 'defence of the religious liberty of the individual',[169] Locke appears as one to whom religious worship is 'essentially a private matter',[170] *Epistola* seems to concern primarily 'the liberty of the individual's

[166] George H. Sabine, *History of political theory* (New York, 1937), ch. 26. The third edition (New York, 1963), revised after the publication of *Essays*, said nothing about the natural duty of worship or about toleration.

[167] e.g. Robert P. Kraynak, 'John Locke: from absolutism to toleration', *American Political Science Review*, 74 (1980), pp. 53–68; George Windstrup, 'Freedom and authority: the ancient faith of Locke's *Letter on toleration*', *Review of politics*, 44 (1982), pp. 242–65; Sanford Kessler, 'John Locke's legacy of religious freedom', *Polity*, 17 (1985), pp. 484–503; Peter C. Myers, 'Locke on reasonable Christianity and reasonable politics', in Douglas Kries, ed., *Piety and humanity: essays on religion and early modern political philosophy* (Lanham, MD, 1997), pp. 145–80, esp. pp. 170–3; Nathan Tarcov, 'John Locke and the Foundations of Toleration', in Alan Levine, ed., *Early modern skepticism and the origins of toleration* (Lanham, MD,1999), pp. 179–95; J. Judd Owen, 'Locke's case for religious toleration: its neglected foundation in *An essay concerning human understanding*', *Journal of Politics*, 69 (2007), pp. 156–68.

[168] George Kateb, 'Locke and the political origins of secularism', *Social Research*, 76(2009), pp. 1001–34, at pp. 1019 and 1026.

[169] A. C. Fraser, *Locke* (Edinburgh, 1890), p. 89, cf. p. 92.

[170] Milton and Milton, 'Introduction', in Locke, *An essay*, p. 32.

conscience',[171] and 'religious worship' figures as 'a private affair of the individual',[172] whilst, more oddly still, it appears that 'ecclesiastical authority lasts only so long as the individual church members continue to give it their consent'.[173] There is a tale that beyond the mist there lies a wholly terrestrial end of diversity and peace—'peace with disagreement is precisely the aim of religious toleration'—which nestles happily with an apocalyptic secularism—for it is added that Locke 'thought that unless religion was excluded from state affairs there was no hope for the survival of the commonwealth'.[174] Here, no doubt, there is a 'distinction between the private and the public'.[175] Conversely, because it is assumed that it is the toleration of worship that is at issue throughout, it is felt that 'privilege' or 'immunity' from state religion is in view.[176] Either way, rights need to be invoked in order to set up claims about toleration. It seems that 'toleration is the expression of a natural rights claim',[177] and that Locke argued about toleration in terms of rights[178]—or at least that we should comment that it is supposed that he did not use them.[179] This Millian simulacrum carries its individual into individualism—Locke's 'account of religion' is said to be 'deeply individualistic'[180] —and even further, into questions about whether Lockean thinking can address difference and diversity successfully.[181] For proponents of this figure, who suppose that the impossibility of willing belief means that there is a 'very important argument in favor of religious toleration', namely that it is 'essentially fruitless' to coerce religious belief,[182] for good measure add that Locke's case for toleration of

[171] Ashcraft, *Revolutionary politics*, p. 499.

[172] John Marshall, *Locke, toleration and early enlightenment culture* (Cambridge, 2006), p. 538.

[173] P. J. Kelly, 'John Locke: authority, conscience and religious toleration', in Horton and Mendus, eds., *John Locke*, pp. 125–46, at p. 143.

[174] Jerome B. Schneewind, 'Bayle, Locke, and the concept of toleration', in Medhi Amin Razavi and David Ambuel, eds., *Philosophy, religion, and the question of intolerance* (Albany, NY, 1997), pp. 3–15, at pp. 4 and 8.

[175] Milton and Milton, 'Introduction', in Locke, *An essay*, p. 32.

[176] Jonathan Israel, *Radical enlightenment: philosophy and the making of modernity, 1650–1750* (Oxford, 2006), p. 266.

[177] Ashcraft, *Revolutionary politics*, p. 499.

[178] A. John Simmons, *On the edge of anarchy* (Princeton, 1993), pp. 123–36; Anthony G. Wilhelm, 'Good fences *and* good neighbors: John Locke's positive doctrine of toleration', *Political Research Quarterly*, 52 (1999), pp. 145–66, esp. pp. 148–52.

[179] Susan Mendus, *Toleration and the limits of liberalism* (Basingstoke, 1991), ch. 2, esp. p. 39.

[180] Milton and Milton, 'Introduction', in Locke, *An essay*, p. 32.

[181] Kirstie M. McClure, 'Difference, diversity, and the limits of toleration', *Political Theory*, 18 (1990), pp. 361–91.

[182] Bernard Williams, 'Deciding to believe', in his *Problems of the self* (Cambridge, 1973), pp. 136–51, and 'Toleration, a political or moral question?', in his *In the beginning was the deed* ed. Geoffrey Hawthorn (Princeton, 2005), pp. 128–38, at pp. 133–4. Williams's claims were made without reference to Locke, but they so exactly express a point of view about him, not least as developed by the literature listed in note 183, that they are placed here.

religious belief consisted in the irrationality of coercing it,[183] so that 'for Locke, the use of force in religion was improper because it was axiomatically inefficacious',[184] and 'Locke's general case' was 'that there is a category mistake in mixing talk of compulsion with talk of mental conviction'.[185] This line even goes so far as the oddly comprehensive claim that 'religious belief cannot be coerced'.[186] Such an approach naturally leads to the view that the attributed emphasis on the irrationality or impossibility of intolerance leaves Locke 'impotent to explain its moral wrongness or injustice'.[187] It finds in Locke's attitude to Roman Catholicism and atheists 'equivocation' and a 'major curtailment' of toleration,[188] even matter of notoriety, matter to shock, doubtless because it presupposes that Locke's 'basic precepts' included 'no state coercion in religious matters' and, in at least one case, it infers that 'the uselessness of coercing conscientious judgment ... applies ... to conscientious religious skeptics': in short, that this attitude should be numbered amongst 'blind spots'.[189] Such exercises achieve wider meaning in a version of Christianity so

[183] Waldron, 'Locke: toleration and the rationality of persecution', pp. 61–86; Susan Mendus, 'Locke: toleration, morality and rationality', in Horton and Mendus, eds., *John Locke*, pp. 147–62; David Wootton, 'Introduction' to John Locke, *Political writings* (Harmondsworth, 1993), pp. 97–106; Richard Vernon, *The career of toleration: John Locke, Jonas Proast, and after* (Montreal, 1997), ch.1; Paul Bou-Habib, 'Locke, sincerity and the rationality of persecution', *Political Studies*, 51 (2003), pp. 611–26; Ryan Pevnick, 'The Lockean case for religious tolerance: the social contract and the irrationality of persecution', *Political Studies*, 57 (2009), pp. 847–65; John W. Tate, 'Locke, rationality and persecution', *Political Studies*, 58 (2010), pp. 988–1008, idem, 'Locke and toleration: defending Locke's liberal credentials', *Philosophy and Social Criticism*, 35 (2009), pp. 761–91; Vernon, 'Introduction', esp. pp. xv–xxvii; and cf. Susan P. Liebell, 'Lockean switching: imagination and the production of principles of toleration', *Perspectives on Politics*, 7 (2009), pp. 823–46. Wootton, Vernon, Pevnick, and Tate widen the focus somewhat, and are critical of Waldron, but take his claim as their central reference. When they go beyond his claims, they remain within the boundaries of an account of Locke framed in terms of contemporary liberalism. For wider commentary on this approach from different points of view, see Micah Schwartzmann, 'The relevance of Locke's religious arguments for toleration', *Political Theory*, 33 (2005), pp. 678–705, and Stanton, 'Locke and the politics and theology of toleration'.

[184] John Marshall, *John Locke: resistance, religion and responsibility* (Cambridge, 1994), p. 360.

[185] Mark Goldie, 'The theory of religious intolerance in restoration England', in Ole Peter Grell, Jonathan Israel, and Nicholas Tyacke, eds., *From persecution to toleration: the Glorious Revolution and religion in England* (Oxford, 1991), pp. 331–68, at p. 366.

[186] Mendus, 'Locke: toleration, morality and rationality', p. 161.

[187] Matt Matravers and Susan Mendus, 'The reasonableness of pluralism', in Catriona McKinnon and Dario Castiglione, eds., *Reasonable tolerance: the culture of toleration in diverse societies* (Manchester, 2003), pp. 38–53, at p. 51.

[188] Israel, *Radical enlightenment*, p. 266.

[189] 'Locke is notoriously willing to deny toleration to atheists': Nicholas Jolley, 'Leibniz, Locke, and the epistemology of toleration', in Pauline Phemister and Stuart Brown, eds., *Leibniz and the English-speaking world* (Dordrecht, 2007), pp. 133–43, at p. 136. For matter to shock, 'given the powerful nature of Locke's case ... it comes as a shock that ... he excludes atheists and Catholics from toleration': Goldie, 'Introduction', in Goldie, ed., *A letter*, p. xviii. For 'basic precepts': Joy Samad, 'John Locke and Muslim liberalism', *Journal of Church and State*, 53 (2010), pp. 84–108,

soaked in liberalism that only terrestrial equality comes out of the wringer.[190] Sometimes, indeed, this Millian image of Locke turns into a Rawlsian one, illustrating toleration as 'political not metaphysical' earlier than Rawls, perhaps better too,[191] or conjuring terms that might justify toleration to theists and atheists alike.[192] Rawls himself supposed that Locke's 'religious doctrine', meaning by that free worship, did lead to 'the political conception' of justice, that being a conception 'worked out for … political, social and economic institutions'—and led, not least, 'to a principle of toleration and … the fundamental liberties of a constitutional regime'.[193] Whatever ghost appears in the mist, not much can be seen clearly, for this watery image cannot survive dry light: some single feature must be picked out, and treated quite without justification (indeed, with marked misidentification) as 'the main line of argument' about toleration,[194] whilst the natural duty of worship is relegated to silence,[195] or treated with the elaborate perversity of evasion.[196]

at p. 84 n.1. For 'religious skeptics': Ronald Beiner, 'Three versions of the politics of conscience: Hobbes, Spinoza, Locke', *San Diego Law Review*, 47 (2010), pp.1107–24, at p. 1123. For 'blind spots': John Christian Laursen, 'Blind spots in the toleration literature', *Critical Review of International Social and Political Philosophy*, 14 (2011), pp. 307–22.

190 Waldron, *God, Locke, and equality*; for toleration, see pp. 208–11, esp. p. 210: 'I think … that the main argument of the *Letter* does have to rest on its distinctively Christian foundations.' He located none there. For criticism of Waldron's account of Locke's natural law, see Timothy Stanton, 'Christian foundations; or some loose stones? Toleration and the philosophy of Locke's politics', *Critical Review of International Social and Political Philosophy*, 14 (2011), pp. 323–47.

191 Vernon, *Career*, ch. 2.

192 Thomas Nagel, *Equality and partiality* (Oxford, 1991), p. 156. Like Williams's argument (n. 182 above), this claim was put forward without reference to Locke; but, again, it exactly encapsulates a point of view.

193 John Rawls, *Political liberalism* (New York, 1993), p. 145 with n. 12; p. 11 for the political conception.

194 Waldron, 'Locke: toleration and the rationality of persecution', p. 61, and idem, *God, Locke and equality*, pp. 209–10. What he had in mind (but misunderstood as an argument for toleration) was only part of the case against extending civil jurisdiction—a third of one case which itself is only a small fraction of the content of *Epistola*. For doubts about Waldron's claim, see Vernon, *Career*, pp. 30–1.

195 e.g. John Rawls, *Lectures on the history of political philosophy*, ed. Samuel Freeman (Cambridge, MA, 2007), devotes pp. 103–21 to Locke's 'doctrine of natural law', but omits entirely the natural duty of worship.

196 Ashcraft, *Revolutionary politics*, p. 493, claimed that 'Locke's argument … depends … upon a natural law framework that limits magisterial authority over matters pertaining to religion', cf. p. 498, but did not recognize that a natural duty to worship is crucial to that and other matters; hence, by p. 499, there is conjured from nowhere the conclusion that 'toleration is the expression of a natural rights claim, when the latter is seen as the fulfilment of the individual's natural law obligations, which is the juridical structure of *all* Lockean natural rights'. One is puzzled to reconcile this last claim with God's *ius* over mankind, e.g. Locke, *Essays*, no. 6, pp. 182 and 186.

It is unnecessary to say much about this simulacrum in relation to free worship and toleration.[197] For instance, the supposition that it is fruitless to change religious belief by coercion is inadequate to show that such belief is free of civil jurisdiction, because it says nothing about the origins, character, and purpose of that jurisdiction. The same is true in relation to toleration by the magistrate and others—there being features of the case besides such futility which might call for coercion. The simulacrum does not even gesture towards the prior question of whether rulers may dispose of beliefs by disposing of believers. This method of proceeding, after all, has had its exponents. As Peirce remarked, 'when complete agreement could not otherwise be reached, a general massacre of all who have not thought in a certain way has proved a very effective means of settling opinion in a country'.[198] It is necessary, however, to say more about the simulacrum in relation to Locke's *Epistola*.

Locke was neither Mill nor Rawls. He did not suppose that 'over himself, over his own body and mind, the individual is sovereign', for that supposition implicitly denies the sovereignty of God.[199] It is to God that there is a natural duty to worship, and it is with God that human destiny is to be found according to Locke. So he was concerned with the bearers of a duty that was everyone's duty—a duty that had to be exercised through societies—and with how each and every one would exercise *cura animae* in *ecclesia*, rather than with the exercise of individualism in a Millian sense, with 'the individual' cultivating a secular destiny understood in terms that contrast with those accepted as norms for societies. It was in terms of duty and its connection with jurisdiction that Locke needed to argue, even in order to ensure the proper exercise of that *cura*. The difference and diversity he countenanced in religion were in the manner of performing one's natural duty to worship God, and these were restricted to the varieties conceivable within the terms of religious society; so, for instance, atheism was not rationally eligible. Neither did the coercion of belief as such trouble Locke, nor the irrationality of the attempt. For Locke, far from declining to juxtapose religious beliefs and coercion, required coercion of practical beliefs that contravened natural law, including religious beliefs, and so ran contrary at once to that law and to a Lockean commonwealth, and he used that same law in generating a duty of mutual tolerance amongst worshippers. He deprecated coercion against the souls who respected natural law, delineated the scope of civil jurisdiction, and pointed to the

[197] The list above is confined to elements structural to this type of thinking; *mere* oddities have not been included, as 'the state is defined in terms of the means at its disposal': Mendus, *Toleration*, p. 25, Mendus, 'Locke', p. 149.

[198] Charles S. Peirce, 'The fixation of belief', in his *Essays in the philosophy of science*, ed. Vincent Tomas (New York, 1957), pp. 3–30, at p. 17.

[199] John Stuart Mill, *On liberty*, ch.1, in *Collected works*, ed. John M. Robson et al. (33 vols., London, 1963–95), XVIII, p. 224.

futility of extending it over worship for the sake of the soul. Neither was he concerned to found the 'reasonableness' of his position in terms that were wholly practical, let alone wholly political, or acceptable to atheists. The latter, he thought, were highly unreasonable, and his account of free worship and toleration implies a natural theology. His commitments, which include an account of the soul, contribute to his account of civil jurisdiction and its ecclesiastical counterpart, and to his account of free worship: the logical sequence is from 'metaphysics' to politics, for natural theology was taken to be part of philosophy, not the other way round. The sequence concludes not in institutional arrangements made by mankind—social, political, economic, constitutional (democratic or otherwise)—but goes beyond these to mankind's destiny of eternal happiness. Locke both understood and required free worship in respect of a duty that looked to God and to that destiny. He sought to mark out a clear path for the natural duty of worship, whether as a duty performed freely or as a manner of performing duty to be tolerated by others, and to indicate how this duty, its end, and the jurisdiction it implied were consistent with other natural duties and ends, and the jurisdiction they implied.

Locke, far from being Mill or Rawls, is better understood as an exponent of natural theology and in particular of natural law. We have seen that he used natural theology as a postulate in thinking about jurisdiction in a way that established freedom of theistic worship in relation to the commonwealth, and generated a duty of mutual toleration amongst worshippers, and also identified as proper objects of coercion those who breached natural law, regardless of whether their anti-social beliefs and activities were religious. Neither modern liberalism nor one of its most persistent opponents has provided a helpful medium for historical scholarship on this subject.

Thus we escape the pull of the stream and the obscurity of the mist. Indeed, in Locke's arguments are not just reasons for action but rather also arguments and facts that Locke understood in terms of his natural theology. Here is not only duty but also duty that is connected with the ends of life—which, in fact, is part and parcel of the end of life which Locke thought the most important. That his account of free worship and toleration can be understood in terms of this area of his thought makes this account and the fact that he was motivated to write about free worship and toleration more transparent. Likewise, we can see that the scope of Locke's arguments in his *Epistola* is much broader than has been recognized, and that their character is not what has been supposed: the reasons that put worship beyond civil jurisdiction, and which made Locke the advocate of mutual toleration amongst theists, also made him the advocate of coercion. Natural theology draws us to a new way of looking at Locke.

5

The Tolerationist Programmes of Thomasius and Locke

IAN HUNTER*

Historical studies of religious toleration are often dogged by the unhistorical assumption that toleration is ultimately grounded in the free individual use of reason, even if other less satisfactory groundings were in play when tolerationist programmes first emerged in early modern Europe. On this assumption, individuals (should) choose their religion by making free use of their conscience and reason to judge which religious doctrines are true of God and which ceremonies are sufficiently pleasing to him to secure their salvation. It is argued that toleration—here, mutual toleration between individuals—arises from this free use of reason in the form of the self-reflexive understanding that it is both impossible and wrong to attempt to coercively impose one's religion on others. This is in part because the inner exercise of reason and conscience is held to be insusceptible of external coercion, and in part because it is believed that to adhere to a religion under duress—hence insincerely or hypocritically—would not be pleasing to God. It is also because the coercion of conduct is supposed to belong to a different sphere of life, politics, where its use is justified by the protection of man's civil interests rather than his spiritual felicity. Concomitantly, and equally unhistorically, it is assumed that the exercise of coercion in religion—'intolerance and persecution'—arises from the failure or denial of man's capacity to govern his religious life on the basis of the free exercise of reason and conscience. This failure or denial of religious reason is thus treated as the source of the attempt by churches to propagate compulsory religious doctrines, and of the illicit recourse to political coercion by the civil magistrate to obtain their acceptance.[1]

* Research for this chapter was made possible by the award of an Australian Professorial Fellowship. I am also grateful to the British Academy for funding my participation in the symposium on Natural Law and Toleration in the Early Enlightenment, and to the symposium's organizers, Professor Susan Mendus, Dr Jon Parkin, and Dr Timothy Stanton.

[1] This double assumption runs throughout John Marshall's otherwise expansively informative *John Locke, toleration and early enlightenment culture* (Cambridge, 2006). For a more succinct statement of the logic, see Timothy Stanton, 'Locke and the politics and theology of toleration', *Political Studies*, 54 (2006), pp. 84–102.

Proceedings of the British Academy, **186**, 107–137. © The British Academy 2013.

In modern academic discussions, this dual assumption of the rationality of religious toleration and the irrationality of religious coercion finds one of its central uses in providing a reception context for a broadly Lockean construction of toleration. In what follows, I will argue that despite this use—and in part because of it—there are several reasons that make this assumption unhelpful for understanding the emergence of tolerationist programmes in early modern Europe. As a point of departure we can observe that alongside the Lockean construction there was a quite different and no less important justification for toleration that was premised on the fundamentally irrational or arational character of religious belief. On this construction—advanced in different ways by the émigré Saxon jurist Christian Thomasius and the Huguenot refugee Pierre Bayle—faith is incapable of rational doctrinal formulation and all public religious ceremonies are indifferent with regard to salvation, which depends wholly on the individual's inner relation to God.[2] On this view, religions should be tolerated not because individuals have the right to rationally pursue religious truth, but because there is no such thing as rational religious truth. If salvation resides in the moral quality of the will rather than the propositional truths of the intellect, then it is vain and illegitimate for any religion to attempt to impose its theological doctrines as true and its public ceremonies as saving. This construction thus gives rise to a form of toleration grounded in man's incapacity for acceding to rational religious truth. It means not only that men have no right to impose their public religions on each other, but also no right of public worship valid against the civil magistrate, the restriction of whose religious powers must come from another source, which turns out to be the purely secular character of politics.

The existence of this alternative Protestant construction of toleration—which Locke also entertained when Charles II was inclined to tolerate dissenters—is a pointer to two historically important features of early modern tolerationist programmes. First, it suggests that tolerationist regimes were not grounded in reason or truth but in particular doctrinal conceptions of reason and constructions of truth, and in the use to which these were put in attacking specific religious and political targets. The modern philosophical doctrine that reason is secular because autonomous and free because formal—not grounded in a 'comprehensive' metaphysical or moral doctrine—is useless for

[2] For pointers to these different constructions of toleration see Sally L. Jenkinson, 'Two concepts of tolerance: or why Bayle is not Locke', *The Journal of Political Philosophy*, 4 (1996), pp. 302–21; Herbert Jaumann, 'Frühe Aufklärung als historische Kritik: Pierre Bayle und Christian Thomasius', in Sebastian Neumeister, ed., *Frühe Aufklärung* (Munich, 1994), pp. 149–70; and Gianluca Mori, 'Pierre Bayle, the rights of the conscience, the "remedy" of toleration', *Ratio Juris*, 10 (1997), pp. 45–60.

understanding early modern constructions of toleration.[3] The central problem around which early modern debates over the role of reason in religion revolved—how far natural reason could penetrate the revealed truths of Christian faith—was itself a theological construct, as reason is only 'natural' and limited in relation to truths conceived of as supernatural and revealed.[4] In grounding religious freedom in a natural theology, that is, in the doctrine that human reason permits natural knowledge of (a non-Trinitarian) God and Saviour, Locke thus based his construction of toleration in a substantive metaphysical or moral philosophical doctrine. This was a construction designed to attack the Trinitarian and hierocratic form of religion—based on a different kind of natural theology—that Locke identified with High Church Anglicanism and Roman Catholicism. Bayle's and Thomasius's rejection of all natural theology was no less substantively based—whether in a Pyrrhonian scepticism (Bayle) or a 'Christian Epicurean' conception of fallen man's ruined faculties (Thomasius)—and designed to reconfigure religion in a manner that prevented its coercive imposition as confessional doctrine and rite.[5] The theological and philosophical divisions unleashed by the splitting of Western Christendom were so far-reaching that they could not be resolved by appeals to universal reason and truth. This is because they were divisions over which uses of the intellect should count as rational, and whether any such uses formed a person capable of acceding to saving religious truth.[6] Religious

[3] When it is applied to the history of toleration this doctrine leads to anachronistic and condescending responses to the historical fact that early modern tolerationist programmes were oriented to such substantive ends as freedom of worship, civil peace, and political stability. Such programmes are treated as at best partial approximations to a future form of toleration conceived as grounded in justice understood as universal respect for the rights of others who are themselves understood as 'justifying rational beings'. For a Habermasian version of this Kant-based approach, see Rainer Forst, *Toleranz im Konflikt: Geschichte, Gehalt und Gegenwart eines umstrittenen Begriffs* (Frankfurt am Main, 2003). For Rawlsian versions, see Jerome B. Schneewind, 'Bayle, Locke, and the concept of toleration', in Mehdi Amin Razavi and David Ambuel, eds., *Philosophy, religion, and the question of intolerance* (New York, 1997), pp. 3–15; and Catriona McKinnon, *Toleration: a critical introduction* (London, 2006).

[4] On this, see Walter Sparn, *Wiederkehr der Metaphysik: die ontologische Frage in der lutherischen Theologie des frühen 17. Jahrhunderts* (Stuttgart, 1976), pp. 5–20.

[5] Thomasius canvasses both ways of suspending religious judgement in the following: 'In übernatürlichen Dingen, die wir nicht genau und deutlich begreiffen, ist es besser und löblicher sein Judicium zu suspendiren, als aus Affecten eine von zweyen einander wiederprechenden Meinungen behaupten wollen.' [In supernatural things that we cannot exactly and clearly conceive, is it better and more praiseworthy to suspend one's judgement than to assert one of two contradictory opinions on the basis of one's passions?]. See Christian Thomasius, *Historie der Weißheit und Thorheit* (Halle, 1693), pp. 146–56. For an account of Bayle's thought which dissents from this view in finding a natural theology at its centre, see Ian Harris, '"And the least sceptical": knowledge, natural theology, and liberty of conscience in Bayle's *Commentaire philosophique*', *Politics and Religion* (forthcoming).

[6] For more, see Ian Hunter, 'The university philosopher in early modern Germany', in Conal Condren, Stephen Gaukroger, and Ian Hunter, eds., *The philosopher in early modern Europe: the nature of a contested identity* (Cambridge, 2006), pp. 35–65.

toleration took its shifting contents from different ways of answering such questions.

Second, for this reason, tolerationist programmes took shape not from the form in which a universal reason recovered its inherent freedom and autonomy, but from the character of the religious and political cultures that they targeted, and from the available intellectual disciplines—theological, juridical, philosophical, and political—on which they drew to attack these cultures. Early modern tolerationist regimes and their modern descendants bear the marks of a distinctly 'regional'—geo-intellectual and geopolitical—emergence. They were fashioned by intellectual groupings located in north-western Protestant Europe in a series of attempts to overcome a distinctively European historical reality: the early modern confessional state. Confessional states (also estates and cities) had begun to emerge in Europe from the middle of the sixteenth century. This occurred when powerful forms of religious pedagogy deployed by rival confessionalizing churches were taken up by state-building dynasties in a manner that would result in the formation of religiously imprinted mutually hostile national populations. Far from being the negative result of the failure to exercise reason in religious affairs, the forms of religious coercion deployed in confessional states were the positive means of securing the superimposition of the religious community on a nascent political nation, the circle of communicants on the encircled territorial citizenry. This superimposition was theorized and underpinned by powerful exercises of theological, juridical, philosophical, and political reason, especially as these were synthesized in the rival scholastic systems of the Protestant and Catholic universities.

The fact that early modern tolerationist regimes were secularizing, in the specific and limited sense of attempting to preclude the exercise of civil power for religious purposes, resulted not from any inherent secularity of reason but from the fact that they emerged as regional cultural–political programmes for undoing the political enforcement of religion in Western European confessional states.[7] The intellectual differences that we have already noted between various tolerationist programmes—particularly with regard to the crucial nexus discipline of natural theology—reflected different strategies for dismantling the scholastic architecture of the confessional state. These strategies

[7] For a powerful argument as to why secularization should be understood as a political–juridcal concept grounded in the programmatic disarticulation of ecclesial and civil authority—rather than as an epochal philosophical concept identified with the onset of 'modernity'—see Martin Heckel, 'Säkularisierung: staatskirchenrechtliche Aspekte einer umstrittenen Kategorie', in Klaus Schlaich, ed., *Martin Heckel gesammelte Schriften: Staat, Kirche, Recht, Geschichte* (4 vols., Tübingen, 1989), II, pp. 773–911. For the alternative view see Jonathan I. Israel, *Radical enlightenment: philosophy and the making of modernity, 1650–1750* (Oxford, 2001); and Marshall, *Early Enlightenment culture*.

were, in turn, reflective of the political and religious forces that anchored such programmes in political reality (or failed to do so). Tolerationist programmes were indeed characterized by hostility towards their targets—by anticlericalism, antisacerdotalism, anti-Catholicism, and the stigmatization of 'papo-caesarism'—and by their own kind of 'sectarian' commitment to substantive theological and political doctrines. This was not the result, however, of some sort of temporary historical mortgaging of their otherwise universal and autonomous rational foundations. It was an inescapable outcome of the historical fact that these programmes were born as combat regimes directed against the intellectual bulwarks of confessional states, states whose very existence was symptomatic of the rivalry among putatively universal theologies and philosophies.

To understand the historical emergence of tolerationist programmes, then, historians cannot afford to assume that religion is free either because of the autonomy of human reason (as Locke argued),[8] or because of the radical incapacity of reason to accede to religious truth (as Thomasius and Bayle insisted). Neither can it be assumed that religious understanding is incapable of compulsion and that coercion belongs to a separate domain of secular politics. For these assumptions or norms were weapons used by tolerationist parties against the defenders of the confessional state in order to attack religious compulsion and secularize the political arena. Their self-evidence to many in the modern West reflects not their universal truth—even today they are rejected by entire religious and political cultures—but their regional success in rationalizing the (protracted and uneven) dismantling of European confessional states and legitimizing their liberal successors. In order to understand the fashioning and deployment of these intellectual weapons, then, it is first necessary to provide an outline of what it is they were deployed against—the early modern European confessional state—which is offered in the next part of the chapter. Following this I will offer an account of Thomasius's construction of toleration as a particular regional programme targeted primarily against Lutheran scholasticism and the Lutheran confessional state. A brief discussion of Locke's tolerationist programme then concludes the chapter, primarily to clarify the differences attendant on his targetting of High Church Anglicanism and the emerging Anglican confessional state.

I

Christian Thomasius developed his tolerationist programme in opposition to the religious, juridical, and political order of his own home state, electoral

[8] But for alternative readings of Locke's position about toleration, see Timothy Stanton, Chapter 3, this volume, and Ian Harris, Chapter 4, this volume.

Saxony.[9] Like several other northern and central territories of the Holy Roman German Empire, Saxony emerged as a confessional state during the second half of the sixteenth century. It was at this time that the Wettin dynasty—in tandem with the reforming Lutheran church and supported by the two universities of Wittenberg and Leipzig—launched a protracted programme to tighten the territory's social governance through disciplined dissemination of the Lutheran religion. This programme included a series of centralizing reforms to the territory's academic, judicial, and ecclesial institutions designed to bring the population under a uniform religious and political order. Saxony thus exemplifies the dual process of religious confessionalization and territorial state-building that historians have identified as central to the religious and political order of the German Empire in the period leading up to the outbreak of the Thirty Years War in 1618.[10]

On the one hand, confessionalization refers to the way in which religious activists such as Luther, Melanchthon, and Bugenhagen drove a process of reforming the church's liturgical, pastoral, and pedagogical structures with a view to achieving something quite momentous: the transfer of forms of spiritual discipline and identity previously reserved for clerical orders into the daily lives of entire populations. On the other hand, confessionalization coalesced with dynastic state-building programmes. This was in part because it offered a powerful form of pedagogy to dynasties intent on the social transformation of their populations, and in part because theological constructions of the Christian prince—mediating divine law via his civil laws as God's viceroy—remained powerful ideological justifications for civil authority. In emerging from this coalescence of religious and political reform, confessional states such as Saxony sought to impose a particular religious culture on a population that was being subjected to more exacting forms of juridical and political governance. A religious community defined by participation in a particular confessional form of the Eucharist was thus superimposed on a civil community defined by the territorial extension and consolidation of a

[9] See in particular Horst Dreitzel, 'Christliche Aufklärung durch fürstlichen Absolutismus: Thomasius und die Destruktion des frühneuzeitlichen Konfessionsstaates', in Friedrich Vollhardt, ed., *Christian Thomasius (1655–1728): neue Forschungen im Kontext der Frühaufklarung* (Tübingen, 1997), pp. 17–50. For a more expansive treatment, see Ian Hunter, *The secularisation of the confessional state: the political thought of Christian Thomasius* (Cambridge, 2007).

[10] For overviews of this process, see Heinz Schilling, 'Die Konfessionalisierung im Reich: religiöser und gesellschaftlicher Wandel in Deutschland zwischen 1555 und 1620', *Historische Zeitschrift*, 246 (1988), pp. 1–45; Heinz Schilling, 'Confessional Europe', in Thomas A. Brady Jr., Heiko A. Oberman, and James D. Tracey, eds., *Handbook of European history 1400–1600: Latin middle ages, renaissance and reformation*. Vol. II: *Visions, programs and outcomes* (Leiden, 1995), pp. 641–82; and Ernst Walter Zeeden, *Konfessionsbildung: Studien zur Reformation, Gegenreformation und katholischen Reform* (Stuttgart, 1985).

single juridical order, which included laws specifying the correct form of Eucharistic participation.[11] This resulted in the emergence of a 'political nation' organized around a confessional identity—a superimposition of political borders and 'frontiers of faith'—and by the end of the sixteenth century had led to the appearance of an array of confessional states that were hostile to each other and to the religious minorities left within them.[12]

The demands posed by the reciprocal defence and tightening of opposed theologies and liturgies intensified the need for larger numbers of more highly trained clergy and teachers.[13] Similarly, the intensification of intrastate administration and the requirements of interstate participation in the juridical institutions of the empire—the Reichskammergericht and the Reichshofrat—produced a demand for well-trained lawyers and jurisconsults as *gelehrte Räte* or political advisers to the court.[14] These demands were met by the reform and expansion of the university faculties of theology, philosophy, and law. From the 1550s to the 1690s there was thus an unprecedented wave of university- and school-building across the German Empire, as state-building dynasties transformed their universities from independent urban corporations into state-funded and administered instruments of the confessionalizing process.[15]

University theology and philosophy faculties fashioned the rival theologies, and trained the orthodox teachers, clergy, and theologians required to disseminate newly confessionalized religions. For their part, law faculties trained jurists, officials, and *politici* in Romano-canon law and the imperial public law that was central to the religious and political order of the empire. They also played a key role in synthesizing a variety of juristic sources into territorial legal codes and in the staffing of emergent centralized judicial systems. Elaborated in a variety of conflicting forms, the discipline of natural law became a central means of organizing the scholastic syntheses required by

[11] Wolfgang Reinhard, 'Zwang zur Konfessionalisierung? Prolegomena zu einer Theorie des konfessionellen Zeitalters', *Zeitschrift für Historische Forschung*, 10 (1983), pp. 257–77.

[12] Heinz Schilling, 'Confessionalisation and the rise of religious and cultural frontiers in early modern Europe', in Eszter Andor and István G. Tóth, eds., *Frontiers of faith: religious exchange and the constitution of religious identities 1400–1750* (Budapest, 2001), pp. 21–35.

[13] Jürgen Bücking, 'Reformversuche an den deutschen Universitäten in der frühen Neuzeit', in Horst Rabe, Hansgeorg Molitor, and Hans-Christoph Rublack, eds., *Festgabe für Ernst Walter Zeeden* (Münster, 1976), pp. 355–69.

[14] Notker Hammerstein, 'Universitäten—Territorialstaaten—gelehrte Räte', in Roman Schnur, ed., *Die Rolle der Juristen bei der Enstehung des modernen Staates* (Berlin, 1986), pp. 687–735.

[15] Anton Schindling, 'Schulen und Universitäten im 16. und 17. Jahrhundert: zehn Thesen zu Bildungsexpansion, Laienbildung und Konfessionalisierung nach Reformation', in Walter Brandmüller, Herbert Immenkötter, and Erwin Iserloh, eds., *Ecclesia militans: Studia zur Konzilien- und Reformationsgeschichte Remigius Bäumer zum 70. Geburtstag gewidmet* (Paderborn, 1988), pp. 561–70.

the new academic order.[16] This was in part because it provided a juridical formulation for moral and political philosophy in keeping with the juridical languages of theology and jurisprudence. It was also because natural law was less a discipline than a matrix for an array of powerful disciplines—theology, positive law, moral philosophy, and political science—whose articulation provided the intellectual architecture for different orderings of the relations among law, religion, and politics, initially in the form of the theocratic order required by the confessional state.[17] Far from reflecting ignorance and superstition, then, the superimposition of religious and civil authority in the confessional state was driven by a massive expansion of higher education and was led by some of the best academic minds of the empire.

In Saxony, the articulation of religious and civil authority via the scholastic synthesis of theology, jurisprudence, and philosophy was given a particular focus and intensity by the state's subscription to the Formula of Concord in 1579.[18] Completed by a team of theologians in 1577, the Formula was intended as the authoritative formulation of the articles of faith for militant Lutheranism, definitively distinguishing it from the rival Protestant faith of Calvinism, which had begun to contest Lutheranism via a 'second Reformation', and from the older but equally detested enemy of Catholicism. Comparable with the tightening of Catholic doctrine in the Tridentine decrees, the Formula consists of a series of authoritative metaphysical–theological explications of the central doctrines of the Trinity and of the manner of Christ's presence in the Eucharist, in addition to a series of other articles dealing with church governance and the status of *adiaphora* or indifferent religious ceremonies.[19] In 1581 academic employment at the two Saxon universities of Wittenberg and Leipzig was made conditional on swearing an oath of adherence to the Formula of Concord and this was gradually extended to the holding of public office more generally. In order to appreciate the depth at which confessionalization transformed Saxony's cultural and political order, however, it is necessary to look at the manner in which the Formula was received in the disciplines of theology, philosophy, and jurisprudence.

[16] For a rare insight into the variety of forms of natural law and some of their conflicting religious and political uses, see T. J. Hochstrasser and Peter Schröder, eds., *Early modern natural law theories: contexts and strategies in the early Enlightenment* (Dordrecht, 2002).

[17] Horst Dreitzel, 'Naturrecht als politische Philosophie', in Helmut Holzhey and Wilhelm Schmidt-Biggemann, eds., *Die Philosophie des 17. Jahrhunderts,* vol. 4: *das heilige Römische Reich deutscher Nation, Nord- und Ostmitteleuropa* (Basel, 2001), pp. 836–48.

[18] Inge Mager, 'Aufnahme und Ablehnung des Konkordienbuches in Nord- Mittel- und Ostdeutschland', in Martin Brecht, Reinhard Schwarz, and Hans-Walter Krumwiede, eds., *Bekenntnis und Einheit der Kirche* (Stuttgart, 1980), pp. 271–302, at pp. 274–6.

[19] A modern English translation can be found in Theodore G. Tappert, ed., *The book of concord: the confessions of the evangelical Lutheran church* (Philadelphia, 1959).

II

In the case of theology and philosophy, it was the speculative Christology lying at the heart of the Formula—its account of the manner in which the exchange of properties between Christ's divine and human natures permitted him to be simultaneously physically present at different iterations of the Eucharist—that drove the changes. As Walter Sparn has shown, this Christology could not be formulated or taught without the utilization of powerful metaphysical doctrines that had in effect been banished from Lutheran universities during the fideist 1520s, but whose return in support of the Formula of Concord at the end of the century marked the onset of Lutheran scholasticism.[20] In his standard *Opus metaphysicum* of 1617, the Giessen metaphysician Christoph Scheibler thus drew on the metaphysics of immaterial and corporeal substance in order to explicate Christ's ubiquitous presence at the Eucharist. This is made possible by the way Christ combines divine immaterial substance (non-temporal, non-spatial, hence omnipresent) and human corporeal substance (physical and locally present) in his single 'person'.[21] Scheibler further argues that this knowledge of Christ's dual nature and Eucharistic ubiquity is accessible to human reason—because the human intellect shares in the same immaterial substance whose originary form is the divine intellect—even if this knowledge can only be acceded to through the discipline of metaphysics itself, acting as a natural theology by permitting man to perfect his intellectual nature.[22] This style of metaphysics or natural theology grounded the elaboration of a distinctively metaphysical form of Christian natural law. On this construction, natural law is the means by which philosophical theologians achieve natural rational access to the divine law via their renovated intellects, and then mediate this law to the civil magistrate—in the form of the Decalogue and Christ's love ethic—who is supposed to enact it as civil law.[23]

There can be little doubt about the confessional purposes of Scheibler's metaphysics, which the author himself points up in his dedicatory preface. Here he commends his work to the Lutheran Duke Ludwig of Hesse as a powerful intellectual weapon against the Socinians and Calvinists, both of

[20] Sparn, *Wiederkehr der Metaphysik*; and Sparn, 'Die Schulphilosophie in den lutherischen Territorien', in Holzhey and Schmidt-Biggemann, eds., *Die Philosophie des 17. Jahrhunderts,* vol. 4, pp. 475–97.

[21] Christoph Scheibler, *Opus metaphysicum, duobus libris universum hujus scientiae systema comprehendens* (Giessen, 1617), bk. II, chs. 1–4.

[22] Ibid., 'Proemium', sections i–v.

[23] For an example, see Balthasar Meisner, *Dissertatio de legibus in quatuor libellos distributa* (Wittenberg, 1616). For a helpful discussion, see Dreitzel, 'Naturrecht als politische Philosophie'.

whom heretically deny Christ's divine presence in the Eucharist. This is a pointer to the fact that this kind of metaphysics was designed as an authoritative natural theology, explicating irrefutable theological truths, and taught to students in the form of apodictic philosophical propositions.

It is no surprise, then, that Locke should have expressed his distaste for Scheibler's metaphysics, which was taught at ante-bellum Oxford, or that Thomasius should have stigmatized this *Schulmetaphysik* as 'sectarian philosophy'. Nonetheless, it is quite implausible to characterize the compulsory teaching of this metaphysics and its use to justify religious coercion as if it were a failure to exercise reason in the pursuit of religious truth. On the contrary, confessional metaphysics of this kind had an exceedingly high regard for human reason, treating it as the *imago Dei* in man through which the human intellect participated in the wisdom of the divine. In combating it, it was Thomasius who adopted an antirationalist stance, arguing that God manifests himself in his will rather than his intellect to which man accedes through faith rather than reason.[24] Rather than treating *Schulmetaphysik* and scholastic learning more broadly as if it represented a culpable failure to make free use of individual reason, it is more helpful to adopt Paul Blum's antianachronistic distinction between 'school philosophy' and 'philosophers' philosophy'. Blum argues that in understanding itself to be founded in a neutral method through which individual philosophers freely reflect on their own thought processes, 'philosophers philosophy' cannot provide the historical basis for understanding *Schulphilosophie*. The latter has a quite different form and function, conceived as the corporate inculcation of authoritative truths, accompanied by their doctrinal refinement and defence, and the pedagogical repulsion of rival doctrines.[25] In comparing the corporate grooming of 'pure minds' for access to authoritative metaphysical truths with individualized philosophical self-reflection, we should be wary of treating the latter as the only true use of philosophical reason, as the two styles in fact represent different constructions of reason and modes of acceding to truth, grounded in different cultivations of a philosophical persona.[26] These are opposed to each

[24] See the clarification of this issue in Thomas Ahnert, *Religion and the origins of the German Enlightenment: faith and the reform of learning in the thought of Christian Thomasius* (Rochester, NY, 2006), pp. 83–106.

[25] Paul Richard Blum, *Philosophenphilosophie und Schulphilosophie: Typen des Philosophierens in der Neuzeit* (Stuttgart, 1998), pp. 1–26. See also, Blum, 'Der Standardkursus der katholischen *Schulphilosophie* im 17. Jahrhundert', in Eckhard Keßler, Charles H. Lohr, and Walter Sparn eds., *Aristotelismus und Renaissance: in Memoriam Charles B. Schmitt* (Wiesbaden, 1988), pp. 127–48.

[26] On the different ways of cultivating a philosophical persona and practising philosophy, see Condren, Gaukroger, and Hunter, eds., *The philosopher in early modern Europe*; Helmut Holzhey, 'Der Philosoph im 17. Jahrhundert', in Jean-Pierre Schobinger, ed., *Die Philosophie des 17. Jahrhunderts,* vol. 1: *allgemeine Themen, Iberische Halbinsel, Italien* (Basle, 1998), pp. 3–30; and Ian Hunter, 'The history of philosophy and the persona of the philosopher', *Modern Intellectual History*, 4 (2007), pp. 571–600.

other on religious, metaphysical, and political grounds in a manner that leaves them incapable of resolution within a unified conception of philosophical reason.

The role of academic jurisprudence in the civil enforcement of confessional Lutheranism is well illustrated in the career and works of the most important Protestant criminal jurist of the seventeenth century, Benedict Carpzov (1595–1666). Carpzov studied philosophy and law at Wittenberg before becoming a doctor of law. In addition to his post as a law professor at Leipzig, he was a political adviser to the Saxon court, and senior or presiding judge of Saxony's most important criminal court, the *Leipzig Schöffenstuhl*. He thus fully embodied the politically important role of academic jurists in the early modern German Empire and its emerging states.[27] In his major juridical work, the *Practica nova imperialis saxonica rerum criminalium* (New imperial Saxon practice of criminal law) of 1635, Carpzov achieved a synthesis of Roman, canon, Saxon, and imperial public law in a practically oriented criminal code that also served as a handbook for inquisitorial trial procedure. This reception and synthesis of positive law was framed by the Christian natural law conception of religious and civil authority. Carpzov thus construes the civil laws of the prince as grounded in divine and natural law, permitting civil infractions to be seen as instances of sinful conduct, and religious heterodoxy to be punished as a civil crime.[28]

Carpzov's multilayered role in mediating the theological, juridical, and political dimensions of the Lutheran confessional state is well reflected in his construction of the crime of heresy in the *Practica nova*.[29] In categorizing heresy as the 'crime of violation of divine majesty', Carpzov was reaching back to the specification of the fourteenth-century canon law jurists. The Italian canonists had themselves reached back to Roman law for the image of affronted majesty and used this to introduce inquisitorial torture and the death penalty for the crime. This conception of the crime had been incorporated into the German imperial legal code of 1530, the '*Carolina*'. It taps into a deep-seated Christian horror of heresy understood as a polluting crime against humanity's common father and lord that threatens the salvation of all members of the community. At the same time, in defining heresy itself as 'an obstinate error in the articles of faith', Carpzov was recovering the patristic-Augustinian construction and activating it in the context of early modern confessionalism. Carpzov incorporated Augustine's stipulation that only obstinate error in a fundamental article constitutes the crime of heresy, and

[27] Peter Landau, 'Carpzov, das protestantische kirchenrecht und die frühneuzeitliche gesellschaft', in Günter Jerouschek, Wolfgang Schild, and Walter Gropp, eds., *Benedict Carpzov: neue perspektiven zu einem umstrittenen sächsischen juristen* (Tübingen, 2000), pp. 227–56.

[28] Benedict Carpzov, *Practica nova imperialis saxonica rerum criminalium* (Frankfurt, 1635), pt. III, qr. ci, pp. 1–7.

[29] Ibid., pt. I, qr. xliv, §§ 1–8.

he used the Formula of Concord to determine which articles of the Christian faith were fundamental. In doing so, he was in effect bringing the long history of canon law proscriptions of heresy to bear as an instrument of juridical governance for a centralizing and in this sense modernizing Protestant confessional state.

What made this confessionalized theocratic judicial code possible, however, was the centralizing and unifying reform of the Saxon court system. In 1574 Elector August (1553–86) had decreed that local judges must send the files for all criminal cases to the *Leipzig Schöffenstuhl* for processing and assessment.[30] Here a panel of legal doctors, sitting as a central legal bureau, would render judgement on them before returning the files to the local judges, who would pronounce it once clearance had been given by the royal court at Dresden. The *Leipzig Schöffenstuhl* thus played a key role in the state-building programme of the Saxon electoral princes. It permitted them to centralize jurisdiction in their own court system, and to establish uniformity of judgement via an institution that assimilated a variety of legal sources—local common law (the *Sachsenspiegel*), consistorial law, imperial public law, and Romano-canon law—in a single judicial practice.

This mix of imperial public law and 'municipal' Saxon law can be seen in Carpzov's second major work, the *Jurisprudentia ecclesiastica seu consistorialis* (Ecclesial or consistorial jurisprudence) of 1649. Like other Protestant territories, Saxony had established a consistory (a mixed lay and theological body for the governance of the church and the exercise of ecclesial jurisdiction) in order to compensate for the loss of episcopal administration following the breach with Rome. This state of affairs was enshrined in imperial public law by the Religious Peace of Augsburg in 1555, which recognized the Protestant prince as both civil ruler and highest bishop in his own territory, thereby giving rise to one of the central doctrines of Protestant *Staatskirchenrecht* (ecclesial public law), the *Zwei-Personen-Lehre* (doctrine of the two persons). In Carpzov's formulation: 'By virtue of the Religious Peace, the episcopal rights of princes and the status of Protestant ruler coincide: by which they represent a double person and exercise a double power, ecclesial and political.'[31] The *Zwei-Personen-Lehre* was accompanied by the *Drei-Stände-Lehre*, or doctrine of the three estates.[32] This doctrine was initially elaborated by Melanchthon as a Lutheran social theory teaching that society consists of three estates: the political, clerical, and oeconomic

[30] Heiner Lück, 'Benedict Carpzov (1595–1666) und der Leipziger Schöffenstuhl', in Jerouschek et al., eds., *Benedict Carpzov*, pp. 55–72.

[31] Benedict Carpzov, *Jurisprudentia ecclesiastica seu consistorialis* (Leipzig: 1649), bk. I, def. 2.

[32] Klaus Schlaich, 'Der rationale Territorialismus: die Kirche unter dem staatsrechtlichen Absolutismus um die Wende vom 17. zum 18. jh.', *Zeitschrift für Rechtsgeschichte*, 85 (1968), pp. 269–340.

(*Wehrstand*, *Lehrstand*, and *Nahrstand*). In the second half of the sixteenth century, though, it was refashioned as a constitutional theory of the church, such that the three estates were renamed as the magistracy, clergy, and people, with the doctrine now being used to treat church governance as divided between the estates. Carpzov could thus use the dual civil–episcopal jurisdiction of the prince to defend the Saxon elector's episcopal right to enforce the Formula of Concord. This also served to justify the delegated competence of the clergy in the consistorial prosecution of religious law—in such areas as marriage, sexual misconduct, church attendance, and heresy—thereby adapting Catholic canon law to the actual practice of the Dresden Superior Consistory.[33] At the same time, Carpzov could use the three-estate doctrine to defend the church against its political secularization, by arguing that the power of church government had to be divided between the secular magistracy, the clergy, and the commons. The prince thus could be treated as a servant of the religious community to which he belonged and prevented from exercising civil authority in 'internal' church matters—doctrine, liturgy, theological controversies—reserved for the clergy.[34]

The exercise of civil authority in religious matters was thus deeply embedded in the theological, philosophical, and juridical culture of the Saxon confessional state. If Saxon philosophers and theologians taught metaphysics as a body of authoritative doctrine designed to support an irrefutable confessional theology, this was not because they failed to make free use of individual reason. It was because they conceived of reason in another way: as a corporate use of the metaphysical intellect as the means of acceding to transcendent theological truths. Similarly, if Benedict Carpzov could use the natural law developed by the Saxon metaphysicians in order to frame a positive jurisprudence in which the prince doubled as bishop, and in which deviation from the Formula of Concord was treated as the punishable crime of heresy, this was not because he failed to understand the inherently free nature of conscience or the essentially secular character of political authority. Religious and civil authority were superimposed in Saxony not as the result of a philosophical mistake but through a dense web of theological, philosophical, and juridical reasoning. Attached on one side to complex metaphysical constructions of man's mode of participation in the saving transcendence of the divine intellect, and on the other to concrete jurisprudential constructions of the Protestant prince's right to enforce his confession under imperial public law, this scholastic web bound the political community to the (Lutheran)

[33] On the consistorial basis of Carpzov's church law, see Landau, 'Carpzov, das protestantische Kirchenrecht und die frühneuzeitliche Gesellschaft'.
[34] Carpzov, *Jurisprudentia ecclesiastica*, bk. I, def. 27, n. 2.

Eucharistic community in a manner that permitted deviation in the ecclesial register to be intelligible as a crime in the civil register. The undoing of this profound articulation would be achieved not through the clean breakthrough to an autonomous philosophical reason, but through a grim and protracted hand-to-hand intellectual combat whose goal was to detheologize jurisprudence and politics and thereby destroy the intellectual infrastructure of the confessional state. Far from being global, this process was not even pan-European, being confined, initially at least, to the northern Protestant states of the Holy Roman German Empire. Here the key role would be played not by dissident philosophers but by extra-ecclesial public law jurists among whom Christian Thomasius was a leading figure.

III

The directness with which Thomasius's conception of toleration emerged from his engagement with the Protestant confessional state can be gathered from the circumstances in which he was exiled from Saxony. This occurred in 1690 as the result of a series of disputations and essays that Thomasius had published while lecturing at the University of Leipzig. The series included an anti-metaphysical natural law work,[35] an anti-scholastic 'civil' philosophy,[36] and a highly controversial public law tract in which Thomasius defended the marriage between Princess Maria Amalia, Calvinist daughter of Friedrich Wilhelm of Brandenburg, and the Lutheran duke, Moritz Wilhelm of Saxon-Zeitz, a brother of the Saxon Elector.[37] In arguing that this match was legitimate under the provisions of the Treaty of Osnabrück (Westphalia)—which awarded Calvinists and Lutherans equal civil rights under imperial public law—and that in any case there should be no significant theological differences between the two Protestant religions, Thomasius outraged Saxon clergy and theologians and offended the royal court. The phalanx of Saxon philosophers and theologians who engineered Thomasius's banning and exile included the metaphysical natural jurist Valentin Alberti, the theologian Johann Benedict Carpzov, and his brother the court pastor Samuel—nephews of the great Benedict Carpzov—indicating the immediacy of Thomasius's

[35] Christian Thomasius, *Institutiones jurisprudentiae divinae* (Leipzig, 1688).

[36] Christian Thomasius, *Introductio ad philosophiam aulicam* (Leipzig, 1688; repr. Hildesheim, 1994).

[37] Christian Thomasius, *Rechtmaßige Erörterung der Ehe- und Gewissens-frage, Ob zwey fürstliche Personen im Römischen Reich, deren eine der Lutherischen di andere der reformirten Religion zugethan ist, einander mit guten Gewissen heyrathen können?* (Halle, 1689). Republished in his *Auserlesene deutsche Schriften, zweiter Teil* (24 vols., Frankfurt and Leipzig, 1714; repr. Hildesheim, 1994), II, pp. 1–102.

engagement with the leading representatives of Lutheran scholasticism.[38] The fact that Alberti and the Carpzov brothers were able to effect his banning and exile by laying a complaint before the Dresden Superior Consistory—leading to a condemnation of Thomasius's 'indifferentism' and 'irreligion' that would be converted into a ducal decree—shows the ease with which academic disputes could become religious and political conflicts in circumstances where academic ideologies were central to a territory's religious and political order. Given that, philosophically speaking, the metaphysical theology and theocratic jurisprudence with which his opponents defended the Saxon confessional state were no less coherent than the civil philosophy and secularized public law with which Thomasius attacked it, then to understand this conflict we must do something more than just explicate the intellectual terms in which it was conducted. We must also clarify the play of political and religious interests that anchored these terms in political reality.

When Thomasius crossed Saxony's northern border in 1690, to begin his life as a successful exile in neighbouring electoral Brandenburg, he entered a Protestant princely territorial state in which the forces of confessionalization had played out in another way, resulting in a configuration of ecclesial and civil authority different from that found in Saxony. The Hohenzollern electors had changed the court religion to Calvinism in 1613 and would formally abrogate Brandenburg's subscription to the Formula of Concord in 1656.[39] With an entirely characteristic mix of genuinely religious and ambitiously political motives, the elector Johann Sigismund (ruled 1608–19) had turned to Calvinism in order to sweep away the 'superstitious' practices of the Lutheran church: such things as baptismal exorcism, the Eucharistic 'ubiquity' doctrine, the 'papist' consecration of the communion host.[40] The reform of the church was also intended as a means of incorporating Brandenburg's Lutheran estates—cities, nobilities, knights' circles—within the emerging princely territorial state of Brandenburg-Prussia. In the event, despite the Hohenzollerns' success in the territorial expansion and military consolidation

[38] On this conflict see Rolf Lieberwirth, 'Christian Thomasius' Leipziger streitigkeiten', *Wissenschaftliche Zeitschrift der Martin-Luther-Universität Halle-Wittenberg (gesellschafts- und sprachwissenschaftliche Reihe)*, 3 (1953), pp. 155–9. See also Frank Grunert, 'Zur aufgeklärten Kritik am theokratischen Absolutismus: der Streit zwischen Hector Gottfried Masius und Christian Thomasius über Ursprung und Begründung der summa potestas', in Vollhardt, ed., *Christian Thomasius*, pp. 51–78. For a helpful discussion of Thomasius's dispute with Alberti, see Ahnert, *German Enlightenment*, pp. 84–93.

[39] On the Hohenzollern dynasty's attempt to use Calvinism as part of an ambitious programme to reform church and society, see the exemplary study by Bodo Nischan, *Prince, people, and confession: the second reformation in Brandenburg* (Philadelphia, 1994).

[40] Bodo Nischan, 'The exorcism controversy and baptism in the late Reformation', *Sixteenth Century Journal*, 18 (1987), pp. 31–52.

of the new state, the planned religious reform ended in a stalemate, with the nobility successfully using their imperial estate rights to resist the Calvinization of the church, aided by a vehemently anti-Calvinist Lutheran clergy and a sometimes riotous populace.[41]

As a result of this impasse, by the time that Thomasius arrived in 1690, Brandenburg was in effect a multi-confessional state in which a Calvinist dynasty ruled over a largely Lutheran nobility and population, in territories that also contained Calvinist and Catholic minorities. Unlike Saxony, the synchronization of confessionalization and state-building had misfired in Brandenburg-Prussia, leading to the emergence of an increasingly powerful and militarized state ruling over an array of religious communities none of whose churches could be endorsed and enforced by law and the state. It was this de facto and unplanned development of political secularization and religious toleration in Brandenburg—the result of political exigency rather than enlightenment philosophy—that provided the political anchorage for Thomasius's tolerationist campaign against the intellectual infrastructure of the Lutheran confessional state.[42]

We have observed that the judicial enforcement of religion exemplified in Benedict Carpzov's heresy statute was attached to the theology of the Formula of Concord that defined Lutheran orthodoxy in Saxony. This theology was, in turn, grounded in an academic metaphysics that supplied it with a rational philosophical explication, including a metaphysical form of natural law that provided a theocratic reception context for positive Romano-canon and imperial public law. It is for this reason that the cutting edge of Thomasius's tolerationist programme was forged not by the discipline of philosophy but by public law jurisprudence (*Staatsrecht*), especially in the form of *Staatskirchenrecht* or imperial public church law. This formed the basis of a string of combative disputations that he launched during the 1690s, on *adiaphora*, judicial torture, heresy law, and the prince's rights of religious supervision, including his right of toleration. At the same time, the deep scholastic roots of Saxon confessional jurisprudence also clarify why Thomasius's juristic programme was supported by a pietistic theology directed against Lutheran metaphysical theology, and a wide-ranging programme of

[41] For an account of the political campaign waged by the estates, see Paul Schwartz, 'Die Verhandlungen der Stände 1665 und 1668 über die Religionsedikte', *Jarhrbuch für brandenburgische Kirchengeschichte*, 30 (1935), pp. 88–115.

[42] See Gerd Heinrich, 'Religionstoleranz in Brandenburg-Preußen: idee und Wirklichkeit', in Manfred Schlenke, ed., *Preussen, versuch einer Bilanz,* vol. 2: *Beiträge zu einer politischen Kultur* (Reinbeck, 1981), pp. 61–88; and Hartmut Rudolph, 'Oeffentliche Religion und Toleranz: zur parallelität preußischer Religionspolitik und josephinischer Reform im Lichte der Aufklärung', in Peter F. Barton, ed., *Im Zeichen der Toleranz: Aufsätze zur Toleranzgesetzgebung des 18. Jahrhunderts in den reichen Joseph II., ihren Voraussetzungen und ihren Folgen* (Vienna, 1981), pp. 221–49.

educational reform designed to free law students from the philosophy, theology, natural law, and jurisprudence of Protestant scholasticism.[43]

Rather than being grounded in philosophy and philosophical reason, then, Thomasius's tolerationist programme drew its intellectual resources from the cultural and political topography of the terrain on which it engaged Protestant scholasticism and the Lutheran confessional state. We can identify three main intellectual resources underpinning his *staatsrechtlich* campaign: a spiritualistic form of lay Protestant theology through which he challenged the doctrine and ritual of the confessional public church; an anti-metaphysical historiography of philosophy and theology that had been pioneered by his father Jacob and that permitted him to suspend the truth claims of metaphysics and theology; and the 'Hobbesian' natural law political philosophy elaborated by his mentor Samuel Pufendorf, which permitted Thomasius to develop a profoundly secular reception of positive law, now understood simply in terms of the pacifying commands of a civil sovereign.

The manner in which Thomasius mobilized these resources can be seen in the two public law disputations that he held on the theme of heresy in 1697. The degree to which Thomasius's agenda was set by his immediate religious and political context is shown by the definition of heresy with which he opens the first of these disputations, *An haeresis sit crimen*? (Whether heresy be a crime?).[44] By sourcing this definition from Carpzov's heresy statute in the *Practica nova*—'Heresy is an obstinate error in the foundations of faith by a person who is or was a member of the church'—Thomasius leaves his readers in no doubt that his prime target is the Lutheran confessional state and, more broadly, the crime of heresy itself, treated as symptomatic of the illicit superimposition of religious and civil authority.[45]

Thomasius begins his systematic dismantling of the elements of Carpzov's definition of the crime by mobilizing a spiritualistic and intensely inward Protestant conception of religion. Against the notion that heresy is deviation by a member of the church, Thomasius invokes the idea that the true church is 'invisible and scattered across the world'.[46] By insisting that the true church is invisible, its membership unknown to all except God, Thomasius denies that the faithful can be brought together in a 'visible assembly'. This is

[43] On this broader campaign, see Hunter, *Secularisation of the confessional state*, chs. 1 and 2.

[44] The disputation was defended by one of Thomasius's doctoral students, Johann Christoph Rube in July 1697, before being translated into German as *Ob ketzerei ein strafbares verbrechen sei?* in 1705, for publication in Thomasius's *Auserlesene deutsche Schriften* (Halle, 1705; repr. Hildesheim, 1994). I will cite from the English version, 'Is heresy a punishable crime?', in *Christian Thomasius: essays on church, state, and politics*, ed. and trans. Ian Hunter, Thomas Ahnert, and Frank Grunert (Indianapolis, 2007), pp. 148–206.

[45] Thomasius, 'Is heresy a punishable crime?', pp. 150 and 160.

[46] Ibid., p. 162.

intended to undermine the notion that any public confessional church could constitute the community of the faithful, deviation from which constitutes heresy. The deconfessionalizing effect of this spiritualist style of Protestantism is further intensified in Thomasius's attack on the concept of faith contained in Carpzov's definition. Faith, he argues, is not a matter of theological doctrines and confessional articles known to the intellect. Rather, it is a matter of acceding to the will of God as revealed to all in the Bible and experienced in the heart of the individual believer.[47] Developing this line of argument in a strongly anti-intellectualist direction, Thomasius ridicules the notion that faith consists in the understanding of, or in intellectual assent to, creeds such as the Formula of Concord—calling this *Hirnglauben* ('brain faith')—insisting instead that faith subsists in the will, and is centrally registered in love of God and love of one's neighbour. Mocking the notion that heresy consists in obstinate deviation from the foundations of faith, Thomasius asks how this can be so when each church and sect has its own version of the fundamental articles and when all have disgraced themselves by their ceaseless quarrels and persecutions over which articles are the true ones.

The final and most radical step in this spiritualistic and fideistic line of argument comes with Thomasius's rejection of the notion of heretical error and, by implication, the notion of theological truth. 'I could easily show', says Thomasius, 'that all heresy arises from nothing other than the pretext of an error in philosophy.'[48] Man's intellectual faculties are so badly damaged, though, and God in any case lies so far beyond them, that it is pointless and presumptuous for any metaphysician or theologian to claim true knowledge of the divine nature, making it unjustifiable to conceive heresy in terms of error in relation to religious truth.[49] The same applies to all of the public religious ceremonies that are claimed to be essential for securing man's salvation. Given that what makes man pleasing to God is the inner condition of his heart and will, known only to God, then external church ceremonies should be regarded as *adiaphora*: as morally indifferent things with regard to salvation. Such ceremonies are thus incapable of forming the sacramental 'keys to the kingdom' from which dissenters might be excluded as heretics.[50] By declaring faith to be independent of intellectual truth, and by denying that any public church ceremony could make man pleasing to God, Thomasius

[47] Ibid., pp. 163–71.
[48] Ibid., p. 160.
[49] Ibid., pp. 175–8.
[50] For a succinct statement of Thomasius's views on the *adiaphora*, see his disputation on this topic: Christian Thomasius, 'The right of Protestant princes regarding indifferent matters or adiaphora', in Hunter, Ahnert, and Grunert, eds. and trans., *Essays on church, state, and politics*, pp. 49–127, at pp. 55–7.

was not grounding his tolerationist rejection of heresy in the free exercise of reason in religious matters, but in the denial that reason allowed man to accede to religious truth or to proscribe religious error.

Considering the spiritualistic and fideistic character of Thomasius's theological assault on heresy law, it might seem odd that his second main source of intellectual weaponry—the historiography of philosophy and theology—should have been both secular and empirical.[51] Yet these two dimensions of his thinking are linked by a strong historical logic. The anti-intellectualist movement of thought that declared God's nature inaccessible to human understanding—thereby removing the divine being from the temporal world—simultaneously opened this world to an array of non-transcendental 'empirical' knowledges which, because they all concerned the temporal world, were generically known as 'history'.[52] For Thomasius, pride of place among these 'historical' disciplines was occupied by the historiography of philosophy and theology that he had learned from the pioneering work of his father, Jacob. This was not least because this historiography provided a powerful means of suspending the truth claims of metaphysics and situating them too in the temporal world. Jacob Thomasius (1622–84) had combined the latest critical philology with a Protestant pietistic distrust of metaphysics in order to show that the central doctrines of Greek metaphysics—the Platonic and Aristotelian doctrines in which a divine mind brings order and meaning to the material world by intelligizing the forms of being—were incompatible with the revealed Christian truth of *ex nihilo* creation.[53] This allowed Greek metaphysics to be removed from the eschatological truth and time of Christian sacred history and viewed as a matter of profane historical fact. In this detranscendentalized temporal domain, the Greek metaphysical doctrines could be treated as products of a wholly pagan time and culture—simply as the teachings of the pagan philosophy schools—divorced from both the redemptive temporality of Christianity and from their own promise of a world illuminated by a divine intellect. It was the illicit combination of these doctrines with the Christian revelation by the Platonizing church fathers that gave rise to the main Christian heresies: the Manichaean teaching that God and matter are two distinct substances, and the pantheistic teaching that God is part of the world that he intelligizes.[54]

[51] See the discussions of this historiography in John Christian Laursen, ed., *Histories of heresy in early modern Europe: for, against, and beyond persecution and toleration* (Basingstoke, 2002).

[52] On this initial conflation of the empirical with the historical, see Arno Seifert, *Cognitio historica: die Geschichte als Namengeberin der frühneuzeitlichen Empirie* (Berlin, 1976).

[53] The best statement of the historical argument is given in Jacob Thomasius, *Schediasma historicum* (Leipzig, 1665).

[54] On this array of issues, see the rare and illuminating discussions by Ralph Häfner, 'Jacob Thomasius und die geschichte der häresien', in Vollhardt, ed., *Christian Thomasius*, pp. 141–64;

Without adding to his father's scholarship, Christian Thomasius put this historiography to a much more radical use by deploying it to repudiate the entire enterprise of metaphysics qua natural theology. This included both the metaphysical theologies of the rival confessional religions and the philosophical theologies of such moderns as Spinoza, Descartes, and the Cambridge Platonists. Thomasius viewed both ancient and modern natural theologies as miscegenations of pagan metaphysics and Christian doctrine—as improper fabrications of philosophizing theologians and theologizing philosophers—thereby treating them as purely historical phenomena whose truth claims are suspended.[55] In the two heresy disputations Thomasius traces the sectarian character of philosophy and theology to this same illicit mixing of pagan philosophy and the Christian revelation. This has led to saving faith being presented in the form of metaphysical doctrines demanding exclusive intellectual adherence, such that those who refuse to subscribe could be condemned as heretics by a clergy acting as philosophical enforcers for pagan teachings:

> Some would find it paradoxical if I said that from the time of Constantine the Great to the Reformation, all of the controversial questions, which were supposed to belong to the Catholic faith, and from which heresies arose, were in fact purely and simply philosophical—metaphysical and logical for the most part; and, therefore, that myriads of men have been butchered and banished not for God's sake, but for the sake of Aristotle's or Plato's metaphysics. Nonetheless, this paradox is only too true.[56]

It was via this historiographic suspension of the truth of metaphysics and theology that Thomasius sought to demonstrate the illicit character of coercion in religious matters, by showing that this arose from the attempt to enforce doctrines grounded in clerical interest. Christian theology and metaphysics should thus be seen as products of a misuse of philosophy, perpetrated by philosophical theologians seeking to supply the clergy with an intellectual weapon of domination. From the viewpoint of this historiography, heretical and orthodox theologies are both products of the pagan philosophical reworking of the Christian revelation, hence neither has any more claim on the truth than the other. Both are regarded as historical phenomena to be

---

and Martin Mulsow, *Moderne aus dem Untergrund: radikale Frühaufklärung in Deutschland 1680–1720* (Hamburg, 2002), pp. 261–307.

[55] See in particular, Christian Thomasius, *Cautelen zur Erlernung der Rechtsgelehrtheit* (Halle, 1713), chs. 6 and 12.

[56] This is from the second heresy disputation, presented at the University of Halle (again by Rube) in November 1697 under the title *De iure principis circa haereticos*. I am citing from my translation (Christian Thomasius, 'On the right of Protestant princes regarding heretics'), presented in the appendix of Hunter, *Secularisation of the confessional state*, pp. 168–205, at p. 178.

understood in terms of their temporal origins and civil effects. This allows Thomasius to present a relativistic historical and political understanding of heresy and orthodoxy: 'Heresy is dissent from the ruling religion', while 'Orthodoxy is the ruling religion.'[57]

The third intellectual resource on which Thomasius drew in his campaign against Protestant scholasticism and the confessional state was the secularized construction of political authority that he found in the natural law political philosophy of his mentor, Samuel Pufendorf. Pufendorf had grounded his construction of civil sovereignty in a powerful anti-metaphysical doctrine that attached duties to imposed moral entities (*entia moralia*). According to this doctrine man is the bearer of obligation not via a moral nature that connects him to rational norms—as in the various moral philosophical conceptions of man's 'rational and sociable nature'—but on the basis of an array of artefactual moral statuses or personae that have been instituted or imposed for the purpose of 'governing his dangerous liberty'.[58] This enabled Pufendorf to effect a radical disaggregation of the moral universe, especially with regard to the relations between man's religious and civil duties, by treating duties as local to distinct moral personae that have been instituted for particular purposes.[59]

For Pufendorf there is no rational and social nature through which man might accede to a level of rational ideas capable of integrating and justifying the forms of his moral governance, and on the basis of which he might possess natural rights as opposed to artefactual obligations. The moral condition (*status naturalis*) through which man acquires the persona and duties of a political subject (*status civilis*)—that of a creature who must be sociable to survive but whose vicious passions wreck sociability—is thus wholly distinct from the status (of biblically revealed fallen man) through which he acquires the persona and duties of a Christian. This produces a radically secularized conception of politics, as the norms of civil life are themselves created by the commands of the sovereign whose authority comes not from God or reason, but solely from the requirement that he coercively forestall the passions and actions that threaten social peace. At the same time it separates and spiritualizes the church by treating it as the custodian of a truth—the salvation promised in the Bible through Christ—to which man is incapable of acceding in his civil personae (as sovereign or citizen) but only via the wholly non-coercive

[57] Ibid., p. 180.

[58] Samuel Pufendorf, *De jure naturae et gentium libri octo* (London, 1672), bk. I, ch. i. In English, Samuel Pufendorf, *The law of nature and of nations in eight books*, trans. C. H. Oldfather and W. A. Oldfather (2 vols., Oxford, 1934), vol. 2.

[59] For a more detailed discussion of this array of issues, see Ian Hunter, *Rival enlightenments: civil and metaphysical philosophy in early modern Germany* (Cambridge, 2001), pp. 163–9.

relations of love and emulation binding the personae of teacher and learner.[60]

Thomasius used Pufendorf's multiple moral personae doctrine as a means of effecting a double disqualification of heresy laws. On the one hand, such laws are symptomatic of the religious abuse of civil authority, emerging when the clergy seek to impose their pagan-tainted theologies as compulsory confessions, persecuting dissenters as heretics, and thereby illicitly seeking to exercise a political authority over Christians by treating them as political subjects of the church.[61] On the other hand, heresy laws are also symptomatic of the political abuse of spiritual authority. This arises when princes who have been seduced by the clergy seek to impose their own personal religion on their subjects, thereby illicitly occupying the persona of teacher, and exercising political coercion to realize an end quite foreign to that role: accession to truth through faith.

This double-sided attack on religious coercion permitted Thomasius a highly distinctive multi-level approach to religious toleration. Mutual toleration is morally required of Christians because as members of the invisible church they are bound together solely by the bonds of love and emulation, and in acute consciousness of the fact that their own salvation depends not on enforceable doctrines and ceremonies but on their individual cultivation of a pure and loving heart. The virtue of mutual toleration thus does not give rise to coercible rights, as these belong to the political domain alone, and pertain to man in his Christian rather than his civil persona.[62] Toleration as a political right, though, arises when men fail to exercise mutual toleration and, seduced by the clericalist desire to rule through religion, engage in mutual persecution, thereby threatening social peace and calling forth the political imposition of toleration among rival churches and sects.[63] For Thomasius, then, toleration as a political right belongs solely to the prince or state, being grounded in the sovereign's duty to exercise coercion in order to maintain the peace between constitutively intolerant confessional religions, which is legitimate to the extent that he does so for this reason alone, without regard to religious truth:

[60] This architecture for separating civil authority and religious pedagogy—state and church—is laid out in Pufendorf's *De habitu religionis christianae ad vitam civilem* (Bremen, 1687). For an English version, see Samuel Pufendorf, *Of the nature and qualification of religion in reference to civil society*, ed. Simone Zurbuchen (Indianapolis, 2002).

[61] Thomasius, 'The right of Protestant princes regarding heretics', §§ 37–41, pp. 180–1.

[62] Christian Thomasius and Enno Rudolph Brenneisen, *Das recht evangelischer Fürsten in theologischen Streitigkeiten* (Halle, 1696), XIV, § 3, p. 171.

[63] For a rare appreciation of Thomasius's views in this regard, see Matthias J. Fritsch, *Religiöse toleranz im Zeitalter der Aufklärung: naturrechtliche Begründung—konfessionelle Differenzen* (Hamburg, 2004), pp. 48–65; also Dreitzel, 'Christliche Aufklärung'.

> The pre-eminent regalian right that a prince possesses in relation to religion is the right to tolerate dissenters, and to protect them against anti-Christian persecutors. Consequently, when fractious clergymen revoke this toleration and wish to introduce coercion of conscience, a prince is bound to fulfil his right and punish those who would hinder him in its exercise, because in doing so they transgress both Christianity and natural law, which teach that no one should be persecuted on account of their religion.[64]

Thomasius did indeed attempt to dissolve the link between religious truth and coercive authority that had been secured by Lutheran scholasticism and a theocratic legal system. This dissolution, though, did not occur in the form of a fundamental philosophical discovery: the discovery of the freedom of reason, or of the inherently secular character of the state. Rather, it took place through the mobilization of a series of intellectual positions that were quite simply inimical to the philosophical, theological, and juridical order of the Lutheran confessional state: a spiritualistic lay theology that undermined its claims to theological truth; a historiography of philosophy that suspended the truth claims of its powerful metaphysics; and a political philosophy that denied the use of civil and juridical authority for religious purposes. The key to the success of this assault on the culture and politics of the Lutheran confessional state was that it found anchorage in the political interests of a de facto multi-confessional state. Elsewhere tolerationist programmes would not be successful, and in other territories the separation of religious truth and civil authority would be seen as neither self-evident nor desirable.

IV

In his second heresy disputation of 1697—'On the right of Protestant princes regarding heretics'—Thomasius makes the following comment regarding the existence of multiple religions within a single state:

> At the same time, this situation need not give rise to great tumult in the commonwealth if, that is, through a compact of peace the laity stipulate mutual toleration—regardless that the clergy murmur against it—such that each religion is held to be orthodox from the juridical viewpoint. From the clerical viewpoint, though, each religion will be orthodox to itself, but heretical to the clergy of the others.[65]

This comment is immediately reminiscent of Locke's more celebrated remarks against the persecution of heretics in his *Letter concerning toleration*—'For every Church is Orthodox to it self; to others, Erroneous or Heretical'—even

[64] Thomasius and Brenneisen, *Recht in Streitigkeiten*, XIV, § 1, p. 167.
[65] Thomasius, 'The right of protestant princes regarding heretics', § 40, pp. 181.

if the distinction between the juridical and clerical viewpoints in Thomasius's formulation is absent in Locke's.[66] This verbal echo is underpinned by a significant overlap in the intellectual sources of the two positions. The two advocates of toleration both adhere to an inward spiritualistic form of Protestantism, with its commitment to a simple ethical faith and its hostility towards elaborate doctrinal confessions enforced as orthodoxy. Not only this, but Thomasius's separation of the offices of prince and teacher—where the prince wields coercive power solely to maintain external peace in the commonwealth, while the teacher edifies solely by preaching the Word, eschewing all force—looks remarkably similar to Locke's way of separating civil government from religious worship.

As with Thomasius, however, then so too with Locke it is misguided to attempt to understand his tolerationist programme as if it were the expression of philosophical principles. Locke too constructed his conception of toleration through programmatic engagement with the looming presence of a Protestant confessional state, even if the distinctive religious and political configuration of the emerging Anglican version—coupled with the peculiarities of Locke's intellectual formation[67]—resulted in a programme that differs significantly from Thomasius's. For our present purposes Locke's situation differed from Thomasius's in two central regards. In the first place, Locke opposed political confessionalism not from the position of an academic jurisconsult to a de facto multi-confessional state, but as an intellectual adviser to a dissenting faction opposed to a state that was fast becoming confessional. Secondly, the cultural nucleus of this emerging confessional state—High Church Anglicanism—had not been subject to the intense metaphysical reworking that Saxon Lutheranism had undergone following subscription to the Formula of Concord, and that imbued Lutheran theology with its highly philosophical character. In England, philosophical theology found its home not in the dominant religion but in such non-confessional academic groupings as the Cambridge Platonists. High Anglicanism focused its attack on Calvinism not in academic metaphysics but in a scriptural Trinitarianism and minimal sacramentalism. This was coupled with a rejection of presbyterial church governance in the name of an episcopal system claiming the authority of the apostolic succession.[68]

The centrality of internal church governance to confessional conflict in England meant that Locke opposed Anglican confessionalism in part by defending a quasi-Congregationalist conception of the church against

[66] John Locke, *A letter concerning toleration*, ed. James Tully, trans. William Popple (Indianapolis, 1983), p. 32.

[67] For one account of these, see Stanton, Chapter 3 in this volume.

[68] Mark Goldie, 'The political thought of the Anglican revolution', in Robert A. Beddard, ed., *The revolutions of 1688* (Oxford, 1991), pp. 102–36.

Anglican episcopalism, in a manner that differed significantly from Thomasius's transfer of church governance to an external public law regime. Perhaps even more importantly, though, the fact that confessional Anglicanism had not been elaborated via an expansive academic metaphysics meant that philosophical or natural theology remained a culturally viable weapon of attack for Locke. He could thus combat the revealed scriptural grounds of Anglican Trinitarian theology on the basis of a non-Trinitarian natural theology or 'reasonable Christianity'.[69] This was quite unlike Thomasius's 'fideist–empiricist' rejection of all natural theology—as symptomatic of the metaphysical miscegenation of philosophy and theology in 'sectarian' scholasticism—and resulted in a decisively different tolerationist programme.

Locke's acceptance of philosophical theology means that he views religious truth as something that may be acceded to through the free individual use of (philosophical) reason and results in what might be called a rationalist Congregationalist conception of the church. If individuals can find religious truth and thus salvation simply by exercising their reason, then the church cannot be a hierocratic organization transmitting supra-rational saving doctrine to the laity via an episcopal hierarchy. Churches must instead be voluntary organizations that individuals rationally choose to enter in pursuit of saving truth—the thought that individuals are born into churches makes salvation unbearably arbitrary for Locke—and through which they publicly proclaim this truth to others: 'A Church then I take to be a voluntary Society of Men, joining themselves together of their own accord, in order to the publick worshipping of God, in such a manner as they judge acceptable to him, and effectual to the Salvation of their Souls.'[70] This construction of an anti-confessional church differs markedly from Thomasius's where the true church is 'invisible and scattered across the world' and where no public church can proclaim (or compel) the true faith because faith is incapable of rational truth. For Locke what prevents a particular public church being established as the true faith is not that religion is incapable of rational truth, but that no one is in a position to judge which of the public churches is the custodian of this truth. Locke's (natural) theological justification for freedom of worship, that all should be free to exercise their reason in pursuit of religious truth, is quite unlike Thomasius's, where faith's insusceptibility of rational formulation makes its public doctrinal formulation intrinsically illicit. It also differs radically from Bayle's, where religious truth is treated as being wholly dependent on religious upbringing and pedagogy, which means that no one can be

[69] Mark Goldie, 'John Locke and Anglican royalism', *Political Studies*, 31 (1983), pp. 61–85.
[70] Locke, *A letter*, p. 28.

blamed for religious error.[71] As we shall see, Locke's rationalist Congregationalist conception of the church has significant consequences when it comes to the question of which churches might not be tolerated.

Locke's rationalism also affects his conception of the state and the manner of its separation from the church. We have noted that Locke's mode of distinguishing the state looks very similar to Pufendorf's and Thomasius's, in that he restricts the exercise of civil power to civil interests—life, liberty, health, property—which means that 'the whole jurisdiction of the Magistrate reaches only to these Civil Concernments; and that all Civil Power, Right and Domination, is bounded and confined to the only care of promoting these things; and that it neither can nor ought in any manner to be extended to the Salvation of Souls'.[72] For Locke, though, these civil interests exist prior to the state, in man's natural condition where they arise as rights of his rational and sociable nature, which means that the state is viewed as a voluntary organization rationally entered by men who delegate to it the powers needed to protect their rights. As the result of a rational decision, men do not delegate their pursuit of saving religious truth to the state—by definition incapable of being delegated—which means that the secularity of the state is grounded in the exercise of reason that forms it.

Again, this differs radically from Thomasius's Pufendorfian construction where men enter the state not through reason but as a result of its absence—that is, through mutual fear. For Thomasius, the secularity of the state arises not from rational insight into the limits of civil authority—and from the decision not to delegate the care of souls to magistrates—but from the fact that such authority answers the compulsive need to secure social peace through the exercise of political coercion. In this regard, the secularity of the Pufendorfian state is inseparable from its 'absolutism', as the compulsive fear-driven entry appointment of the civil sovereign means that only he can determine the laws required to maintain social peace, thereby constituting the sole source of civil obligation and right. By comparison, Locke's conception of a state limited by the rights that it is rationally delegated to protect is much closer to the tradition of Christian natural law, in which the state is held accountable to supra-political natural rights arising from man's rational and sociable nature. We shall see that the moral contractarian character of Locke's conception of the state, in tandem with this rationalist Congregationalist conception of the church, has unexpected consequences for his construction of citizenship.

[71] Pierre Bayle, *A philosophical commentary on these words of the gospel, Luke 14.23, 'Compel them to come in, that my house may be full'*, ed. Chandran Kukathas and trans. John Kilcullen (Indianapolis, 2005), pp. 473–8.

[72] Locke, *A letter*, p. 26. Compare Harris, Chapter 4 in this volume.

It thus becomes clear that Locke's construction of toleration as an individual right of religious freedom arises directly from his natural theological conception of the church and his rational natural right conception of the state. On one side, a multiplicity of churches must be tolerated because churches are the product of man's free use of his reason to pursue saving religious truth, and no one can determine which among the churches has arrived at this truth. On the other side, it is illicit for the state to enforce a particular religion because the state itself is the product of man's free use of reason, and man has determined only to delegate protection of his civil interests to the magistrate, reserving the pursuit of saving religious truth for individuals as voluntary members of Christian congregations. Locke thus constructs toleration as a lawful right possessed by individual church members against both a state church and the state itself, as churches are nothing more than the corporate form in which individuals exercise their reason in pursuit of saving truth, thereby giving rise to religious freedom as a natural right:

> These Religious Societies I call Churches: and these I say the Magistrate ought to tolerate. For the business of these Assemblies of the People is nothing but what is lawful for every man in particular to take care of: I mean the Salvation of their Souls: nor in this case is there any difference between the National Church, and other separated Congregations.[73]

The philosophical rationalist character of this way of cleaving church from state is particularly apparent in Locke's treatment of the *adiaphora*. Despite having earlier defended the magistrate's right to determine indifferent religious ceremonies, in the *Letter* Locke insists that once an action—washing a baby—has been incorporated into religious worship, it ceases to be indifferent and passes beyond the authority of the civil magistrate.[74] There can be no blurring the boundary because reason itself shows that the baptismal use of washing for salvation is utterly distinct from those matters for which the magistrate might exercise coercive authority, for example washing for health reasons. Conversely, the existence of religious ceremonies or doctrines that disturb civil society cannot be envisaged as part of a rational order at all, and must be regarded as 'rare' and perhaps even as 'madness'.[75] This means that the civil chaos and carnage wrought by religions must be sheeted home not to their essential nature—intrinsically benign because rational—but to the maddening effects of their irrational repression by confessionalized states: 'What else can be expected, but that these men, growing weary of the Evils under which they labour, should in the end think it lawful for them to resist

[73] Locke, *A letter*, p. 39.
[74] Ibid., pp. 39–41.
[75] Ibid., p. 49.

Force with Force, and to defend their natural Rights (which are not forfeitable upon account of Religion) with Arms as well as they can?'[76] At this point the programmatic character of Locke's rationalism becomes particularly clear, as few would have doubted that religious doctrines and ceremonies had indeed given rise to enormous civil carnage. Even in the example that Locke chooses to illustrate his point, Baptism, differences over infant versus adult and over the use of baptismal exorcism had caused great conflict, because the religious ritual itself gave rise to a contested civil identity and rights.[77]

Here we have reached the point of maximum difference between Locke's tolerationist programme and Thomasius's. For Thomasius, we recall, membership of the 'invisible church' does not give rise to rights, as these arise only as protection from mutual injury—which is impossible in the spiritual community—so that the individual pursuit of salvation does not translate into rights for the public church. It has not been sufficiently observed that in Thomasius's account it is the *absence* of rights in the religious domain that gives rise to a duty of mutual toleration among members of the Christian community. This absence also ensures that toleration as a duty among Christians remains moral, private, and unenforceable. A civil or juridical right of toleration only emerges where the members of rival public churches engage in mutual persecution, thereby threatening social peace. This activates the civil sovereign's duty and right to compel their mutual toleration, not as Christians but as political subjects. For Thomasius, then, the juridical right of toleration is possessed by the civil sovereign alone.[78] The sovereign exercises this right in relation to the public churches not out of respect for their pursuit of religious truth, but on the condition of his complete indifference to such truth, purely in order to maintain social peace. Thomasius thus viewed rights as a public-law jurist, tying them to the legal personality of the citizen, not as a moral philosopher tying them to the Christian's responsibility for his own salvation or to man's rational capacities for understanding and free action. Further, in Thomasius's account the state's character and prerogatives derive not from its contractualist origins—the protection of the liberties and security of those who delegate their (moral) sovereignty to it—but from its political function: to preserve domestic peace and external security through the exercise of a power that must be sovereign to achieve these ends. For Thomasius, the state finds limits to its right of religious supervision not in a moral consensus or natural right that it was formed to uphold, but in a quite different source: namely, in the fact that if it is to end its clerical captivity then it must on no account seek to govern its subjects' consciences, restricting itself solely to their external conduct as this affects social peace.

[76] Ibid., p. 55.

[77] Nischan, 'The exorcism controversy and baptism'.

Seen from a Lockean perspective, therefore, Thomasius's arguments for the toleration of heretics and dissenters have a decidedly limited and ambivalent character. As toleration for Thomasius is not grounded in the universal rights of the tolerated, but in a historical campaign to establish a desacralized political authority, the rights and liberties of all churches, dissenting and orthodox, are circumscribed by the sovereign's absolute right to settle all disputes capable of impacting on civil peace. If dissenters and heretics are to be tolerated and allowed to proclaim their faith, this is not because it might be true, and hence must be respected by the prince as a right. Rather, it is because coercion is futile in matters of faith and the prince must on no account attempt this on the basis of a religious judgement. He has the right, though, to restrict dissenters from engaging in disputations and proselytizing to the extent that these disturb the civil order.[79]

Notwithstanding this difference, however, it is by no means clear whether Locke's construction of toleration in terms of a natural right against the prince gives rise to a more expansive and secure form of toleration, or one more in tune with enlightenment and modernity.[80] In fact, there is an important sense in which Locke's attribution of political rights to church members opens the door to the denial of such rights to those who are not church members, or who belong to the wrong kind of church.[81] Locke thus denies toleration to members of theocratic churches and to those requiring loyalty to a foreign prince, by which he means Catholics pre-eminently.[82] It is historically unrevealing, though, to characterize Locke's denial of toleration to Catholics as merely 'political'—as if Locke were not in any danger of grounding this exercise of civil authority in religion—not least because Locke's arguments were designed to determine the contents of the political and the religious domains. In this regard it is important to recall that to count as a Lockean church and qualify for civil toleration, a congregation must be engaged in the free rational pursuit of saving truth, which means that to the extent that they accept their faith in the form of authoritatively imposed doctrine, Catholic congregations are not churches and should not be tolerated. We thus find Locke arguing in *c.*1674 that the condition of tolerating Catholic priests in England is that they abjure papal infallibility and the right of church councils to establish true doctrine.[83] Somewhat unexpectedly, Locke's conception of the free pursuit of religious truth itself thus assumes a political–confessional

[78] Thomasius and Brenneisen, *Recht in Streitigkeiten*, XIV, § 1, p. 167.
[79] Thomasius, 'Is heresy a punishable crime?', pp. 286–7.
[80] But compare Harris, Chapter 4 in this volume.
[81] For a different gloss, see Stanton, Chapter 3 in this volume.
[82] Locke, *A letter*, pp. 49–51.
[83] John Locke, *Political essays*, ed. Mark Goldie (Cambridge, 1997), p. 223.

role, because he deploys it as the (philosophical) theological qualification for civil rights. This has quite different consequences to restricting toleration on the basis of an independent political secularist norm: the maintenance of domestic peace and external security.

The nature of this difference becomes clearer when we examine the second category of (non-) believer to whom Locke denies political toleration, atheists. He does this on two interrelated grounds: because atheists cannot keep the covenants and oaths necessary for human society, and because in lacking a religion they lack the right on which toleration is based: 'Promises, Covenants, and Oaths, which are the Bonds of Humane Society, can have no hold upon an Atheist. The taking away of God, tho but even in thought, dissolves all. Besides also, those that by their Atheism undermine and destroy all Religion, can have no pretence of Religion whereupon to challenge [that is, claim] the Privilege of Toleration.'[84] Here we see the unexpected political costs associated with Locke's grounding of toleration in a subjective right based on the pursuit of religious truth. In making the pursuit of religious truth into the source of binding oaths and covenants, hence of civil society, Locke ends up asserting that those who do not belong to the assemblies of religious truth-seekers are incapable of holding to such oaths. This means that he views civil duties as grounded in the rights associated with church membership, so that civil rights will be denied to those who are not members. Those who hold to no religion, then, may not be tolerated, as political rights in this regard come from membership of churches as the corporate form in which individuals pursue religious truth and salvation. Locke's refusal of toleration to Catholics and atheists is thus not an anomaly or historical detour within his philosophical construction of religious freedom on the basis of individual natural rights. On the contrary, it is the direct result of this construction, arising as the flipside of his attempt to ground toleration in a 'lawful' rational natural right against the state.

V

Somewhat unexpectedly, then, the Lockean doctrine designed to set limits on the exercise of civil authority—namely, that there is a natural right to pursue religious truth on the basis of the freedom of reason of conscience—is also the doctrine that permits civil coercion to be used against those who refuse to pursue religious truth in this manner. Equally unexpectedly, in refusing to ground civil authority in the natural rights of reasonable Christians—in

[84] Locke, *A letter*, p. 51.

grounding it wholly and solely in the maintenance of social peace—Thomasius is not compelled to exercise it against those who refuse to be reasonable or who deny Christ. It was this chain of consequences that eventually allowed Thomasius to argue for the toleration of both Catholics and atheists:[85]

> religions as such do not disturb external peace, and where their teachings are so disposed [to tranquility], then the prince can well tolerate them. For those who deny the Trinity do not immediately disturb the state. Where, though, such people do disturb the state, then the prince's duty requires that he expel them from the commonwealth. In fact, in the past I maintained that nothing could be more injurious to the commonwealth than atheism. Now, however, I recognize this to be false. Who then may not be tolerated in the republic? Our Lutherans answer: the papists, because they say publicly that the subject of a prince who belongs to another religion may kill him in good conscience, and that heretics may not defend the faith. These principles are contrary to the state and disturb the commonwealth, as one has seen in France, and should therefore not be tolerated. I do not want to go into the facts here ... but we must nonetheless not impute the principles of the Jesuits to everyone. And if a prince wishes to act as if turmoil could arise from an opinion simply by probable consequence, then he would tolerate no religion, for the Lutheran religion can also give occasion to turmoil by consequence. ... This then is the wisest counsel: that a prince should tolerate all religions. No turmoil arises from diversity of opinion as such, but arises rather when those who disagree feud. Then the prince must bravely punish them, so that afterwards they will live quite peacefully.[86]

More generally, we can say that in refusing to view the state in Lockean terms—as a contractual expression of a moral agreement among Christian subjects—Thomasius could go much further than Locke in freeing the state from the need to enforce any kind of morality, religious or otherwise, eventually resulting in a more secularized conception of toleration. Thomasius's position in this regard was supported by his rejection of the view that good conduct depends on having the right religious or moral ideas, which permitted him to support the Dutch government's toleration of Spinoza's atheism in much the same way as Bayle had. Paradoxically, it is the prince's indifference towards religion and morality that best guarantees the freedom of Christians in this regard, even if it lies entirely at the prince's disposition to determine when the threshold of civil disturbance has been crossed and freedom ceases.

[85] In arguing that Thomasius refused to accept the toleration of atheists, Fritsch (*Religiöse Toleranz*, p. 65) would appear to have overlooked Thomasius's final views on the matter.

[86] Christian Thomasius, *Vollständige Erläuterung der Kirchenrechts-gelahrtheit* (Frankfurt and Leipzig, 1740), pp. 349–51.

6

Leibniz's Doctrine of Toleration: Philosophical, Theological, and Pragmatic Reasons

MARIA ROSA ANTOGNAZZA*

LEIBNIZ IS NOT COMMONLY NUMBERED amongst canonical writers on toleration. One obvious reason is that, unlike Locke, he did not write a treatise specifically devoted to that doctrine. Another is the enormous amount of energy that he famously devoted to ecclesiastical reunification. Promoting the reunification of Christian churches is an objective quite different from promoting the toleration of different religious faiths—so different, in fact, that they are sometimes even construed as mutually exclusive. Ecclesiastical reunification aims to find agreement at least on the most important doctrines. Religious toleration involves accepting and respecting disagreement even on the most important doctrines. If one regards these two projects as alternative rather than complementary strategies for dealing with religious diversity, Leibniz might more readily be characterized as an ecumenist rather than a tolerationist.[1] Such appears to be the conclusion, at any rate, implicit in the balance of critical literature on these topics: whereas a steady stream of studies has discussed Leibniz's project of ecclesiastical reunification, only a meager trickle has been devoted to his views on toleration;[2] and

* I would like to thank Howard Hotson for many insightful comments on earlier drafts of this chapter. A date accompanied by an asterisk indicates the period from which a text probably dates; a double date indicates the difference between the Julian calendar (old style) and the Gregorian calendar (new style). When not otherwise identified, translations are my own.

[1] Cf. Nicholas Jolley, 'Leibniz, Locke, and the epistemology of toleration', in Pauline Phemister and Stuart Brown, eds., *Leibniz and the English-speaking world* (Dordrecht, 2007), pp. 133–43, esp. p. 133.

[2] To the best of my knowledge, the most substantial discussions are Yves Charles Zarka, *Philosophie et politique à l'âge classique* (Paris, 1998), pp. 245–55; my own essay, 'Leibniz and religious toleration: the correspondence with Paul Pellisson-Fontanier', *American Catholic Philosophical Quarterly*, 76 (2002), pp. 601–22; Jolley, 'Leibniz, Locke, and the epistemology of toleration'; and Mogens Laerke, 'Leibniz et la tolerance', *Bulletin de l'institut de l'histoire de la Reformation*, 28 (2008), pp. 29–47. To these contributions should be added accounts in the following: Aloys Pichler, *Die Theologie des Leibniz* (Munich, 1869–70), II, pp. 59–64; Lucy

some of these studies go so far as to conclude that Leibniz had no doctrine of toleration at all.[3]

This chapter will attempt to show, on the contrary, that a robust, many-layered, and unusually inclusive doctrine of toleration can be gleaned from Leibniz's writings. The fragmentary, occasional nature and relative paucity of passages expressing his views on toleration—although far less immediately impressive than the mass of texts specifically devoted to the project of ecclesiastical reunification—are by no means an indication of the lack of importance of religious toleration in Leibniz's general outlook. It is not in fact unusual for significant Leibnizian doctrines to be buried in his general correspondence or in occasional writings tackling a vast array of disparate issues; and as Leibniz scholars have become aware of this fact, they have needed to become increasingly adept at teasing out statements on particular issues from a multiplicity of diverse texts and then carefully comparing and contrasting them to work out the consistent though often complex doctrines underlying them. Applying such an approach to Leibniz's scattered statements on the topic of this chapter allows us to reach at least four fresh and significant conclusions.

First and most generally, it can be documented that Leibniz had, in fact, a doctrine of toleration and frequently employed and developed it in writings on a wide range of subjects throughout his long intellectual life. A second conclusion is the discovery that this doctrine operated at least at three different levels: philosophical, theological, and pragmatic. As this implies, thirdly, the doctrine of religious toleration, rather than being in collision with Leibniz's core project of ecclesiastical reunification, was an essential element of that very project: it should be seen, in other words, not as a competing goal, but as a necessary first step towards ecclesiastical reunification. Yet at the same time it will also emerge, fourthly, that Leibniz's doctrine of toleration was no mere

Prenant, 'L'esprit de tolerance chez Leibniz', *Cahiers d'Histoire*, 4 (1959), pp. 61–2; Miguel Beltrán, 'Leibniz on tolerable religious dissidence', in *Leibniz und Europa: VI Internationaler Leibniz-Kongress* (Hanover, 1994), I, pp. 57–64; and Wilhelm Totok, 'Der Toleranzbegriff bei Leibniz', in *Leibniz und Europa: VI Internationaler Leibniz-Kongress* (Hanover, 1995), II, pp. 299–303. Louis Lanoix, 'Le Hanovre, l'Angleterre et la naissance de la tolérance: la correspondance de Gottfried von Leibniz avec Caroline von Anspach, Princesse de Galles (1705–1716)', in Paul-Gabriel Boucé, ed., *Evolution et révolution(s) dans la Grande-Bretagne du XVIIIe siècle: actes des colloques tenus en 1989–1990 à la Sorbonne nouvelle / Centre d'études Anglais du XVIIIe siècle* (Paris, 1993), pp. 51–67 touches tangentially on the issue of religious toleration in the context of the author's sweeping assumption that 'la liberté de conscience' is 'le fondement même du protestantisme' and therefore all sorts of 'Protestants'—'Sophie de Hanovre, la duchesse d'Orléans, John Toland, Leibniz et Caroline'—'marquent bein l'aube du Siècle des Lumières, le siècle d'or des Protestants' (pp. 56, 66). Such generic lumping together of 'Protestants' as the holders of the banner of freedom does not seem to me either illuminating or accurate.

[3] Mogens Laerke doubts the existence of a Leibnizian concept of toleration: see Laerke, 'Leibniz et la tolerance'.

function of this intra-Christian project of reunification: rather it pointed towards a still more fundamental principle which extended beyond the ecumenical project as well. It had the resources, in other words, for accepting and respecting irreducible religious diversity and disagreement on points of importance not only between Christian communities, but also between Christians and non-Christians, including, in principle, even the atheists. These conclusions should emerge from a discussion of statements on the philosophical, theological, and pragmatic justifications of religious toleration scattered throughout Leibniz's sprawling corpus of writings.

I

Leibniz's doctrine of toleration rests on a range of philosophical premises. From an epistemological point of view, Leibniz shares with Locke the thesis that to change beliefs or opinions is not within the power of the will, but only within the power of the intellect. This is apparent, for instance, in his epistolary exchange of 1690–1 with Paul Pellisson-Fontanier, a French Huguenot who had converted to Catholicism. In a memoire addressed to Pellisson in response to the French thinker's *Reflexions sur les différends de la religion* (1686) Leibniz writes: 'Opinions are not voluntary, and are not dismissed at will; this is why (absolutely speaking) they are not subject to orders.'[4] The same position had already been presented in a letter of 11 January 1684 to another convert from Calvinism to Catholicism, Leibniz's trusted friend Landgraf Ernst von Hessen-Rheinfels, who repeatedly tried to convince him to embrace the Catholic faith. Writing to Landgraf Ernst, Leibniz maintains that 'opinion is not something which depends on the Empire of the will and which can be changed as one pleases'.[5] In turn, in a letter to Marie de Brinon of 23 October 1693 he repeats: 'opinions [les sentimens] are not arbitrary, it is not up to us to adopt them'.[6] Likewise, in his *Remarques sur un petit livre traduit de l'Anglois, intitulé Lettre sur l'enthousiasme* written around 1711 in response to Shaftesbury's *Letter concerning enthusiasm* (1708), we read: 'one

[4] G. W. Leibniz, *Sämtliche Schriften und Briefe*, ed. by the Academy of Sciences of Berlin, series I–VIII (Darmstadt, Leipzig, and Berlin, 1923f.) [cited by series, volume, and page] I. 6, p. 117. See also idem, *Nouveaux essais sur l'entendement humain*, IV.xx.17, in Leibniz, *Sämtliche Schriften*, VI. 6, p. 520. Pellisson published his epistolary exchange with Leibniz as the fourth part of his *Reflexions* (Paul Pellisson-Fontanier, *Reflexions sur les differens de la religion. Quatrième partie. Ou réponse aux objections envoyées d'Allemagne, sur l'unité de l'eglise, et sur la question, si elle peut tolérer les sectes*. Paris, 1691).

[5] Leibniz, *Sämtliche Schriften*, I. 4, p. 320.

[6] Leibniz, *Sämtliche Schriften*, I. 9, p. 192.

does not have a belief at will, but acts as one wills; it is not the lack of belief which deserves properly to be punished, but malice and obstinacy'.[7]

If belief is intellectual in origin rather than voluntary, it follows that nobody should be condemned or punished for believing (or not believing) any particular doctrine, since to do otherwise is not within the power of their will. It is true that belief can be obliquely influenced by the will, as Leibniz admits in the *Nouveaux essais*:

> what we believe is never just what we want to believe but rather what we see as most likely … nevertheless we can bring it about indirectly that we believe what we want to believe. We can do this by turning our attention away from a disagreeable object so as to apply ourselves to something else which we find pleasing; so that by thinking further about the reasons for the side which we favour, we end up by believing it to be most likely.[8]

But this is precisely an *indirect* intervention of the will by which we focus our attention on the *reasons* in favour of a belief so that we are, eventually, convinced by them. The only way to bring a person to change opinion therefore ultimately remains persuasion based on reasons regarding the falsity (or truth) of the doctrine in question.[9] As an example Leibniz uses the most consequential clash between religion and science of his time: the condemnation by the Roman church of the Copernican system:

> to believe or not to believe is not a voluntary thing. If I believe I see a manifest error, all the authority of the world could not change my view if this [authority] is not accompanied by some reasons capable of satisfying my difficulties or of overcoming them. And if the whole Church were to condemn the doctrine of the movement of the Earth, the able astronomers of this opinion [ce sentiment] could certainly dissimulate, but it would not be in their power to give up [their view].[10]

[7] G. W. Leibniz, *Die philosophischen Schriften*, ed. C. I. Gerhardt (7 vols., Berlin, 1875–90, repr. Hildesheim, 1960–1), III, p. 415.

[8] Leibniz, *Nouveaux essais*, IV.xx.16, in *New essays on human understanding*, ed. and trans. Peter Remnant and Jonathan Bennett (Cambridge, 1981) p. 517. This point is rightly noted by Jolley, 'Leibniz, Locke, and the epistemology of toleration', p. 139, where this passage from the *Nouveaux essais* is quoted.

[9] Cf. Leibniz to Ernst von Hessen-Rheinfels, 4/14 August 1683, in Leibniz, *Sämtliche Schriften*, II. 1, p. 535, and G. W. Leibniz, *Lettre de Monsieur de Leibniz à l'auteur des Reflexions sur l'origine du Mahometisme*, 2 December 1706, in Leibniz, *Opera omnia, nunc primum collecta, in classes distributa, praefationibus et indicibus exornata*, ed. L. Dutens (6 vols., Geneva, 1768), V, p. 483.

[10] G. W. Leibniz, *Textes inédits d'après les manuscrits de la Bibliothèque Provinciale de Hanovre*, ed. G. Grua (2 vols., Paris, 1948), vol. 1, p. 216 (July 1703). During his extended stay in Rome in 1689, Leibniz joined his voice to those who urged the Vatican to lift the ban on the Copernican system. For details see André Robinet, *G. W. Leibniz iter Italicum* (Florence, 1988), esp. p. 102, and Maria Rosa Antognazza, *Leibniz: an intellectual biography* (Cambridge, 2009), pp. 301–2.

The only rule of faith is therefore to believe that, for which reasons have been given: 'In order to believe, faith must be presented in a credible way: otherwise there is no obligation to believe.'[11] Belief—any belief—must be based on reasons, as Leibniz writes in 1690 commenting on Pellisson's *Reflexions sur les différends de la religion*: 'it is obvious that nothing can be believed if one does not think that one has some proof or ground for it. Therefore it must be acknowledged that we all have need of some examination, otherwise religion would be arbitrary.'[12]

However, as this response to Pellisson continues, the reasons required for (any) belief can be of two different kinds. They can be either 'explicable' or 'inexplicable':

> the *reasons* of our persuasion are of two kinds, those of one kind are explicable; those of the other kind are inexplicable. Those which I call *explicable* can be proposed to other people by distinct reasoning; but *inexplicable reasons* consist only in our conscience or perception, and in an experience of an interior feeling into which others cannot enter, if one does not find a way to make them feel the same things in the same manner. For instance, it is not always possible to tell others what one finds pleasing or disgusting in a person, in a painting, in a sonnet, in a ragout; for this reason it is said that tastes should not be disputed. It is for the same reason that one could not make a person born blind comprehend what colour is. Now, those who say that they find in themselves a *divine internal light*, or a ray [of light] which makes them feel some truth, base themselves on some inexplicable reasons. And I see that not only the Protestants but also the Roman Catholics use this *ray* [*of light*]: since—in addition to the *motives of belief or of credibility* (as they call them), that is to say, in addition to the explicable reasons of our Faith, which are nothing else than a collection of arguments of different degrees of force, and which even taken all together can only ground a *human faith*—they demand a light of grace from heaven capable of producing a full conviction, and which forms what is called *divine Faith.*[13]

Explicable reasons can provide the basis merely of human faith. Reasons of this kind are nevertheless extremely important precisely because they can be

[11] Leibniz's marginal note published in *Sämtliche Schriften*, I. 6, p. 145.

[12] Leibniz, *Sämtliche Schriften*, I. 6, p. 76.

[13] Leibniz, *Sämtliche Schriften*, I. 6, p. 76. Leibniz's use of this distinction is found in the context of his exchange with Pellisson. I do not see why Zarka, *Philosophie et politique à l'âge classique*, p. 252 claims that Leibniz criticizes 'la distinction opérée par Pellisson entre raison explicable et raison inexplicable de la croyance, et, corrélativement, celle de la distinction entre foi humaine and foi divine'. Leibniz clearly embraces these distinctions not only in his exchange with Pellisson but also in the *Examen religionis christianae (Systema theologicum)*, April–October 1686*, in *Sämtliche Schriften*, VI. 4, p. 2362; the *Nouveaux essais*, IV.xviii.9, in *Sämtliche Schriften*, VI. 6, p. 497; and the *Theodicy*, 'Discours preliminaire', § 29, in *Die philosophischen Schriften* VI, pp. 67–98. For an illuminating discussion of divine faith in Leibniz, see Paul Lodge and Benjamin Crowe, 'Leibniz, Bayle, and Locke on faith and reason', *American Catholic Philosophical Quarterly*, 76 (2002), pp. 575–600.

'explained', that is, they can be communicated to other people, providing a sort of objective common ground on which rational beings can meet and discuss. Examples of explicable reasons might therefore be the defence against the charge of contradiction; the historical and philological verification of the authenticity of Scripture and of the authenticity of testimony; and the 'explanation' of the mysteries 'so much as is necessary to believe them', that is, by providing at least an 'analogical understanding' of the meaning of the mysteries since (according to Leibniz) one cannot consider as true 'words entirely devoid of meaning' or 'sounds without meaning (*sine mente soni*)'.[14] In other words, explicable reasons are those normally called by Leibniz the 'motives of credibility' which can and should be provided in support of the Christian faith. These motives do not amount, however, to a rational demonstration of Christian doctrines. According to the metaphor used by Leibniz in the 'Discours preliminaire' of the *Theodicy*, they are like the 'Letters Patent' which must be presented to the tribunal of reason, before reason can yield to revelation as a new light superior to it.[15]

Inexplicable reasons, on the other hand, are those which ground faith in the full sense of the term, that is, as a divine faith which is the fruit of God's grace and of his illumination. Due precisely to their 'inexplicability', however, this second kind of reasons must be subject to caution in order to avoid the danger of illusion.[16] The bottom line is that religious belief can only be grounded in reasons—either reasons that can be provided by human beings or reasons that come directly from God as a product of divine illumination. In neither case can belief be the result of a mere act of human will.

II

From the epistemological view that beliefs are not voluntary, there follows quite naturally Leibniz's distinction between the errant and the error. In essence, this distinction implies that, whereas one has a duty to fight error through the means of rational persuasion, one must not persecute those who

[14] See Leibniz, *Theodicy*, 'Discours preliminaire', §§ 5, 54, 55, 66.

[15] Leibniz, *Theodicy*, "Discours preliminaire" § 29, in *Die philosophischen Schriften*, VI, p. 67: 'les *motifs de credibilité* justifient, une fois pour toutes, l'autorité de la S. Ecriture devant le Tribunal de la Raison, afin que la Raison luy cede dans la suite, comme à une nouvelle lumière, et luy sacrifie toutes ses vrai-semblances. C'est à peu près comme un nouveau Chef envoyé par le Prince doit faire voir ses Lettres Patentes dans l'Assemblée où il doit presider par apres ... car il faut bien qu'elle [the true religion] ait des caracteres que les fausses religions n'ont pas.'

[16] See Leibniz, *Sämtliche Schriften*, I. 6, pp. 76–7.

are in error, since coercion is in itself an enemy of truth.[17] The penalty for the errant, Leibniz therefore insists, is simply 'to be taught'.[18] Leibniz's attitude towards anti-Trinitarianism offers a particularly good insight into the way in which he weds the unyielding defence of what he regards as objective religious truth with the rejection of violent means of propagating or defending it. Throughout his life, from his earliest writings to the *Theodicy*, Leibniz consistently opposed anti-Trinitarianism, leaving behind a wealth of texts in which he engaged in a sophisticated intellectual duel especially against the chief anti-Trinitarians of his day, the Socinians.[19] At the same time, however, he consistently opposed the persecution and universal ban of these same Socinians.[20] In particular, he describes as 'inexcusable' the violent repression of anti-Trinitarians emblematically represented by the condemnation and execution of Michael Servetus (*c.*1511–53) in Calvin's Geneva: 'the severity exerted against them [the anti-Trinitarians], and particularly against Servetus, is inexcusable, since it is only the bad will, and not the error in itself that can be punished. *The penalty for one who is mistaken is to be taught.*'[21] Writing in 1698 to Hiob Ludolf, Leibniz claims that 'refutation can exist together with ecclesiastical toleration'.[22] Leibniz recognizes that it is often difficult in practice to combat error without harrying those who propagate it; but instead of using this difficulty as a justification of religious persecution, he derives precisely the opposite conclusion from it: namely, that a tolerant attitude be adopted towards an error if it cannot be eradicated without causing great harm to those who hold it or to the society in which they live.[23]

[17] *Remarques sur un petit livre traduit de l'Anglois, intitulé Lettre sur l'enthousiasme, publiée à la Haye en 1709* [French translation of Anthony Ashley Cooper, 3rd earl of Shaftesbury, *A letter concerning enthusiasm* (London,1708)], in *Die philosophischen Schriften*, III, p. 410: 'Il faut avouer que ceux qui sont persuadés comme il faut, qu'un autre est dans le chemin de la perdition, ont droit et même obligation de tâcher de l'en retirer: mais il faut que ce soit par des voies permises … la contrainte est ennemie de la vérité.'

[18] See Leibniz, *Sämtliche Schriften*, II. 1, p. 535; Leibniz, *Opera omnia*, V, p. 483.

[19] For details see Maria Rosa Antognazza, *Leibniz on the Trinity and the Incarnation: reason and revelation in the seventeenth century* (New Haven and London, 2007).

[20] Cf. Leibniz to Ernst von Hessen-Rheinfels, mid-May 1687, in *Sämtliche Schriften*, I. 4, p. 433, and Leibniz to Thomas Burnett of Kemney, 8 (18) April 1698, in ibid., I. 15, p. 489. See also Leibniz, *Lettre de Monsieur de Leibniz à l'auteur des Reflexions sur l'origine du Mahometisme*, 2 December 1706, in *Opera omnia*, V, p. 483.

[21] Leibniz, *Lettre de Monsieur de Leibniz*, in *Opera omnia*, V, p. 483.

[22] Leibniz, *Sämtliche Schriften*, I. 15, p. 629.

[23] Ibid.: 'Equidem tecum sentio, odia inter dissentientes abesse debere, sed scis quam difficile sit in praxi, personas separare a causis, et moderationem justam obtinere. Plerique dicunt se haereses odio habere non homines; sed ubi aliter non possunt solent haeresin tollere cum haeretico … Ita sentientibus non facilius persuaderi potest moderatio, quam si ostendatur ipsis, falli eos opinione, et pejores alios putare, quam sunt. Potest sententia alicujus falsa esse, ita tamen ut non sit tam prava et noxia, quam alii praejudiciis affectibusque occupati judicant. … Quanquam ut dixi optem ego et suadeam etiam zizaniam ferri quoties sine magno malo evelli non potest. Et hoc

The inexcusability of the use of violence against people who profess opinions regarded as erroneous but believed by them in good conscience to be true is ultimately justified by appeal to natural law and natural rights, that is to say by appeal to the primary, inalienable moral qualities of human beings the violation of which define what is an unjust action. Since it is 'a natural right [droit naturelle] to express what one believes to be the truth', Leibniz doubts that one could have the 'right to proceed … to the ultimate punishment' even in the case of recognized atheists.[24] On the contrary,

> it is against natural right [droit naturelle] to punish someone because he is of some opinion, no matter which, as opposed to punishing someone for some actions; *for the penalty for one who is mistaken is to be taught* [*nam errantis poena est doceri*]. And again, I do not believe that we have the right to punish someone with corporal pains for actions which he undertakes in accordance with his opinion, and which he believes his conscience obligates him to perform.[25]

Indeed, it is nothing less than 'a crime' to abjure what one believes to be true.[26] Therefore 'it is necessary to be very careful in matters of retractation to avoid forcing people to act against their conscience'.[27]

III

In addition to Leibniz's general epistemological doctrine of the involuntariness of beliefs, his epistemology of toleration can also be seen as specifically grounded in his views regarding the epistemic status of faith. As he writes in the early *Commentatiuncula de judice controversiarum* (*c.*1669–70), '[f]ides est credere. Credere est verum putare',[28] that is, faith is to believe and to believe is to hold something as true as opposed to *knowing* that something is true. Faith, in other words, belongs in the domain of opinion (broadly conceived) based

inprimis faciendum quoties data est tolerandi fides. Ut igitur concludam: utrumque tolerandi genus, quoties cum ratione id fieri potest, utiliter inculcari arbitror, majoremque esse efficaciam suadentis, ubi conjungi possunt.' See also Leibniz to Des Bosses, 21 July 1707, in *Die philosophischen Schriften*, II, p. 337.

[24] Leibniz to Ernst von Hessen-Rheinfels, 4/14 August 1683, in *Sämtliche Schriften*, II. 1, p. 535.

[25] Ibid.

[26] Leibniz to Des Bosses, 21 July 1707, in *Die philosophischen Schriften*, II, p. 337.

[27] Leibniz to Ernst von Hessen-Rheinfels, 29 June / 9 July 1688, in *Sämtliche Schriften*, I. 5, p. 182: 'On n'a pas droit de condamner toutes les erreurs, ny d'obliger tousjours les gens à les desavouer. … Il faut estre fort circomspect en matiere de retractation[s], pour n'obliger personne à agir contre sa conscience.'

[28] G. W. Leibniz, *Commentatiuncula de judice controversiarum*, § 20, in *Sämtliche Schriften*, VI. 1, p. 550.

on reasons for credibility,[29] and not in the domain of demonstration. As such, belief (any belief) is exposed to the possibility of error. From an epistemological point of view, faith admits the possibility that a doctrine believed to be true might on the contrary be demonstrated to be false. 'I challenge', Leibniz continues in the *Commentatiuncula*, 'those who deny that faith [fidem] exists together with the fear of its opposite or that it is an opinion [opinionem esse], if they are telling the truth, to try to explain why such faith has room for the notion of "more or less". However, that it does admit of it, the witness of Christ shows.'[30] Since, 'due to the obscurity of the human mind',[31] the truth of revealed propositions cannot be demonstrated, one must hypothetically admit that the contrary of these propositions could be demonstrated. The task of the defender of the mysteries is therefore to dispel 'the fear of the opposite', repelling time and again attempts to prove the contrary.

To be sure, in the case of a genuine divine revelation, the believer is certain that no such proof exists. Moreover, for Leibniz faith does not simply reduce to believing a proposition to be true. To be truly faithful, the will as well as the intellect must be involved. Leibniz does distinguish between a theoretical opinion which one can embrace on purely rational grounds, and the wholehearted practical assent and unshakable conviction which is the fruit of the supernatural grace of God and marks faith in the full sense of the term, that is divine faith.[32] Nevertheless, as long as there is no demonstration or adequate knowledge, the possibility of error cannot be excluded; that is to say, the possibility cannot be excluded of having mistakenly believed as divine revelation some doctrine that is later demonstrated to be false and therefore not of divine origin at all. Although believers will hold firm to their beliefs and are rationally justified in doing so as long as there is no proof that they are mistaken, the epistemology of faith described above naturally opens the faithful to a more humble attitude towards what they believe to be true—and '*humility*', as Leibniz remarks, 'does not imagine that reason is always on its side'.[33]

Indeed, according to Leibniz, fragments of truths are present everywhere, and the same universal truth is expressed by different people and traditions from different perspectives. As he tells Nicolas Rémond on 10 January 1714, 'I have tried to unearth and reunite the truth buried and dispersed under the

[29] Cf. Leibniz, *Commentatiuncula*, § 32, in *Sämtliche Schriften*, VI. 1, p. 522.

[30] Ibid.

[31] G. W. Leibniz, *De demonstratione possibilitatis mysteriorum eucaristiae*, in *Sämtliche Schriften*, VI. 1, p. 515.

[32] I fully agree with Lodge and Crowe who insightfully make these points in 'Leibniz, Bayle, and Locke', esp. pp. 597 and 599.

[33] Leibniz, *Sämtliche Schriften*, I. 6, p. 87 (Leibniz's remark on a letter by Paul Pellisson-Fontanier of 4 September 1690).

opinions of the different sects of philosophers, and I believe I have added to that something of my own in order to advance a few steps further … I have found that most sects are right in a good part of what they affirm, but not so much in what they deny.'[34] Likewise, at the beginning of 1708, pouring water on the fire of a sterile controversy in which he had become involved against his will, Leibniz confides:

> I am more inclined to excuse than to accuse, and to praise rather than to blame; and I prefer to note the good in people to benefit from it and to encourage them, than to point out their defects and do them wrong … There are many true and certain things, but sometimes this truth is only known in a confused way until one begins to doubt it. And it is then that it is developed and demonstrated as it should be … [I]nsightful objections are always useful, and serve to clarify truth the better.[35]

This typically conciliatory outlook—substantiated by his doctrine of universal harmony, according to which diversity and multiplicity should not be feared but celebrated since it can ultimately be traced back to unity—could not but foster a tolerant attitude.

IV

These epistemological views grounding toleration, and his appeal to natural law, are complemented at the metaphysical level by Leibniz's conviction of the conformity between divine and human justice and love. In the *Méditation sur la notion commune de la justice* of 1703, rephrasing Plato's celebrated 'Euthyphro dilemma', Leibniz asks the vexed question of whether there is an objective standard of goodness and justice:

> It is agreed that whatever God wills is good and just. But there remains the question whether it is good and just because God wills it or whether God wills it because it is good and just: in other words, whether justice and goodness are arbitrary or whether they belong to the necessary and eternal truths about the nature of things, as do numbers and proportions.[36]

Following in the footsteps of Plato, Leibniz thinks that justice and goodness belong to 'eternal truths about the nature of things', which as such have the same kind of absolute necessity as the truths of logic and mathematics. Divine justice and human justice must therefore be of the same kind, differing from

[34] Leibniz, *Die philosophischen Schriften*, III, pp. 606–7.
[35] Hanover, Niedersächsische Landesbibliothek / Gottfried Wilhelm Leibniz Bibliothek, Leibniz-Handschriften, I 20 Bl. 132.
[36] G. W. Leibniz, *Méditation sur la notion commune de la justice*, in *The political writings of Leibniz*, trans. and ed. with an introduction by Patrick Riley (Cambridge, 1988), p. 45.

one another only in degree of perfection. Against Pellisson, who advocates the incommensurability of human and divine justice,[37] Leibniz therefore argues for the opposite thesis, in a way reminiscent of his defence in the *Theodicy* of the conformity of human and divine reason, despite the finitude of the former and the infinitude of the latter:[38]

> There are certain universal principles of justice which suit both God and man; otherwise God's justice would be actually denied or we would not have any idea of it. To distinguish the principles of divine justice from those of human justice, would amount to saying that the principles of our geometry are not good for God or the angels.[39]

What would seem to be deeply unjust in the human domain could not be just for God. Therefore 'one should not imagine that God is capable of doing what would be tyranny if done by human beings',[40] and

> one should not say either that what we call justice is nothing in relation to God, who is the master of all things to the point that he could condemn innocent people without violating his justice; or finally that justice is something arbitrary in respect to him; [these are] bold and dangerous expressions to which some people have let themselves be dragged to the prejudice of God's attributes: since in this case there would be no point in praising his goodness and justice; and everything would be as if the most wicked spirit, the Prince of evil spirits, the evil principle of the Manicheans, were the only Master of the Universe.[41]

This position leads, in turn, to a cluster of theological reasons for religious toleration grounded in key aspects of Leibniz's soteriology and ecclesiology.

V

According to Leibniz, it would be against God's justice and love to condemn those who search for the truth in a sincere way even if they are objectively in error. Writing to his friend Ernst von Hessen-Rheinfels on 4/14 September 1690, he remarks:

[37] Cf. Pellisson's remarks published in Leibniz, *Sämtliche Schriften*, I. 6, p. 144. See also Pellisson, *Reflexions*, p. 36: 'Nos lumieres sont trop courtes pour percer la profondeur de la justice divine; nous n'en connoissons pas même les fondemens et les principes.'

[38] Leibniz, *Theodicy*, 'Discours preliminaire', § 61, in *Die philosophischen Schriften*, VI, p. 84.

[39] Leibniz's marginal note on his copy of the fourth part of Pellisson's *Reflexions*, in *Sämtliche Schriften*, I. 6, p. 144. See also Leibniz to Ernst von Hessen-Rheinfels, 4/14 September 1690, in *Sämtliche Schriften*, I. 6, p. 108, and Leibniz, *Theodicy*, 'Discours preliminaire', § 37, in *Die philosophischen Schriften*, VI, pp. 71–2.

[40] Leibniz to Ernst von Hessen-Rheinfels, 4/14 September 1690, in *Sämtliche Schriften*, I. 6, p. 108.

[41] Leibniz, *Theodicy*, 'Discours preliminaire', § 37, in *Die philosophischen Schriften*, VI, pp. 71–2.

> I am not entirely of the opinion of Mr Arnauld who … finds it strange that so many millions of pagans have not been condemned; I would find it much stranger if they had been: I don't know why we are so inclined to believe that people are damned or sunk in eternal miseries, even if they could not help it; but this leads to thoughts hardly compatible with the goodness and justice of God … I don't believe that the opinion of the eternal damnation of so many virtually innocent people is so edifying and so useful in preventing sin as is imagined. It leads to thoughts hardly compatible with the love of God.[42]

In the *Nouveaux essais*, recalling his exchange of 1690–1 with Pellisson, Leibniz notes,

> I once showed M. Pellisson that many eminent doctors of the Roman Church, far from damning lax Protestants, have been willing to save even pagans … I adduced the view of a Portuguese teacher, Diego Payva de Andrada, who was very famous in his day and had been one of the theologians at the Council of Trent. He went so far as to say that those who took the opposite view of the matter were making God supremely cruel—'For', he said, 'there can be no worse cruelty.'[43]

After disapproving of Augustine's view, according to which unbaptized children are damned, Leibniz concludes: 'we are fortunate that God is more charitable than men'.[44]

Leibniz, in fact, finds reasons internal to the Christian revelation for proposing toleration as the most consistent way of following the teaching of Jesus Christ. Persecution and condemnation are against the very spirit of Christianity since 'it is clear that the spirit of Christianity should lead to mildness',[45] and toleration is 'necessary on account of the principle of Christian charity'.[46] As a young man, countering the accusation by his half-brother that he had abandoned Lutheranism to embrace the hated heresy of Calvinism (vehemently condemned by the hardline Lutherans who dominated his immediate family), Leibniz replies: 'I hold and with God's help will continue to hold fast to the Evangelical [that is, Lutheran] truth as long as I live, but I am deterred from condemning others both by my own personal inclination and by the stern command of Christ: "Judge not, that ye be not judged."'[47] Later on he launches a heartfelt appeal to Christian charity and the evangelical love of peace as the basis for ending the division amongst Christians:

[42] Leibniz, *Sämtliche Schriften*, I. 6, pp. 107–8.

[43] Cf. Diego Payva Andradius, *Orthodoxarum explicationum libri decem* (Cologne, 1564).

[44] Leibniz, *Nouveaux essais*, IV.xviii.9, in *New essays*, pp. 500–2.

[45] Leibniz, *Sämtliche Schriften*, I. 4, p. 341.

[46] Ibid., I. 14, p. 691.

[47] Paul Schrecker, ed., 'G.-W. Leibniz: lettres et fragments inédits', *Revue philosophique de la France et de l'Étranger*, 118 (1934), pp. 5–134, at p. 82 (quoting Matthew 7.1).

> Charity (which is the highest of virtues), the love of peace, so recommended by Jesus-Christ, and the proofs of Christian moderation given for such a long time by this side [that is, the Lutherans], demand that we omit nothing now which is in our power and which could serve to remove or diminish the unfortunate schism which is so harmful to souls and which has rent the West for over a century and a half.[48]

As shown by this passage, the well-being of Christian souls themselves is endangered by the conflict amongst the Christian churches. Indeed, in Leibniz's view, a central feature of Christian soteriology points to toleration as something required by the very nature of salvation. Although he firmly maintains the objective truth of the Christian religion, he also identifies the subjective sincerity or insincerity of conscience as the ultimate ground of salvation or condemnation; and in this, he is eager to stress, he is in agreement with prominent theologians in the Roman Catholic church. One of the key reasons presented by Leibniz in support of religious toleration both of other Christians and of non-Christians is precisely this distinction between the objectivity of truth and the subjectivity of salvation.[49] This distinction, in turn, goes hand in glove with the traditional distinction between material and formal heretics proposed by Roman Catholic theologians. Material heretics are those who embrace a doctrine that is objectively erroneous and against the teaching of the truly universal or catholic church. Formal heretics are those who not only embrace an objectively erroneous doctrine, but are also conscious of their opposition to the teaching of the universal church and nevertheless continue to hold to what they know to be condemned by it. Material heretics are excused by their invincible ignorance of their error and, in particular, by their invincible ignorance of being opposed to the teaching of the catholic church. As a consequence they are not excluded from salvation, as are formal heretics.[50] Those who have not been reached by the Christian revelation are not excluded from salvation provided that they search for the truth in good faith and strive towards a morally good life.[51]

The difficult case, however, is represented by those who *are* reached by the teaching of the catholic church but do not embrace it.[52] This category of

[48] *Oeuvres de Leibniz*, ed. A. Foucher de Careil (7 vols., Paris, 1861–75; 2nd edn, 2 vols., Paris, 1867–9), II, p. 173.

[49] I have discussed this soteriological foundation of toleration in more detail in my 'Leibniz and religious toleration', from which I am drawing here.

[50] See for instance the entry 'Hérésie. Hérétique' in Alfred Vacant, Eugène Mangenot, Emile Amann, Bernard Loth, and Albert Michel, eds., *Dictionnaire de théologie catholique* (Paris, 1903–50), vol. 6, part 2, columns 2208–57. Cf. *De haeresi formali et materiali*, 1695* in Leibniz, *Sämtliche Schriften*, IV. 6, p. 337.

[51] Cf. Leibniz, *Sämtliche Schriften*, I. 6, pp. 79, 82–3, 119, 101 (Leibniz's marginal note); Leibniz, *Sämtliche Schriften*, IV. 6, pp. 370–2 (*De dissertatione Thomasiana an haeresis sit crimen*, July 1697–May 1698).

[52] Cf. Pellisson's remarks published in Leibniz, *Sämtliche Schriften*, I. 6, p. 143.

people can include both non-Christians, such as Muslims and Jews, and Christians from other confessions such as—from the point of view of the Roman church—Protestants or Christian heresies such as Socinianism. It is at this point that the full inclusiveness of Leibniz's doctrine of toleration appears. According to Leibniz, the category of material heretic can be extended also to these people.[53] Muslims and Jews, even when presented with the definitive revelation from God, do not realize its true status. As long as there is not conscious disobedience to God's revelation, they can only be considered material heretics.[54] Moreover, following the principles of Roman Catholic theologians themselves, Leibniz insists, the same applies to Protestants and even to Socinians and other radical movements since, from their point of view, what they refuse to follow is not in fact the doctrine of the truly universal or catholic church but only the teaching of a particular church.[55] Referring in particular to the case of the Protestants, Leibniz argues:

> Mr Pellisson … admits amongst material heretics only those who do not know, or do not believe, that the dogmas in matter of faith which they reject are the doctrine of the Catholic Church. If we apply this restriction to the Protestants we will find that they are of this number … So it is not easy to prove to the Protestants that they deny what they know to be decided by the Catholic Church.[56]

The consequences for toleration are clear. None of these people can be rightfully condemned and it should be assumed that they are saved as long as there is no conscious rebellion against what they know to be the true church or the

[53] Cf. Leibniz, *Sämtliche Schriften*, I. 6, p. 91: 'il faut estre effectivement de bonne foy et sans opiniastreté, et alors on ne sera qu'hérétique matériel'.

[54] Cf. for instance § 96 of the *Theodicy* (*Die philosophischen Schriften*, VI, p. 156), where, mentioning his exchange with Pellisson, Leibniz writes: 'l'Eglise Romaine allant plus loin que les protestants, ne damne point absolument ceux qui sont hors de sa communion, et même hors du Christianisme'.

[55] In his response to Leibniz, Pellisson writes (*Sämtliche Schriften*, I. 6, p. 143): 'ne faut-il pas dire tout au contraire; Je sçay la decision [de l'Eglise], et j'y resiste, donc je suis un de ces heretiques formels qui ne se peuvent sauver'. Leibniz replies in a marginal note to his copy of the fourth part of Pellisson's *Reflexions* (ibid.): 'Si je sçay la décision de ceux qui se vantent d'estre l'Église, je ne sçay pas pour cela que c'est l'Église qui l'a décidé.'

[56] Leibniz to Marie de Brinon for Pellisson, second half of January 1691, in *Sämtliche Schriften*, I. 6, pp. 164–5. Cf. also ibid., pp. 165–8: 'Je sçay que des Docteurs Catholiques Romains habiles ont avoué, qu'un Protestant, qui seroit porté à se sousmettre aux decisions de l'Eglise Catholique, mais qui se trompant dans le fait ne croiroit pas, que le Concile de Trente eust esté oecumenique, ne seroit qu'un heretique materiel … Mettant donc le Concile de Trente à part par les raisons susdites, on peut dire que l'Eglise Catholique n'a pas excommunié les Protestans. Si quelque Eglise Italienne le fait, on luy peut dire qu'elle passe son pouvoir … [Les Protestants] ne rejettent que ce qu'ils croyent contraire à la doctrine de l'Eglise de Dieu.' See also Leibniz to Pellisson, 19 (29) November 1691, in *Sämtliche Schriften*, I. 7, pp. 192–3, and *Nouveaux essais*, IV.xviii.9 (ibid., VI. 6, p. 500).

true divine revelation.[57] From very early on Leibniz maintains, in fact, that to be in error (that is, to believe something false) cannot be confused with acting against conscience and should not, therefore, be taken as a ground of condemnation. In a letter responding to the attack against Calvinism and Syncretism by his strictly Lutheran half-brother,[58] the twenty-three-year-old Leibniz writes:

> To err against conscience [Errare contra conscientiam] implies contradiction. In fact, from the beginning of the world, nobody has erred against conscience. Someone errs who believes as true that which is false [Errat qui putat verum esse quod falsum est]. Whoever believes, this person is not otherwise convinced; whoever is not otherwise convinced, does not know better; who does not know better, does not feel against conscience. Or, in short, the contradiction could be shown as follows: to err against conscience is to err knowing the very thing in which one is in error. To err knowing the very thing in which one is in error is to err in the very thing in which one is not in error. In fact, who knows, to the extent in which he knows, does not err. Therefore, if someone errs against conscience, two contradictory things—to err and not to err—belong to him in the same respect, which is absurd. We can act against conscience but we cannot believe [sentire non possumus] against conscience. So you see that, if only those who err against conscience are to be damned, nobody is to be damned for his error.[59]

Some twenty years later, Pellisson is clearly troubled by Leibniz's position and does not hesitate to define toleration as 'the greatest of all errors because it agrees with all errors'.[60] Indeed, the point Leibniz is trying to advance seems to be precisely the one that Pellisson finds so scandalous. For all that we know or can judge, there are no heretics in the sense of people certainly excluded

[57] Cf. Leibniz to Marie de Brinon for Pellisson, second half of January 1691, in *Sämtliche Schriften*, I. 6, p. 164: 'il me semble que la question est tout decidée par l'aveu de ceux qui reconnoissent des heretiques materiels, ou des heretiques de nom et d'apparence … c'est à dire des Gens qui paroissent estre hors de l'Eglise et y sont pourtant en effect, ou bien, qui sont hors de la communion visible de l'Eglise, mais estant dans une ignorance ou erreur invincible, sont jugés excusables, et s'ils ont d'ailleurs la charité et la contrition, ils sont dans l'Eglise virtuellement, et *in voto*, et se sauvent aussi bien, que ceux qui y sont visiblement.'

[58] Strict Lutherans rejected efforts at Protestant reconciliation as a dangerous syncretism which threatened to pollute the true Lutheran faith with Calvinism.

[59] Leibniz to Johann Friedrich Leibniz, 5 October* 1669, in Schrecker, ed., 'G.-W. Leibniz: lettres et fragments inédits', pp. 68–9.

[60] Pellisson to Madame de Brinon for Leibniz, 4 September 1690, in *Sämtliche Schriften*, I. 6, p. 92: 'Je croi, à vous dire la verité, Madame, que ceux qu'on appelle Sociniens, et après eux ceux qu'on nomme Deistes et Spinosistes, ont beaucoup contribué à répandre cette doctrine, qu'on peut appeller la plus grande des erreurs, par ce qu'elle s'accorde avec toutes. Car craignant de n'être pas soufferts, et que les loix civiles ne s'en mélassent, ils ont été bien aises d'établir qu'il falloit tout souffrir: delà est né le dogme de la *Tolerance*, comme on l'appelle, et un autre mot encore plus nouveau, qui est l'*Intolerance*, dont on accuse l'Eglise Romaine, comme d'un grand crime.'

from salvation on the grounds of their objectively erroneous beliefs.[61] The reason for this is that we cannot see the secrets of their hearts and the ways in which the grace of God can work within them.[62] Leibniz clarifies in the *Nouveaux essais* (firmly rejecting as a good Protestant any Pelagian interpretation of the claim that people could also be saved outside Christianity):

> Nor are those who accord salvation to pagans, or to others who lack the ordinary aids, thereby obliged to rely for this on natural processes alone ... One can, after all, maintain that, when God gives them grace sufficient to call forth an act of contrition, he also gives them before their death, even if only in the final moments, all the light of faith and all the fervour of love which they need for salvation; this being given to them either explicitly or dispositionally, but in any case supernaturally ... Let me add that none of this gives this doctrine anything in common with the special views of the Pelagians and Semipelagians ... Contrary to the Pelagians, all three of the accepted religions[63] ... agree in teaching that there is a supernatural grace in all who possess faith.[64]

As we have seen, for faith in the full sense of the term—that is, divine faith as opposed to a merely human faith based on explicable 'rational grounds for beliefs'[65]—a supernatural light and 'fervor of love' are necessary, which can only be given by God's grace. Precisely because these are 'inexplicable reasons' which 'consist only in our conscience or perception', 'those who base themselves on this light, cannot demand another examination from others who base themselves on a contrary light than the examination of one's own individual conscience; namely whether one says the truth and really feels the light of which he boasts'.[66] As the Jesuits themselves maintain, Leibniz concludes, the last instance of judgement regarding the salvation of any individual can therefore only be the sincerity of his or her conscience, no

[61] Cf. the passage quoted above from the young Leibniz's response to his half-brother, in Schrecker, ed., 'G.-W. Leibniz: lettres et fragments inédits', pp. 68–9.

[62] See in particular Leibniz, *Nouveaux essais*, IV.xviii.9, in *Sämtliche Schriften*, VI. 6, pp. 500–2, and *Theodicy*, §§ 93, 95–6, in *Die philosophischen Schriften*, VI, pp. 155–6. In both cases Leibniz refers explicitly to his exchange with Pellisson. Cf. also *Sämtliche Schriften*, I. 6, p. 121: 'M. Pellisson dit luy-mesme fort judicieusement dans un endroit de son premier Tome [Pellisson, *Reflexions*, 36], que *nos lumieres sont trop courtes pour percer la profondeur de la justice divine*. Ne prononçons donc pas si hardiment des sentences condamnatoires contre nos freres' (emphasis original).

[63] Leibniz means Roman Catholics, Lutherans, and Calvinists.

[64] *Nouveaux essais*, IV.xviii.9, in *New essays*, p. 502.

[65] Leibniz, *Nouveaux essais*, IV.xviii.9, in *New essays*, p. 497. See also *Sämtliche Schriften*, I. 6, p. 76.

[66] Leibniz to Duchess Sophie for Paul Pellisson-Fontanier, early August* 1690, in *Sämtliche Schriften*, I. 6, p. 76.

matter how objectively erroneous his or her beliefs may be.[67] 'People are not excommunicated for their error,' Leibniz writes, 'but for their obstinacy or bad disposition of heart. One can be of bad faith and obstinate even if he asserts the truth, that is to say when this is maintained without foundation on the basis of a bad principle.'[68] So it is this subjective sincerity or insincerity of conscience (together with God's grace) that is, ultimately, the ground of salvation or condemnation.[69] Yet since we cannot enter into the conscience of other people, it is God's business alone to decide who is saved or condemned. Leibniz stresses forcefully that it would be extremely arrogant to assume otherwise: 'I do not know how one can be humble when he sets himself up as a judge of souls to the point of condemning them to eternal fire. There is nothing more presumptuous than that.'[70]

The question nevertheless arises as to what this sincerity of conscience (on which salvation ultimately rests) consists of, given that it cannot be identified with believing a corpus of true doctrines. Asserting his agreement with the 'views of several very celebrated Doctors of the Roman Church', Leibniz claims that for the salvation of an individual 'no revealed article is absolutely necessary, and therefore *it is possible to be saved* in every Religion, *provided that one truly loves God above all things*'.[71] It should be noted that this is not, for Leibniz, a super-fundamental article of faith which on its own could be sufficient for salvation.[72] On the contrary, Leibniz explicitly distances himself from the well-known and controversial Protestant doctrine of fundamental and non-fundamental articles of faith, which famously came to be used as a basis for toleration.[73] The point that is controversial in this doctrine is not, strictly speaking, the *distinction* between fundamental and non-fundamental

[67] Leibniz's marginal note on his copy of the fourth part of Pellisson's *Reflexions*, in *Sämtliche Schriften*, I. 6, p. 94: 'Les jésuites ont soutenu que l'ignorance invincible excuse, et qu'ainsi la conscience sincère d'un chacun est tousjours le dernier juge icy-bas, *in conscientiae foro*.'

[68] Leibniz's marginal note to Pellisson's remarks, in *Sämtliche Schriften*, I. 6, p. 141. See also *De haeresi formali et materiali*, 1695* in Leibniz, *Sämtliche Schriften*, IV. 6, p. 337: 'si quis malo animo veritatem amplecteretur, is posset dici haereticus formalis non materialis; dignus poena; etsi non erravit'.

[69] In support of this thesis Leibniz quotes the sentence, 'facienti quod in se est Deus non denegat gratiam'. Cf. Leibniz's marginal note on his copy of the fourth part of Pellisson's *Reflexions*, in *Sämtliche Schriften*, I. 6, p. 144, and *Theodicy*, § 95, in *Die philosophischen Schriften*, VI, p. 155.

[70] Leibniz's marginal note on his copy of the fourth part of Pellisson's *Reflexions*, in *Sämtliche Schriften*, I. 6, p. 88. Cf. also Leibniz to Ernst von Hessen-Rheinfels, 4/14 September 1690, in ibid., pp. 107–8: 'je ne sçay pourquoy nous prenons tant de plaisir à croire les gens damnés. N'y at-il pas un peu de vanité et de la corruption du coeur humain, qui trouve une joÿe secrete dans les maux d'autruy.'

[71] Leibniz, *Sämtliche Schriften*, I. 6, pp. 78–9. Cf. also Leibniz's marginal note on his copy of the fourth part of Pellisson's *Reflexions*, in ibid., p. 101.

[72] I disagree on this point with Zarka, *Philosophie et politique à l'âge classique*, p. 252.

[73] I discuss this point in detail in 'Leibniz and religious toleration', pp. 605–12.

articles as such. Rather, the crux of the controversy is whether these necessary or fundamental articles of faith can be determined by Scripture alone without appeal to a principle of authority. Leibniz does not deny that an infallible authority is needed in order to decide at least some controversies regarding fundamental matters. More specifically, in the passage quoted above, he is not proposing some sort of 'single necessary article of faith', on belief in which alone salvation depends. Instead he is reiterating that salvation, ultimately, does not rest on the correctness of one's beliefs but on a practical attitude: that is, a sincere love of God.

If salvation depends on the sincere love of God above all things bestowed by the supernatural and mysterious operation of God's grace, the further conclusion follows that compulsion in religious affairs undermines rather than advances the aim of salvation. To force someone to embrace a religion that he or she cannot sincerely believe could put in danger the soul of that person, even if the religion in question is the true one. As Leibniz writes in March 1685 to the Catholic convert from Calvinism, Landgraf Ernst von Hessen-Rheinfels, 'One should not create hypocrites, since a true Huguenot is incomparably more worthy than a false Catholic and will sooner be saved without any doubt.'[74] It is clear that Leibniz rejects the tradition of the *compelle intrare*.[75] This position has obvious consequences for toleration, since he deems it unacceptable to try to convert people with tools other than persuasion on the grounds that to do otherwise, far from propelling them through the gates of Heaven, could instead close those gates to them forever.

VI

Leibniz's ecclesiology also naturally leads to toleration amongst the main Christian churches. In his view, each particular Christian church has some fragment of truth, and none can claim to possess the truth in its totality. Against Pellisson's denial that the truth might be distributed amongst churches, Leibniz replies in no uncertain terms: 'this is possible'.[76] The truly universal (or catholic) church is not one of the particular churches and its

[74] Leibniz, *Sämtliche Schriften*, I. 4, p. 352. Cf. also Leibniz to Ernst von Hessen-Rheinfels, 23 February / 5 March 1691, in ibid., I. 6, pp. 177–8, and 24 December 1684 (8 January 1685), ibid., I. 4, p. 341: 'Le Roy T. C. a dit à ce qu'on m'a conté, qu'il fait à la verité de mauvais convertis, mais que leur enfans seront bons catholiques. Cependant je doute que cela se puisse approuver, car c'est vouloir faire damner quelques uns pour sauver d'autres.'

[75] Cf. Leibniz, *Remarques sur un petit livre traduit de l'Anglois, intitulé Lettre sur l'enthousiasme*, in *Die philosophischen Schriften*, III, p. 410.

[76] Leibniz's marginal note on his copy of the fourth part of Pellisson's *Reflexions*, in *Sämtliche Schriften*, I. 6, p. 141.

true doctrine can be discovered only by respectful listening to the entire ecclesiastical tradition from apostolic times onward.[77] In a letter of 30 January 1692 to Landgraf Ernst, Leibniz summarizes the positions of the main parties—the Roman Catholic and the Greek Orthodox churches, the Protestants, and the more radical Christian movements emblematically represented by the theological rationalism of the Socinians—giving in a nutshell his own view on the matter:

> One might say that the parties have three principles: 1.) the authority of traditions, 2.) Scripture [and] 3.) philosophy. Authority leads principally the Greeks and the Romans, Scripture the Protestants, and philosophy the Socinians. All three principles are good, but one can abuse each of them, and this [abuse] causes the errors.[78]

In a typically conciliatory way, Leibniz acknowledges the merits of all three approaches while taking his own stand. Despite his own allegiance to Protestantism, he admits the legitimacy of a recourse to 'the authority of traditions' against a rigid application of the Protestant rule of 'Scripture alone'. Moreover, he rejects, on the one hand, irrationalistic positions barring all 'philosophy' or rational motives from the realm of faith, while criticizing, on the other hand, the Socinian abuse of reason as the ultimate criterion of religious truth. The view that no particular Christian church has a monopoly of a truth that needs to be retraced in the entire ecclesiastical tradition has immediate consequences for toleration amongst the Christian confessions. No particular church can claim to be the true Church to the exclusion of the others, and none has the right of excommunicating those who do not follow all of its doctrines.

VII

The ecclesiology just described might leave the impression that Leibniz was impossibly naive when it came to assessing the extent and depth of the disagreement among the Christian churches, as well as the willingness of their armies of theologians and prelates to restore harmony by sitting around a table serenely reviewing the entire ecclesiastical tradition in search of the doctrine of the truly catholic church. Far from dissolving into such Panglossian

[77] See for instance Leibniz, *Sämtliche Schriften*, I. 6, p. 147: 'les Églises d'Italie ou de France n'ont aucun avantage sur celles d'Alemagne ou d'Angleterre, et n'ont aucune raison de se croire plus dans l'Église qu'elles'; and ibid., p. 148: 'Les dogmes de Trente n'ont aucun avantage sur ceux d'Augsburg ou de Dordrecht pour estre attribués à l'Église. On ne réformera que les dogmes des églises particulières.' Cf. also p. 167.

[78] Leibniz, *Sämtliche Schriften*, I. 7, p. 261.

optimism, however, Leibniz's approach to church reunification was in fact markedly pragmatic.[79] Regarding reunification between Protestants (notably Lutherans) and Roman Catholics, he embraced the plan proposed by the Roman Catholic negotiator, the Franciscan Cristobal de Rojas y Spinola (*c.* 1626–95), who toured the courts of Protestant German princes on behalf of the (Catholic) Holy Roman Emperor seeking an understanding with Rome. Basically Rojas's reunion strategy was twofold: first it envisaged a preliminary reunion of the Protestants with the Roman church before full agreement was reached on controversial issues, at which point, secondly, a truly ecumenical council would be summoned. Having been recognized at the outset as truly ecumenical, the council would therefore be endowed with the authority to settle controversial issues. Both Catholics and Protestants would agree in advance to abide by its decisions. By consistently supporting this strategy over the years until finally confronted with its failure, Leibniz showed himself fully aware that theological agreement could not, in all probability, be reached through learned discussion alone. It was for this reason that a pragmatic, preliminary reunification would need to be achieved before controversial issues could be settled by a principle of authority recognized as such at the outset by all parties.

After these plans for a comprehensive reunion of Protestants and Catholics became unworkable, Leibniz, from the late 1690s onwards, concentrated primarily on the more limited project of reunifying the Lutheran and Reformed confessions; and here too he was equally aware of the difficulty of reaching full theological agreement. For instance, when in the autumn of 1699 a small group of Lutheran and Reformed theologians proposed to convene a broad Protestant theological conference involving England, Scotland, Brandenburg, Braunschweig-Lüneburg, and, possibly, Denmark and Sweden, Leibniz opposed the idea. According to him, such an initiative was more likely to exacerbate divisions than to mend them: inter-Protestant reunification needed to be prepared in advance through the careful negotiation of agreement on controversial points by a small, select, but representative group of theologians working in private. In his view, to plunge straight into a large, international conference without a fairly firm platform on which theological differences had already been mediated was only likely to provoke intransigent confrontation. In fact, when towards the end of 1702 the Prussian king decided to take matters into his own hands and pursue the union between Lutheran and Reformed churches within his own dominions by convening a *Collegium Irenicum*, Leibniz's warnings proved more than justified, since a

[79] I discuss Leibniz's efforts toward ecclesiastical reunification in more detail in Antognazza, *Leibniz: an intellectual biography*.

barrage of polemical pamphlets began from both sides even before the work of the *Collegium Irenicum* could begin.[80]

Without entering into the details of Leibniz's lifelong ecumenical efforts, for present purposes it is enough to note that in both projects—the pursuit of comprehensive reunification of Catholics and Protestants and the narrower pursuit of inter-Protestant reconciliation—toleration is seen by Leibniz as an essential ingredient of the whole process. It is true that in his earlier years he sounds almost dismissive of toleration in observing that it addresses only 'the most pressing symptoms' rather than being a proper cure for the malaise gripping the Christian churches. On the other hand, he also grants that 'the way of dispute or discussion', in which controversial points are examined in detail by the opposing parties, has proven of 'little effect' in these matters.[81] For all his indefatigable efforts towards the development of a *characteristica universalis* which would have settled all controversies including religious ones,[82] Leibniz is realistic enough to see that the solution of the religious conflicts raging across Europe could not wait for the creation and universal acceptance of his wonderful formal language. Instead a bold pragmatic move of the sort indicated by Rojas was needed, the first step towards which could only be establishing religious toleration amongst the churches that agreed to the preliminary reunification while awaiting the final verdict of a truly ecumenical council on controversial points. Later, with the insight gained from years of difficult negotiations, Leibniz comes to estimate more highly the value of toleration amongst the Christian churches, despite its falling short of being a definitive solution of their conflicts. In 1697, addressing the task of re-establishing Protestant unity, he identifies three different degrees of increasing difficulty: political unity or 'a good civic understanding', 'Ecclesiastical toleration', and finally theological agreement or 'concord of views'. 'The first and the second degree', Leibniz concludes,

> seem to me necessary and achievable, and sufficient. The first degree is necessary on political grounds for the conservation of both parties. The second degree is necessary on account of the principle of Christian charity, and in consequence is more than feasible. The third degree does not seem attainable, but it is also not necessary. It would nevertheless be good if some able theologians were to work at it at least as regards certain points where, I believe, the disputes consist in fact more in formulations than in realities.[83]

It is clear that his target remaines theological agreement whenever this seems possible. A prime example of this is his negotiations of 1697–1699 with the

[80] Ibid., p. 401.

[81] Leibniz, *Sämtliche Schriften*, I. 5, p. 11. Cf. also ibid., I. 4, p. 380.

[82] See for instance Leibniz, *Sämtliche Schriften*, II. 1, pp. 490–1 and I. 2, 226–7.

[83] Leibniz, *Sämtliche Schriften*, I. 14, pp. 690–1.

Brandenburg court chaplain, Daniel Ernst Jablonski, on the reunion of the Reformed and Lutheran churches in Brandenburg and Hanover.[84] Leibniz shows himself aware of how, historically, the legal enforcement of toleration by rulers had led to forced conversions.[85] His rejection on this occasion of the model of toleration proposed by Jablonski, should be interpreted not as a rejection of toleration as such but as the judgment that on the matter at hand proper theological agreement could be reached. However, as shown by the passage quoted above, when a full 'concord of views' did not seem attainable Leibniz regards a 'good civic understanding' and 'Ecclesiastical toleration' as sufficient as well as necessary 'on account of the principle of Christian charity'.

VIII

Finally, let us turn to Leibniz's pragmatic reasons for toleration and to his view that the alternative to toleration—that is, persecution—is futile and counterproductive. In 1687 Leibniz brushes aside the 'way of rigour' as of dubious legitimacy and uncertain results.[86] When in 1693–4 news reaches him that the English parliament has ordered the public burning of an anti-Trinitarian pamphlet by William Freke, he comments dryly that the anti-Trinitarians could reasonably reply that 'it is easier to burn such things than to refute them: the truth, indeed, cannot be burned'.[87] Around 1711 he also observes that persecution has proven to strengthen rather than weaken the convictions of its victims: 'I acknowledge that in general persecution is not at all desirable, and that it has wronged the faith of many people but gives relief to that of some others: more zeal is never noted than in these occasions of trial, and greater examples of a great conviction are never found.'[88]

His own pragmatic advice is that it is often better to leave heterodox doctrines alone, especially when they have no bad practical consequences. In many cases they will die down on their own, while attempting to exterminate them more often ends up inflaming them. As he explains to Duchess Sophie in a letter of 26 October 1691,

[84] See especially *Erste Fassung des Unvorgreifflichen Bedenckens* (c. January 1699) and *Unvorgreiffliches Bedencken über eine Schrifft genandt Kurtze Vorstellung* (written before 11 February 1699) in Leibniz, *Sämtliche Schriften*, IV. 7, pp. 424–648.

[85] See *Erste Fassung des Unvorgreifflichen Bedenckens* in Leibniz, *Sämtliche Schriften*, IV. 7, p. 248, in which the case of Hesse-Kassel is discussed.

[86] Ibid., I. 5, p. 11.

[87] Cf. Leibniz, *Sämtliche Schriften*, I. 11, p. 123. On this episode see Antognazza, *Leibniz on the Trinity*, ch. 9.

[88] Leibniz, *Die philosophischen Schriften*, III, pp. 413–14.

> under the pretext of preventing heresies, they have been engendered. Normally these things fade away on their own when they lose the attraction of novelty; but when one wants to suppress them with noisy denunciations, persecutions, and refutations, it is like wanting to extinguish a fire with a pair of bellows ... For fear of being short of heretics, Messieurs the theologians sometimes do everything they can to find some.[89]

It is not necessary to believe everything that is true, and there are things that are not true and are nevertheless tolerable.[90] In some cases, he argues, a heterodox theology can positively enhance the moral stand of a person, and abstaining from intervention is definitely advisable when incorrect beliefs have a good practical effect. A noteworthy example is Leibniz's reaction to Baron Franciscus Mercurius van Helmont. While taking issue with the strange and (in Leibniz's view) dubious elements that peppered van Helmont's thought,[91] Leibniz deeply appreciates the baron's commitment to the common good which inspired a number of practical schemes for the improvement of the human condition. As Leibniz writes on 20 December 1696 to Andreas Morell, 'the touchstone of true illumination is a great eagerness for contributing to the general good'. This is, in his view, what really distinguishes van Helmont from other millenarians and promoters of controversial religious movements. 'Among those who had extraordinary ideas,' Leibniz concludes, 'I have hardly found anyone beside van Helmont who shared this great principle of charity with me and who had a true eagerness for the general good, although in other respects we often had very different opinions about different matters.'[92] In short, van Helmont's belief in universal salvation, combined with a radically optimistic eschatology expecting a future millennium and a final restoration of all things, although supported by shaky arguments and contrary to ecclesiastical tradition, plays an important role in inspiring his love of God and his commitment to the common good.[93] Leibniz acknowledges and admires this aspect of van Helmont's thought despite his own distance from many of the baron's 'extraordinary ideas'.

Leibniz's criterion for not tolerating certain religious doctrines is also practical: doctrines should not be tolerated if they lead to dangerous actions

[89] Leibniz, *Sämtliche Schriften*, I. 7, p. 38. See also Leibniz to Des Bosses, 21 July 1707, in *Die philosophischen Schriften*, II, p. 337.

[90] Cf. Leibniz, *Sämtliche Schriften*, I. 6, p. 118.

[91] See for instance Leibniz's entries in his *Tagesbuch* of August 1696, in G. W. Leibniz, *Gesammelte Werke*, ed. Georg Heinrich Pertz, series I (Hanover, 1847; repr. Hildesheim, 1966), vol. 4, pp. 193 and 198.

[92] Leibniz, *Sämtliche Schriften*, I. 13, pp. 399–400; trans. by Howard Hotson in 'Leibniz and millenarianism', in Maria Rosa Antognazza and Howard Hotson, eds., *Alsted and Leibniz on God, the Magistrate and the Millennium* (Wolfenbütteler Arbeiten zur Barockforschung, Wiesbaden, 1999), pp. 187–8.

[93] See Hotson, 'Leibniz and millenarianism', pp. 189 and 192.

which are clearly against precepts of natural law. Likewise, the use of violence against the state for religious principles cannot, according to Leibniz, be tolerated. This is evident from the passage mentioned above, in which Leibniz writes: 'it is against natural right to punish someone because he is of some opinion, no matter which, as opposed to punishing someone for some actions; *for the penalty for one who is mistaken is to be taught*. And again, I do not believe that we have the right to punish someone with corporal pains for actions which he undertakes in accordance with his opinion, and which he believes his conscience obligates him to perform.' This passage continues with the following caveat: 'apart from the case in which these actions are evil in themselves, manifestly contrary to natural right. As if someone wanted to trouble the State and use violence and poison for a religious principle.'[94]

On the other hand, doctrines that do not teach criminal behaviour should not be persecuted. As Leibniz writes to his Jesuit friend, Bartholomew Des Bosses, on 21 July 1707:

> what I find worst of all is persecution on account of opinions that do not encourage criminal acts, a practice from which honorable men should not only refrain, but which we should also abhor and work against so that others, over whom we have some authority, are discouraged from it … And indeed, if it were within my powers of persuasion, Gerberon[95] and others like him would enjoy complete freedom … let them write, let them defend their opinions. Their errors should be overturned with equal arms, not by force and fear … It is extremely harmful that freedom of thinking [sentiendi libertatem] be restrained from day to day within unnecessary limits.[96]

Mentioning explicitly the Socinians, he remarks in 1698: 'I am delighted that authors whose views are dangerous are refuted but I am not sure it is appropriate to establish against them a kind of inquisition when their false opinions have no influence on morals; and although I am very far from the views of the Socinians, I don't believe it is right to treat them as criminals.'[97]

To sum up, in Leibniz we find no blanket exclusion from toleration of broad categories of people: certainly not the Catholics, but also not the Socinians or other heretical movements. It is not beliefs as such that are not to be tolerated, but the actions deriving from these beliefs that harm other

[94] Leibniz to Ernst von Hessen-Rheinfels, 4/14 August 1683, in *Sämtliche Schriften*, II. 1, p. 535. Cf. also 'Réflexions de Leibniz sur un Écrit Irénique de Fétizon' (August 1700), in Schrecker, ed., 'G.-W. Leibniz: lettres et fragments inédits', p. 107: 'Et quand il s'agit de la Tolerance, il ne faut point estre promt à condamner, mais il ne faut pas estre negligent non plus lors qu'une doctrine est dangereuse.'

[95] Gabriel Gerberon (1628–1711) was a Jansenist author. He was arrested in 1703.

[96] Leibniz, *Die philosophischen Schriften*, II, p. 337; Brandon C. Look and Donald Rutherford, trans., *The Leibniz–Des Bosses correspondence* (New Haven and London, 2007), pp. 95–7.

[97] Leibniz to Thomas Burnett of Kemney, 8 (18) April 1698, in *Sämtliche Schriften*, I. 15, p. 489.

people. The measures to be taken for dealing with such potentially or actually harmful beliefs should, however, be as restrained as possible. As he writes in 1706, 'One has some right to take measures to prevent the propagation of a pernicious error, but that is also all one has a right to do, and these measures must be the mildest possible.'[98] In concrete terms, what Leibniz normally proposes, besides active refutation, is moderate censorship or, in some cases, a ban; but even the latter should not be universal, since a universal ban would be equivalent to a sentence of death.[99]

IX

To conclude, Leibniz does not ground toleration in the separation between church and state (as Pufendorf and Locke do).[100] His doctrine of toleration is also not grounded in indifference towards the content of revealed religion, in favour of natural religion. Nor is it even grounded in the distinction between the fundamental and non-fundamental articles of faith. He is convinced of the objective truth of the Christian religion and of the duty to uphold and propagate it; but he denies that it should be upheld or propagated by means other than persuasion, and this for philosophical, theological, and pragmatic reasons, not least by appealing to natural law and to the very nature of that salvation one has in sight when setting off to spread the good news. In short, in his thought, belief in what is regarded as objective truth does not and must not yield intolerance. On the contrary, when the expressions of Leibniz's view have been collected from a broad sample of his correspondence and other writings, they yield one of the most inclusive doctrines of toleration of his time.

It cannot be denied that Leibniz devoted far more energy to the pursuit of ecclesiastical reconciliation than to the formulation of a doctrine of religious toleration. But this does not imply that he regarded the one as far less important than the other. Rather, this concentration of effort reflects the balance of opportunities and necessities in seventeenth-century Germany, a balance that

[98] Leibniz, *Opera omnia*, V, p. 483.

[99] On Leibniz's moderate censorship see the following contributions by Mogens Laerke, 'Leibniz, la censure et la libre pensée', *Archives de Philosophie*, 70 (2007), pp. 373–88, and idem, 'G. W. Leibniz: moderation and censorship', in Mogens Laerke, ed., *The use of censorship in the Enlightenment* (Brill's Studies in Intellectual History, Leiden, 2009), pp. 155–78. On Leibniz's criticism of the universal ban see his letter to Landgraf Ernst von Hessen-Rheinfels of mid-May 1687 (*Sämtliche Schriften*, I. 4, p. 433), which refers specifically to the case of the Socinians.

[100] See, for Pufendorf, Simone Zurbuchen, Chapter 1, and Thomas Ahnert, Chapter 2, this volume; for Locke, compare Timothy Stanton, Chapter 3, Ian Harris, Chapter 4, and Ian Hunter, Chapter 5, this volume.

can perhaps best be revealed when contrasted with the more familiar situation in contemporary England. In England—a large, politically unified but religiously rather diverse polity—the dominant issue was how to get Protestants of different shades of opinion to tolerate one another. This was the problem addressed by Locke. In the Holy Roman Empire, on the other hand—a vast entity divided into a large number of internally more religiously homogeneous territorial states which, in turn, formed three main confessional blocks—the crucial political issue was how to regain sufficient unity to allow the empire to defend itself against confessionally unified neighbours who sought to exploit these confessional differences and thereby to divide the empire against itself. In this respect, as in so many others, Leibniz's intellectual priorities can only be properly assessed by putting them back in the unfamiliar context of the Holy Roman Empire; and his dogged pursuit of ecclesiastical reconciliation should not be interpreted as a lack of commitment to the still more basic need for religious toleration. Since Leibniz never published a major synthetic statement of his views on this latter subject, it would be unjustified to regard him as a major contemporary advocate of religious toleration, alongside his celebrated English contemporary. Yet this conclusion is also not without irony, since Locke—unlike Leibniz—won his reputation as an apostle of religious toleration despite excluding from toleration by far the largest single confessional community in Europe: the Roman Catholic church. Locke's famous formulations, addressed as they were to insular conditions, were utterly inadequate for dealing with the religious divisions of continental Europe as a whole, half the population of which they excluded from toleration. Leibniz's softly spoken and hitherto overlooked reflections on the subject, on the other hand, originating as they did from the juxtaposition of all the main branches of Latin Christianity within the microcosm of the Holy Roman Empire, expanded to embrace the entire population of Europe.

7

Toleration as Impartiality? Civil and Ecclesiastical Toleration in Jean Barbeyrac

PETTER KORKMAN

TOLERATION IS AN AMBIGUOUS TERM. Some would insist on the importance of defining toleration as a grudging acceptance, a willingness to suffer the existence of some evil. Viewed as such, toleration is part of a hierarchical relationship. Toleration is granted from a position of superiority. In other cases, the concept of toleration is used for theories that defend a right to freedom of religion or freedom of thought. On such a picture, toleration denotes a set of equal universal rights. A third possibility is to think of toleration more as an attitude in the individual, as an open-mindedness, a willingness to encounter different viewpoints. That would make toleration a virtue.

This chapter is concerned with Jean Barbeyrac's views on toleration and, more specifically, with how natural law theory and toleration relate to one another in Barbeyrac's writings. Barbeyrac is known to posterity as an influential translator of, and commentator upon, the natural law theories of Samuel Pufendorf and Hugo Grotius amongst others. Of the numerous European editions made in the eighteenth century of Pufendorf's major opus, *De jure naturae et gentium*, over two-thirds contained Barbeyrac's footnotes and commentary.[1] It is safe to say that natural law, in the Enlightenment era, came in a package devised by Barbeyrac.[2] What makes this fact particularly interesting in the context of a volume on natural law and toleration is Barbeyrac's lasting interest in the question of toleration.

[1] Samuel Pufendorf, *De jure naturae et gentium libri octo* (London, 1672). For details of subsequent printings incorporating Barbeyrac's notes and commentary, see Sieglinde Othmer, *Berlin und die Verbreitung des Naturrechts in Europa: kultur- und sozialgeschichtliche Studien zu Jean Barbeyracs Pufendorf-Übersetzung und eine Analyse seiner Leserschaft* (Berlin, 1970), p. 141. All translations are mine unless otherwise stated.

[2] For different aspects of Barbeyrac's place in the history of natural jurisprudence, see, *inter alia*, Othmer, *Berlin*, passim; David Saunders, 'The natural jurisprudence of Jean Barbeyrac: translation as an art of political adjustment', *Eighteenth-Century Studies*, 36 (2003), pp. 473–90; Gabriella Silverstrini, 'Rousseau, Pufendorf, and the eighteenth century natural law tradition', *History of European Ideas*, 36 (2010), pp. 280–301.

Proceedings of the British Academy, **186**, 165–182. © The British Academy 2013.

Barbeyrac discusses toleration in all three of the senses distinguished above: as a privilege or concession, as a right to freedom of religion, and as a virtuous attitude conducive to a better and more open society. Before exploring the relationship between toleration and natural law in these three areas, however, it may be helpful to say a few words about how Barbeyrac's interest in toleration relates to his life and career.

I

Jean Barbeyrac was born in France in 1674, into a family of Calvinists. When the revocation of the Nantes edict was issued at Fontainebleau in 1685, Barbeyrac was eleven years old. The revocation forced Barbeyrac's father, a Huguenot minister, to leave the country, but did not allow him to take his children with him. The children were later smuggled out of France—in direct contravention of the king's orders.[3]

The debate about the French persecutions remained lively among the Huguenot refugees throughout Barbeyrac's life. Barbeyrac himself often referred to the revocation and the events surrounding it. He was particularly eager to prove, first, that the state—any state—has a duty to tolerate any peaceful religious minority, and, secondly, that the French persecutions injured the inalienable rights of the Huguenots and gave them a right to resist or disobey.

From the beginning of his career, Barbeyrac argued that the right to self-governance in religion is clear to all impartial persons. Thus in the *Préface du traducteur sur les deux discours de Mr Noodt* from 1707, Barbeyrac views the fact that so many seem unconvinced about the validity of the demand for toleration as proof that many are unwilling to use their rational faculties impartially. The problem is not that these people would not be able to understand the proofs adduced for the illegitimacy of persecution. It is a problem of will rather than intellect. Persecutions happen not because the need for toleration is obscure and hard to grasp, but because the impartial demands of reason are trampled by worldly interests, passions, prejudice, and blind attachment to tradition, all of which contribute to making persons partial.[4]

[3] Barbeyrac's life and career have been described in Philippe Meylan, *Jean Barbeyrac et l'enseignement du droit dans l'ancienne académie de Lausanne* (Lausanne, 1937). See now also Fiammetta Palladini, *Die Berliner Hugenotten und der Fall Barbeyrac: Orthodoxe und 'Sozinianer' im Refuge* (1685–1720) (Leiden, 2011).

[4] Jean Barbeyrac, 'Préface du traducteur sur les deux discours de Mr Noodt', in *De pouvoir des souverains; et de la liberté de conscience. En deux discours, traduits du Latin de Mr. Noodt, professeur en droit dans l'université de Leide: par Jean Barbeyrac* (Amsterdam, 1707), p. 5.

Barbeyrac inserted a very similar remark in the preface to his French translation of Pufendorf, *Le droit de la nature*, which was published one year earlier.[5] To acquire a correct understanding of one's natural law duties, Barbeyrac writes, one 'almost does not have to go outside one's own self, or consult any other master than one's own heart'.[6] Natural law and toleration are equally available to all impartial persons, and in fact they are not distinct things. Religious toleration, as I will argue in this chapter, is, for Barbeyrac, a principle of natural law.

The French persecutions remained an important issue for Huguenot refugees, but life (usually) went on. When Louis XIV died in September 1715, Barbeyrac received an anonymous request from Bordeaux, asking him to take part in preparing a message to Louis's successor, his great-grandson Louis XV. The idea was to petition the new king and court for increased toleration towards Huguenots in France. Barbeyrac declined the request.[7] For him, Catholics were intolerant by definition, and the Catholic regime in France seemed to him quite beyond the reach of rational argumentation.[8] The Reformation, on the other hand, was for Barbeyrac a tolerant movement. Protestants whose actions or words defended intolerance expressed a *sentiment particulier*; they deviated from the true cause of the Reformation.[9] Barbeyrac, perhaps somewhat amusingly, recognized that Luther, Calvin, and many other central Reformation figureheads, had in this respect deviated from the real Reformation, that they had in fact failed the test of the true Protestant.[10]

Barbeyrac's original life plan had been to serve as pastor in the Huguenot community in Berlin. He encountered considerable resistance from influential

[5] Samuel Pufendorf, *Le droit de la nature et des gens, ou, systeme general des principes les plus importans de la morale* (2 vols., Amsterdam, 1706). For the list of impediments to knowledge of natural law, see p. vii in the preface. This first paragraph of the preface remained the same in the reworked editions of the *Le droit de la nature* that Barbeyrac published in 1712 (Amsterdam), 1732 (Basle), and 1734 (Amsterdam). The 1734 edition only differs in mentioning prejudice (in addition to passions) as a potential obstacle to an understanding of natural law. Compare Pufendorf, *Le droit de la nature … nouvelle edition, revûë de nouveau & augmentée* (Paris, 1740), I, préface, p. xv.

[6] Pufendorf, *Le droit de la nature* (1706 edn), préface, p. ii. One must admit, Barbeyrac adds, that it is 'less because of the prejudices of the mind than because of the illusions of the heart, and the tyranny established in the world as regards sentiments, which forms the gravest hindrance to a serious study of morals, and an exact knowledge of our duties' (p. xviii).

[7] Meylan, *Jean Barbeyrac*, pp. 113–14.

[8] Jean Barbeyrac, *Traité de la morale des pères de l'Église* (Amsterdam, 1728), ch. 12, §42, p. 186.

[9] Jean Barbeyrac, ed., *Bibliotheque raisonnée des ouvrages des savans de l'Europe* (50 vols., Amsterdam, 1728–53), I. 2, §9.

[10] Barbeyrac, *Traité de la morale*, ch. 12, §43, pp. 186–7. For Barbeyrac, the real heroes of the Reformation are, rather, Grotius and Erasmus: the latter is a recurrent reference and is affirmed to be a greater reformer than Calvin or Luther in e.g. *Bibliotheque raisonnée* I. 1, §4, p. 43.

elements in the clergy there, and was soon decried as an Arminian and Socinian. In 1699, Barbeyrac gave up his plans for an ecclesiastical career. Instead, he taught classical languages, wrote journal articles, and translated.[11] His first translation was Samuel Pufendorf's massive *De jure naturae et gentium* (1672), mentioned above, which he published as *Le droit de la nature et des gens*, and which appeared in print in 1706. The preface to this book was a book-length account of the history of moral thought, which gave a dark picture of priests and Church Fathers as engaged in a project of deceiving and confusing people so as to gain power over them. Barbeyrac's other translations included Gerhard Noodt's defence of freedom of conscience (also mentioned), as well as several volumes of Archbishop Tillotson's *Sermons*.[12] Barbeyrac also translated juridical treatises on more specific issues,[13] as well as the natural law treatises of Grotius and Cumberland,[14] but throughout, work on natural law was for him closely related to discussion of a reasonable approach to religion, both in itself and as a social phenomenon.

Natural law theory provided Barbeyrac with a discourse to use against the intolerance of both Catholic persecutors and Protestant guardians of orthodoxy. It provided him with a secular-rational theory of morality which was, he insisted, also the core of true Christian belief. Or, as Barbeyrac explained in his first independently published book, the *Traité du Jeu* (1709), the morality taught by Jesus was the very same that reason could have found unaided, and this morality was only given in broad outlines in Scripture, with the intention that men should use their reason to elaborate a solid science of morality.[15]

Barbeyrac thus has a double interest in natural law as a source for ideas on religious toleration. On the one hand, he remains interested in discussing the civil toleration that French Catholics failed to show to the Huguenot minority. On the other hand, he is eager to use natural law as a basis for a rationalist rethinking of Christian and reformed ideals, and, in this connection, he was keen to emphasize the need for more toleration in the Protestant community. As a university professor and Rector in Lausanne, Barbeyrac was

[11] Barbeyrac's first publications appeared in 1697 and 1698 in the *Nouveau Journal des Sçavans* published in Berlin by Etienne Chauvin, who a few years later became Barbeyrac's father-in-law.

[12] John Tillotson, *Sermons sur diverses matieres importantes … traduit par J Barbeyrac* (2 vols., Amsterdam, 1744).

[13] See e.g. Cornelis van Bijnkershoek, *Traité du juge competent des ambassadeurs: tant pour le civil, que pour le criminel, traduit … par Jean Barbeyrac* (The Hague, 1723) ; Abraham Westerveen, *Dissertation, ou l'on prouve le droit exclusif de la Compagnie Orientale des Provinces Unies, au commerce & a la navigation des Indes Orientales traduite du latin* (The Hague, 1728).

[14] Hugo Grotius, *Le droit de la guerre et de la paix Nouvelle traduction par J Barbeyrac* (Amsterdam, 1729) ; Richard Cumberland, *Traité philosophique des loix naturelles, traduit … par Jean Barbeyrac* (Amsterdam, 1744).

[15] Jean Barbeyrac, *Traité du jeu* (Amsterdam, 1709), I. 3, §2, pp. 32–3.

also concerned about the imposition of religious conformity in that context. He defended, in both words and actions, the right of professors and students to search for the truth freely and without being restrained by (religious) thought-policing from the authorities. Barbeyrac's arguments concerning ecclesiastical toleration should be understood, as they are in the next section of this chapter, against this background.

II

Pufendorf's natural law theory was self-consciously secular.[16] The foundation for natural law, Pufendorf argued, was the observation that the human species cannot survive and prosper unless humans behave sociably towards one another. While the duty to act sociably stems from God's will, the contents of natural law are defined by a secular logic. Natural law aims at producing the survival of the human species: obedience to this law is not a step towards salvation, nor does knowledge of natural law require any special revelation. The political implications of Pufendorf's secularism are a core theme in Barbeyrac's discussions of civil toleration.

In his *De habitu religionis christianae*, Pufendorf had set out the fundamentals of the case for toleration, or so Barbeyrac argued.[17] But Pufendorf had nevertheless failed to draw the appropriate inferences from his main thesis. When men decided to form states, Pufendorf had suggested, they had in view only the safeguarding of their external security. The state was thus originally an institution unrelated to religion. This, Barbeyrac claimed, implies a clear limit to the state's authority. The civil authority was created to provide security for men's lives and external possessions, and this is the only legitimate aim of its power. That authority must not be used to impose religious beliefs.[18] Religious beliefs are internal affairs, as are virtuous dispositions, and as such they are not the concern of the state. The purpose of this authority and its laws 'is not to render truly virtuous those on whom the laws are imposed', but simply 'to prevent citizens from doing each other some considerable harm, whether in their persons or in their property; and with this aim, to curb the external actions of vice which tend towards such wrong, to the extent that

[16] For an interpretation that emphasizes this aspect of Pufendorf's natural law theory particularly strongly, see Ian Hunter, *Rival enlightenments: civil and metaphysical philosophy in early modern Germany* (Cambridge, 2001).

[17] Samuel Pufendorf, *De habitu religionis christianae ad vitam civilem* (Bremen, 1687). For discussion, compare Simone Zurbuchen, Chapter 1, and Thomas Ahnert, Chapter 2, in this volume.

[18] Pufendorf, *Le droit de la nature* (1706 edn), VII. 4, §11, n. 2.

society's peace demands and permits'.[19] This is what Pufendorf should have concluded, but, according to Barbeyrac at least, he had failed to do so.

Barbeyrac did not see Pufendorf as a consistent proponent of either secularism or toleration. Even in his works on natural law, where typically he declined to discuss the question of toleration in any great detail, Pufendorf sometimes argued in ways that seemed quite incompatible with a secular understanding of the state. Thus when Pufendorf does provide a limited defence for toleration in the *De jure naturae*, this comes in the form of a religious argument rather than a precept of natural law. The sovereign, Pufendorf argues, may have a duty to tolerate a religious minority, if (and apparently only if) the minority has the true religious faith—in such a case the sovereign in fact has a duty to embrace the true faith and to further its cause.[20] Barbeyrac protests, of course. Toleration was evidently an issue for sovereigns to ponder when they ruled over minorities whose beliefs they did not consider to be true. Barbeyrac argues, in his second note to the same paragraph, that the sovereign has a duty to tolerate all religious opinions irrespective of their truth or untruth, as long as these do not constitute an immediate threat to public safety. Heterodox beliefs are not in themselves against natural law, nor can the state, which exists to promote external security only, have any legitimate jurisdiction over such beliefs.

Barbeyrac's secularism is in many ways more marked than either Pufendorf's or Locke's. Atheism, on Barbeyrac's view, is not a crime, since it does not constitute an injury against civil peace. An atheist who converts simple folk to his cause so as to make them into unscrupulous and fearless criminals can indeed be punished. But as long as the atheist is content to keep his terrible truth to himself, there is no reason to persecute him.[21] Atheism and religious beliefs should be treated alike in this: if either the atheist or a religious person finds in his beliefs a reason for criminal behaviour, then that person should be punished as a criminal, and persons teaching a doctrine that embraces a right to crime should likewise be punished. But this punishment

[19] Pufendorf, *Le droit de la nature* (1706 edn), 'What is Permitted by the Laws', pp. 316 and 318.
[20] Pufendorf, *Le droit de la nature* (1706 edn), VII. 4, §11.
[21] Ibid., III. 4, §4, n. 2. Even Jean Le Clerc was critical of Barbeyrac's claim that toleration extends to atheists: see *Bibliotheque choisie, pour servir de suite a la Bibliotheque universelle par J Le Clerc* (28 vols., Amsterdam, 1703–18), IX (1706), p. 405. Interestingly, Barbeyrac's emphasis on virtue seems to open up the possibility that freethinkers and even virtuous atheists might be saved, since virtue, which does not as such demand adherence to any religious dogma, constitutes the core of all religion: 'La Vertu est la principale chose, le but de la Foi même: & ce que l'on peut faire de mieux, en matiére d'Opinions, c'est d'examiner sincérement & sans partialité.' ['Virtue is the most important thing and [is] the same end of faith: and the best that we can do, in matters of opinion, is to examine sincerely and impartially']: Barbeyrac, *Bibliotheque raisonnée* VII. 2, §3, p. 353.

would be meted out for a secular crime, not for a thought-crime, not for heresy or atheism as such.[22]

In some respects, then, Barbeyrac seems to embrace a more consistently secularist conception of the state than Pufendorf did. Yet secularism as such is not incompatible with intolerance. Pufendorf had in fact argued on several occasions that public tranquillity is better served by religious unity, and that the Dutch model of tolerating several denominations in one state was messy.[23] Barbeyrac responded by claiming that toleration as such was generally conducive to peace and public tranquillity. The main question is not, however, as Jean Le Clerc had also pointed out against Pufendorf, whether religious unity or pluralism is better. The question is, what should be done about the pluralism that in fact exists: should we tolerate or persecute? Of the two solutions, toleration accords far better with the interests of the state, Barbeyrac argues. Toleration will also lead to increased population and prosperity.[24] Even if persecuting a religious minority in the state might offer advantages in the short term, there is a strong likelihood that it will lead to worse problems and divisions later on.[25] There are thus good 'reason of state' grounds for supporting a tolerant policy, and for tolerating all sorts of Protestants, including heterodox thinkers and even atheists. The same grounds, however, imply that tolerance has its limits and that to some sorts of religious position intolerance is the proper response. The outstanding example of a religion that must not be tolerated, for Barbeyrac, is Roman Catholicism.

A responsible ruler will fear Catholics for at least two familiar reasons. First, because Catholics believe that they can obey the Pope against their own ruler: this view leads to war.[26] Second, because Catholic doctrine includes a principled support for intolerance and for religious violence.[27] Such doctrines are therefore 'contrary to Order & Civil Tranquillity'.[28]

A purely pragmatic secularist account of civil authority is not without its problems. Many proponents of intolerant measures (Pufendorf amongst others) defended oppression against minorities in secularist terms.[29] Does a sovereign who genuinely believes his actions serve public tranquillity, or who

[22] See also Jean Barbeyrac, *Recueil de discours sur diverses matières importantes* (Amsterdam, 1731), p. 204.

[23] Pufendorf commented on the Dutch model in his *Introductio ad historiam praecipuorum regnorum et statuum modernorum in Europa* (Frankfurt, 1688) and in some letters. See Le Clerc, *Bibliothèque choisie*, VII (1705), pp. 391–8; idem, *Bibliotheque universelle et historique* (26 vols., Amsterdam and The Hague, 1686–1738), XII, pp. 475–83.

[24] Barbeyrac, *Traité de la morale*, ch. 12, §31, pp. 180–1.

[25] Ibid., §33, pp. 181–2.

[26] Ibid., ch. 12, §23, pp. 177–8.

[27] Ibid., ch. 12, §42, p. 186.

[28] Ibid., ch. 12, §23, p. 178.

[29] See Ahnert, Chapter 2, and Zurbuchen, Chapter 1, in this volume.

at least claims such a belief for his justification, have a right to impose religious unity? Barbeyrac is clearly committed to answering this question in the negative. The state has a duty to tolerate peaceful religious minorities, that is, minorities whose actions and principles are not in themselves opposed to a tranquil public life. This duty remains, Barbeyrac adds, even if pluralism sometimes does entail inconveniences for the state.[30] The state thus has a duty to tolerate that is not reducible to reason of state arguments. This brings us to freedom of conscience.

III

For Barbeyrac, it is important to insist that the state, when it interferes with the peaceful religious life of a citizen, does a real injury to that person. Every person, Barbeyrac explains, has an 'honest liberty' to serve God 'in accordance with the light of his own Conscience'.[31] This 'freedom of conscience' (*liberte de conscience*) thus forms an inalienable part of man's natural liberty.

What does inalienability mean for Barbeyrac? There are two different answers to this question. One is that, even if men had wanted to, they would not in fact have been able to give away certain portions of their self-governance. Thus Barbeyrac sometimes argues, in a Lockean vein, that

> A Man can never give to another Man an arbitrary power over his own life, of which he is not himself the Master. But he is even less the master of his own Conscience, over which God holds empire to a point where other Men, whatever they will or do, could in reality exercise none. The greatest efforts of Violence do not here amount to anything more, than to making Hypocrites.[32]

This emphasis on men's psychological inability to submit their opinions to another's rule is not Barbeyrac's main argument, however. The inalienability of certain rights, he explains elsewhere, consists in this, that renouncing them is forbidden by a higher law.[33] This is the second sense in which natural liberty is inalienable.

[30] Barbeyrac, *Traité de la morale*, ch. 12, §33, p. 181.
[31] Barbeyrac, *Traité de la morale*, p. xiv. Barbeyrac sometimes writes about 'rights of conscience' (Grotius, *Le droit de la guerre*, II. 26, §5, n. 2, p. 1181), but mostly he writes about 'liberty of conscience', which implies 'a natural and inalienable right to a full liberty of acting in accordance with one's conscience, especially as regards one's greatest interests' (Pufendorf, *Le droit de la nature* (1712 edn), I. 3, §11, n. 1). It is this right that explains why the state has no authority to hinder 'that each serves God peacefully in accordance with the lights and movements of his own conscience'. See Pufendorf, *Le droit de la nature* (1706 edn), VII. 8, §5, n. 7; ibid., VII. 2, §21, n. 1.
[32] Barbeyrac, *Traité de la morale*, ch. 12, §29, p. 180.
[33] Pufendorf, *Le droit de la nature* (1706 edn), I. 7, §17, n. 1.

For Barbeyrac, the 'higher law' that forbids me from alienating certain portions of my natural liberty is the law of nature. Natural law, he holds, derives from three separate sources. One of these is sociability, which Pufendorf explains as necessary for the survival of the human species. Another is self-love, which entails the rational care for one's own well-being. A third, which, in order of importance, is the first and highest, is the duty of religion, or of serving God peacefully in accordance with one's conscience. This tripartite deduction of natural law has important consequences for how natural law is applied in Barbeyrac's political theory. The principle of sociability results in an obligation to obey the civil sovereign, but if the civil sovereign misuses this authority by extending it beyond its secular-rational limits, then duties of religion and self-care may sometimes trump that duty of obedience. Natural law itself imposes a duty to obey, but at the same time implies a right to life and to liberty of conscience.[34]

Under normal circumstances, conscientious protests cannot justify disobedience, Barbeyrac admits. In ordinary cases, the citizen, soldier, and subject in general, do have a clear duty of conscience to obey civil law and the sovereign's commands, even against conscientious scruples. Conscience commands obedience to civil law.[35] Some Christian groups, Barbeyrac notes, may believe that a war they are enlisted to take part in is unjust. If their doubts were cause enough for disobedience, then the sovereign could not do his job. Forcing these subjects into the army does not constitute an injury against their inalienable right to freedom of conscience. The French persecutions, however, are quite another matter.[36]

Occasionally Barbeyrac writes as if freedom of conscience were based on a duty to serve God. This first account is sometimes (but not always) articulated by referring to the idea of God as my owner. I cannot alienate what does not belong to me.[37] Such an approach sits uncomfortably with Barbeyrac's desire to extend this freedom to atheists. Some of his arguments for a liberty of conscience therefore rely on a more general reasoning. Obedience to conscience is a kind of meta-duty upon which all other duties are based.[38] Demanding that persons reject the voice of their conscience in matters that have no bearing on external peace is a clear case of wanting to deny their moral responsibility. Persecuting the unorthodox, Barbeyrac thus argues, is

[34] Ibid., II. 3, §15, n. 1 and 5.
[35] Ibid., VIII. 1, §1, n. 2.
[36] Ibid., VIII. 1, §6, n. 4.
[37] Ibid., VII. 8, §6, n. 2.
[38] Already in 1706, Barbeyrac argued that the right to freedom of conscience is particularly important because it connects to the most foundational duty of all, namely 'the indispensable necessity under which every person is to follow the lights of his own conscience' : Pufendorf, *Le droit de la nature* (1706 edn), VII. 8, §5, n. 7.

'clearly a case of wanting to force them into disobeying their conscience, & of thereby putting them in a disposition to crush beneath their feet all respect for Truth & Virtue'.[39] This seems to make liberty of conscience into a general liberty to think what one will, as long as one's thoughts are not immediately harmful to public tranquillity.

Barbeyrac does impose restrictions on what conscience can possibly demand. The duty to obey conscience is always articulated as a duty to think and do peacefully what one believes is right. All intolerant principles are naturally excluded. 'The right to act in accordance with the movements of one's conscience', Barbeyrac writes, 'is founded on the very nature of man, and since this nature is the same for all, none of them in particular could be accorded the slightest thing that would tend to the diminution of such a shared right. Thus the right to obey one's conscience carries in itself this exception: barring cases where it would constitute an injury against the conscience of another.'[40] Barbeyrac's argument is that demands of conscience have to submit to a test of universality dictated by the moral equality of men as equally agents with a conscience. It would be inconsistent to demand a right to freedom of conscience for oneself as equally entitled to self-government if one's demand at the same time constituted an injury against another person's similar right. I cannot, in other words, have a right of conscience to injure *your* right of conscience. This constitutes Barbeyrac's version of the formula that all beliefs should be tolerated, except intolerant ones.

Barbeyrac's main discussion of civil toleration thus revolves around the concept of liberty. Pufendorf and Grotius had failed to discuss the right that each person has to defend his liberty against unjust attacks from the sovereign, Barbeyrac complains. To rectify this problem, he argues that in some cases, when the sovereign's orders clearly and obviously injure the liberty of conscience of some citizens, this entails a right for the victims to resist and a duty for others to assist them. The Catholic dragoon should have perceived clearly that it was wrong to harm Huguenots whose only crime was seeking to serve God peacefully—as they had every right to do. The dragoon should have disobeyed the sovereign's orders because the inalienable right of the Huguenots in this case trumped the duty to obey the sovereign.[41] Barbeyrac even gives his account of a right to freedom of conscience an application in the international arena by arguing that Protestant powers could legitimately band together to wage war on countries that allow the Inquisition.[42]

[39] Barbeyrac, *Traité de la morale*, ch. 12, §55, p. 197.
[40] Pufendorf, *Le droit de la nature* (1712 edn), I. 3, §11, n. 1.
[41] Ibid. (1706 edn), I. 5, §9, n. 1.
[42] Pufendorf, *Le droit de la nature* (1706 ed.), VIII. 6, §3, n. 1.

For Barbeyrac, then, civil toleration is not simply a policy that the state should observe. Civil toleration also denotes a duty to respect the inalienable liberty of citizens to be self-governing in religious matters that are not directly harmful to social peace. A serious injury against this duty is not only bad policy, but a crime that can and should be hindered by all parties involved, even foreign powers. And such injuries can, Barbeyrac believes, be recognized by all human beings. This last point can be further elucidated by looking at how Barbeyrac's views on the epistemology of natural law evolved over time.

IV

Pufendorf had made a sharp distinction between natural law as science and natural law as social reality. As a science, natural law depends on a calculation of the various sorts of norms that human beings need to obey in order for a sociable coexistence between them to be possible. Pufendorf clearly regarded such calculations as requiring both higher education and a good deal of intelligence.[43] Neither did ordinary citizens gain insights into the natural laws from some sort of moral intellection. Moral distinctions are learned through a process of socialization in which individuals see some actions praised and others punished. Natural laws are also imposed on people from above by the authorities. It is thus tradition and authority that together bring morality and natural law to ordinary men, and individuals themselves have practically no capacity or inclination for critical reflection on these norms.[44]

Barbeyrac was not happy with Pufendorf's approach here. For a victim of persecution to have a right in any efficacious way, he needs an ability to perceive this right even when tradition and authority deny it; for a persecutor to violate a right in the appropriate sense, he must be able to know about that right without relying on instructions from his corrupt superiors. Through consecutive editions of *Le droit de la nature*, Barbeyrac tends to de-emphasize the difference between natural law as science and natural law as everyday knowledge. Already in 1706, Barbeyrac insisted that humans recognize actions as 'morally honest or dishonest, because of the '*convenance* that they have with a Rational & Sociable nature'.[45] Elsewhere he insists that one can think of some actions as honest or dishonest in themselves because they accord

[43] We do need to think of people as able to grasp the basic laws of nature, Pufendorf explained, but this was never more than a *de jure* principle: we need to assume that people are capable of this, otherwise it would be unjust to punish them for their crimes. See Pufendorf, *De jure naturae*, I. 3, §3, and for discussion Kari Saastamoinen, *The morality of the fallen man: Samuel Pufendorf on natural law* (Studia Historica 50, Helsinki, 1995), p. 132.

[44] Pufendorf, *De jure naturae*, II. 3, §3, and Saastamoinen, *Morality of the fallen man*, pp. 132–5.

[45] Pufendorf, *Le droit de la nature* (1706 edn), II. 3, §4, n. 5.

with the nature of the agent to whom the actions are imputed. Some actions are naturally honest for men to do towards other men, others are dishonest. Already the language is sliding away from Pufendorf's, and this tendency is further extended as time goes on.

In later editions of *Le droit de la nature*, Barbeyrac made a significant addition to the passage in which Pufendorf discussed the moral insights of common people. To Pufendorf's account, Barbeyrac insists, we must add 'the manifest proportion that these maxims [the maxims of natural law] have with the lights of right reason; for it makes itself felt to the simplest folks, from the moment that the principles are proposed to them, and that they consider them well; although they would perhaps never succeed in discovering them by themselves'.[46] This does not mean that the 'simplest folks' would be capable of calculating the long-term advantages of sociable behaviour. It is rather that they naturally recognize some actions as honest and as being consonant with human nature, irrespective of either divine commands or utility. Barbeyrac further insists that Pufendorf was 'too enlightened' to think that lying or ingratitude, for example, would be as beautiful as truthfulness and gratitude. Some actions have a certain dignity that others lack, and 'our Author [Pufendorf] recognized in the honest and dishonest things, a relation of harmony (*convenance*) or disharmony (*disconvenance*), independently of the will of God'.[47] This is how both common man and the learned know the fundamental laws of nature. We all recognize that some actions are in harmony with reason and sociability, not because we would be able to calculate the long-term advantages, but simply because we recognize the natural uprightness of those actions.[48]

> When I say: one must repay good with good but not with evil; men ought to obey God their Creator; there is in these propositions such an evident and clear harmony (*une convenance si Claire & si évidente*), that one cannot but assent, however little attention one pays to the matter, and to find beautiful and honest what they contain, without having to consult in any manner the advantage that comes from their observation. One is agreed from thence on, that whoever acts against these maxims, sins against reason, and one is brought to make reproaches to oneself. From this alone arises the idea of Duty, and the reasonable aim of observing it.[49]

As Barbeyrac's views on moral epistemology evolved, so too did his thoughts on sociability itself. In his footnotes to Grotius's prolegomena, Barbeyrac

46 Ibid. (1712 edn), II. 3, §13, n. 7.

47 '[N]ôtre Auteur reconnoissoit dans les Choses Honnêtes ou Deshonnêtes, un rapport de convenance ou de Disconvenance, indépendamment de la Volonté de DIEU' : Pufendorf, *Le droit de la nature* (1732 edn), I. 2, §6, n. 1; see also ibid. (1706 edn), II. 3, §4, n. 5.

48 Pufendorf, *Le droit de la nature* (1734 edn), II. 3, §19, n. 2, I, pp. 230–2.

49 Ibid. (1732 edn), II. 3, §10, n. 6.

argued that human beings have a natural benevolence towards other humans. This natural benevolence precedes and is independent of any views of interest. The human individual, as the Stoic philosophers had explained, naturally has a willingness to help other humans. 'Such Dispositions as are contrary to Humanity,' Barbeyrac explains, 'are rather the Result of a bad Education and Custom, than of a natural and invincible Inclination.' The natural sentiments of Humanity drive humans to act sociably towards each other without reflecting on either advantage or God. In this connection, Barbeyrac also refers approvingly to Shaftesbury, whom he regards as an 'ingenious and penetrating Author'.[50] Barbeyrac's moral epistemology moves in an increasingly sentimentalist direction, with an emphasis on innate moral sentiments and a natural moral rectitude.

Barbeyrac expresses agreement with Pufendorf and Locke as regards innate ideas, but he is also in agreement with the views that Shaftesbury presented against Locke on this issue.[51] Thus he fully accepts 'that there is a natural proportion between the ideas of a divinity, and of virtue, and the constitution of our understanding, so that one easily assents to these ideas and finds in them harmony, beauty, and dignity'.[52] We are preprogrammed, as it were, to recognize or develop in ourselves a set of basic notions of what common sense and decency demand of us in our actions towards other human beings. This general benevolence is based only on common human nature, or Humanity.[53] It is in this sense that Barbeyrac describes the principles of toleration as being easily within the grasp of all human beings. To come up with a correct understanding of the principles of toleration it is enough that one refrains from 'renouncing the simplest and purest notions of common sense, & does not divest one-self, I do not say of charity, but of the most vulgar Humanity'.[54] So long as a person does not dehumanize himself on purpose, he will easily be able to perceive the immorality of persecution.

[50] Grotius, 'Prolegomena', in *Le droit de la guerre*, §7, n. 4 and n. 6.

[51] For which, see Daniel Carey, 'Locke, Shaftesbury, and innateness', *Locke Studies*, 4 (2004), pp. 13–45.

[52] Cumberland, *Des loix naturelles*, pp. 7–9, n. 1.

[53] Pufendorf, *Le droit de la nature* (1732 edn), II. 3, §18. The term Humanité is used several times: 'General benevolence towards all men' is based on 'nothing but common human nature or Humanity … a general friendship (amitié generale)', and it is 'always to our advantage too', and yet when one looks for the foundation for that general friendship, 'one should not look to the advantage'. But that is not what the 1706 edition says: there, Barbeyrac translated: 'quand il s'agit d'en établir le fondement, on ne le cherche pas d'ordinaire dans l'utilité qu'on en retire ; mais dans la conformité d'une même nature'. And the same passage in 1732 says: 'le fondement, il ne faut pas le chercher dans l'utilité'. [This is throughout the question … is Humanity a calculated advantage-oriented general love or an inclination (or duty) to love all men because of shared humanity.]

The overall picture that emerges from Barbeyrac's various comments is the following one. Humans have a natural inclination to benevolence towards each other; they possess what Barbeyrac terms 'sentiments of Humanity'. These sentiments come with a more or less distinct idea of which actions are consonant with human nature, which actions one human being can legitimately do to another. The actions are not now regarded as consonant with human nature in the Pufendorfian sense, where some actions have deplorable consequences at a societal level. Instead, certain actions are thought of as incompatible with the benevolence and respect that every human being should have for other human beings.

The shift in moral epistemology also impacts on Barbeyrac's discussion of equality, or more precisely, Barbeyrac's rethinking of sociability entails a reconfiguration of how equality and sociability relate to one other. In Hobbes and Pufendorf, the impression is generally that citizens should grant each other an equal status in proceedings because a failure to do so would endanger sociability when people's injured pride would prompt them to wreak vengeance on those who fail to show due respect. According to Barbeyrac, it would be a misunderstanding to think that the duty to treat others equally derives from impractical social consequences. The real foundation for the duty to treat others equally lies in the self-evident and simple recognition of other human beings as equally human.[55] Natural equality, Barbeyrac argues, implies a perfect right to demand that one is regarded and treated as a Human. This means that one's inalienable human rights must be respected. A person who does not respect my freedom of conscience thus injures both my natural and inalienable liberty and my natural equality. This is against Christian teachings and against natural law in equal measure.[56] To treat you as my equal in the relevant sense, I must regard you as entitled to form your own opinion about the deity and His wishes. This takes us much of the way to a comprehensive view of toleration, but not the whole way; what of the third and final aspect of toleration identified at the start of this chapter, toleration as a virtue?

V

According to Barbeyrac, the main problem in Protestant countries is not the lack of civil toleration as such, but rather a lack of ecclesiastical toleration.

[54] Barbeyrac, *Bibliotheque raisonnée*, I. 2, §5, p. 321.

[55] Pufendorf, *Le droit de la nature* (1706 edn), III. 2, §2, n. 3.

[56] Ibid., III. 2, §1, n. 1. See also idem, *Bibliotheque raisonnée*, IV. 1, §6, p. 21.

Protestants of various denominations are too eagerly denouncing various opinions as dangerous for salvation and as grounds for exclusion from their churches. Such ecclesiastical intolerance also spills over into civil intolerance.

Barbeyrac had become the victim of ecclesiastical intolerance himself, as I noted earlier. In Berlin, he was accused of Arminianism and Socinianism; later, his professorship at Lausanne was delayed because the authorities in Berne needed to examine similar accusations. Later still, when Barbeyrac was Rector of the Lausanne Academy, he was involved in a vicious struggle concerning the imposition of the *Confessio helvetica* on students and teachers. Basically, Barbeyrac argued that teachers and students should be left free to work out their own convictions without having to sign a confession imposed from above. The quarrel over the confession brings to light an important fact: ecclesiastical toleration was not only about participating in the same church, but also about the freedom to teach and think in schools and universities. Ecclesiastical toleration is about tolerating within a church people who do not share all of the views defined as orthodox, but it is also by implication about tolerating unorthodox thinkers within universities and schools.

Barbeyrac, it is clear, holds that the churches should make room for dissent within.[57] Allowing unorthodox thinkers in the church simply means that one does not regard their opinions as dangerous to salvation—and we should, Barbeyrac stresses, be extremely cautious about declaring any opinions to be hindrances to salvation.[58] Barbeyrac's own approach is cautious indeed in this sense. Thus he speculates, in an anonymous review article in the *Bibliothèque raisonnée des savans*, that virtuous freethinkers and atheists may well find a place in Heaven, since virtuous action is the main aim of religion. Virtue and good conduct are the core of Christian religion and indeed of all religion; speculative dogma is in itself irrelevant to salvation.[59]

Barbeyrac's views on the inviolability of conscience and of salvation did not make the role of the church altogether redundant. But they did imply significant revisions to the character imputed to it. Thus, if Barbeyrac called for an open, inclusive and united Protestant church, he did so on grounds that embodied his wider prepossessions. Open debate and communing together, Barbeyrac writes, is the only way to overcome the inconveniences attached to a plurality of religious beliefs.[60] Plurality will never go away: it is a constant

[57] Barbeyrac, *Traité de la morale*, ch. 12, §22, p. 177.

[58] Ibid., ch. 12, §24, p. 178.

[59] Barbeyrac, *Bibliotheque raisonnée*, VII. 2, §3, p. 353. Similar but less radical views are expressed in e.g. Hugo Grotius, *De veritate religionis Christianae* (Oxford, 1675), Bk. II. §12, pp. 43–45, and idem, *Meletius sive de iis quae inter Christianos conveniunt epistola*, ed. and trans. Guillaume H. M. Posthumus Meyjes (Leiden, 1988), §§89–91, pp. 132–4.

[60] Barbeyrac, *Traité de la morale*, ch. 12, §33, pp. 181–2.

feature of human history, and one intended by God. Plurality has a lesson for us: it is God's way of encouraging the two most important Christian virtues, namely moderation and charity.[61] The true believer and the true Christian is tolerant in the sense of ecclesiastical toleration. Such a person, Barbeyrac holds, is ready to discuss religious issues patiently with those who think differently, and even to question his own convictions in light of new knowledge. Open and free debate will thus take away some of the causes of partiality; it will lessen the force of passionate prejudice. This is why ecclesiastical toleration is also the only road to increasing civil toleration further.

When Barbeyrac enters the fray to reform the Reformation, his main point is to combat authoritarianism and intolerance. These 'remnants of Papism' must, he argues, be eradicated for the Reformation to reach its true fruition.[62] Such a reform does not appear likely to come from pastors and priests. The ecclesiastics, as Barbeyrac wrote in 1707, are no longer the most competent people at rethinking Christianity: religion is not safe in their hands.[63] The true reformers of the day, as Barbeyrac also argued in the preface to *Le droit de la nature*, are thinkers like Grotius, who make natural law and ethics the core of religion.[64] Barbeyrac thus sees natural law as a tool with which to rework reformed religious thought in a more tolerant direction. At the same time, he views this work for a more tolerant Reformation as a prerequisite for a fuller realization of civil toleration.

VI

Barbeyrac's turn from an ecclesiastical career to work on natural law was inspired specifically by two strong motives. One was to criticize Protestant orthodoxy and to argue for a more tolerant, inclusive, and less authoritarian Protestant Christianity. The other was to clarify, as the Huguenots constantly tried to do, what conclusions Europe and the world should draw from the French persecutions. Civil and ecclesiastical toleration were arguably the primary issues that natural law was called upon to address. If this is the case, then it would not be surprising to find that Barbeyrac allowed his concern with toleration to influence his ideas of natural law. Barbeyrac's later, increasingly sentimentalist approach to the epistemology of natural law was dictated, at least in part, by his need to explain how natural law's demand for toleration would be obvious to ordinary soldiers and citizens just as much as to experts

[61] Ibid., ch. 12, §34, p. 182.
[62] Barbeyrac, *Traité de la morale*, ch. 12, §42, p. 186. See also Tillotson, *Sermons*, I, p. vii.
[63] Barbeyrac, 'Préface générale', in *Recueil*, p. xxx.
[64] Pufendorf, 'Prolegomena', in *Le droit de la nature* (1712 edn), §11.

on the subject. In the end, this concern led Barbeyrac to make quite substantial modifications to the Pufendorfian theory he had started out with. Not only did natural law theory have an impact on debates concerning toleration, the need to defend toleration also contributed to the development of early Enlightenment conceptions of natural law.

Barbeyrac established a set of connections between toleration in all the three senses that I distinguished at the start of this chapter, and natural law theory. First, the state is created to secure external tranquillity and it therefore entails a right for the sovereign to impose laws that serve this end. By the same token, the sovereign ought not to interfere with the peaceful religious life of minorities, but must defend these from unwarranted aggression. Natural law thus establishes toleration as a unilateral and hierarchical relationship between the sovereign and peaceful religious minorities. Second, minorities, and indeed individual persons, have a formal right to freedom of conscience. This is of particular importance for understanding what happens when religious groups succeed in turning the state against a harmless minority, or when the authorities fail to intervene in defence of a religious minority. This is not only a case of the state failing to fulfil one of its duties, but constitutes an injury against a formal human right. The demand for toleration is now articulated in terms of self-evident inalienable natural rights of men. Third, both universal sentiments and Scripture urge men to respect each other as persons endowed with a conscience and a right to exercise it freely: both recommend the virtue of Humanity, which in turn builds on other virtues such as humility and charity.

When Barbeyrac's defence of religious toleration draws on universal sentiments of humanity, it makes natural law into a set of more or less self-evident maxims. This transition is important for understanding how the Pufendorfian tradition of natural law as divine socially useful commandments handed down by tradition and authorities could become, in the eighteenth century, a resource for a language of self-evident inalienable rights. The right to freedom of religion, and thus the moral idea of toleration, is evident to all. As a counterpoint to this optimistic epistemology, Barbeyrac provides a rather darker picture of history and especially of the influence of self-serving religious authorities and competing religious orthodoxies. Power-hungry priests are for Barbeyrac the ones who have a real interest in creating partisan groupings and in fostering a spirit of intolerance. Instead of only limiting the damage by declaring that the church can wield no worldly power, nor the state aim at salvation—claims that Barbeyrac did assert and defend—one must reshape religion from within, in a more tolerant direction.

For Barbeyrac, toleration, and the lack of it, was a concrete reality shaping his life and activities. One aspect of how Barbeyrac worked for toleration was his fight against the imposition of the *Confessio helvetica* during his rectorate at the Lausanne Academy. Another was his activity in the learned journal *Bibliothèque raisonnée des ouvrages des savans de l'Europe* (1728–1753), a journal which explained that it kept the names of its journalists anonymous so as to make it possible for them to reason impartially, without having to fear attacks from religious orthodoxy. Viewed from this perspective, Barbeyrac's writings on ecclesiastical toleration are part of a wider project, the main aim of which was to make room for impartial public reasoning. Toleration would, Barbeyrac believed, follow as a matter of course, as soon as freedom of judgement was guaranteed. It would be easy, he asserts, to 'clear away the false ideas of the partisans of despotic power and intolerance, if one established everywhere a full liberty of judgement'. Until such a time, all one can do is to defend 'honest liberty' in places where one is allowed 'to say what one thinks'. Perhaps by this means, Barbeyrac speculates, the truth will find its way to those countries where darkness and tyranny reign, and perhaps it will open the eyes of a great number of people, 'and bring them either to throw off that yoke, or to retire one after the other to countries of freedom, and thus to leave the incorrigible tyrants to rule with their supporters over vast empty spaces'.[65] Perhaps.

[65] Barbeyrac, 'Préface sur les deux discours', *Recueil*, pp. 5–6.

8

Natural Rights or Political Prudence? Francis Hutcheson on Toleration

KNUD HAAKONSSEN*

THE RELATIONSHIP BETWEEN Francis Hutcheson's moral philosophy and his views on religion has attracted the attention of modern scholarship. It has been suggested that he saw the moral life of humanity as part of the providentialist dispensation that can be discerned by natural and moral philosophy.[1] More specifically, it has been argued that his idea of a moral sense that constitutes the basis for moral judgement and moral virtue is intimately connected with his providentialism, for unless the possibility of gratifying the moral sense reaches into eternity, it cannot be expected to sustain the stability of moral virtue that humanity is capable of.[2] For Hutcheson, the moral life transcends our earthly existence, so that the 'theological perspective is ... the completion of morality'.[3] I want to take these arguments further in this chapter by showing that something that is commonly taken to be as central to Hutcheson's philosophical endeavour as the idea of the moral sense, namely his idea of a natural right and the associated theory of toleration, is crucially dependent upon religious assumptions.

* I am grateful for comments made by audiences at the British Academy conference on toleration and at a public lecture at the University of Glasgow, and I thank Professor M. A. Stewart for many helpful suggestions.

[1] David Fate Norton, *David Hume: common-sense moralist, sceptical metaphysician* (Princeton, NJ, 1982), pp. 87–92.

[2] James A. Harris, 'Religion in Hutcheson's moral philosophy', *Journal of the History of Philosophy*, 46 (2008), pp. 205–22.

[3] Knud Haakonssen, *Natural law and moral philosophy: from Grotius to the Scottish Enlightenment* (Cambridge, 1996), p. 71. For Hutcheson's later work, see especially James Moore, 'Hutcheson's theodicy: the argument and the contexts of *A system of moral philosophy*', in Paul Wood, ed., *The Scottish Enlightenment: essays in reinterpretation*, (Rochester, NY, 2000), pp. 239–66.

I

Hutcheson's reputation as a protagonist of natural rights in general and of a right to toleration in particular needs some important modifications. Paradoxical though it may seem to us, it is Hutcheson's remarkably inclusive—as we might say, liberal—view of the Christian religion that implies a less than straightforward tolerationist standpoint. Closely connected with this are two further features of Hutcheson's thought; one is the well-known moral philosophy that centres on the idea of a moral sense; the other is his attempt to square a circle in contemporary debate by rejecting ministerial subscription to creeds or confessions enforced by the church which was established by law, while maintaining an Erastian view of the relationship between state and church. This complicated Hutchesonian argument was clearly developed as a forceful contribution in the continuing struggle over the direction that the Scottish kirk should take. For although Presbyterianism had been re-established by law in 1690 as the national form of church government, this could mean different things to different people—and it did. During the second quarter of the eighteenth century, Hutcheson's philosophy became a force in the articulation of an anti-orthodox line of argument on most of the central questions in these controversies. It must thus be seen as part of the prehistory to the dominance of the Moderate party in the church that came about in the third quarter.

The public debate involving Hutcheson reached something of a crescendo in 1738, when a veritable pamphlet war engulfed him.[4] A self-proclaimed but anonymous former student directed an epistolary pamphlet to him, entitled *Shaftesbury's ghost conjur'd; or, A letter to Mr. Francis Hutcheson Professor of Moral Philosophy in the University of Glasgow, wherein several gross and dangerous errors, vented by him in the course of his teaching, are brought to light, and refuted.*[5] In forty-two densely printed pages the disenchanted student, now secure in orthodoxy, ascribes eleven propositions to Hutcheson and then

[4] I am greatly indebted to James Moore and M. A. Stewart for references to the pamphlets mentioned in the following couple of pages. I am using these pieces only as scene setters. Full analyses must await the work of these two scholars, but see for a start James Moore, 'Presbyterianism and the right of private judgement. Church government in Ireland and Scotland in the age of Francis Hutcheson', in Ruth Savage, ed., *Philosophy and religion in Enlightenment Britain* (Oxford, 2012), pp. 141–68; and the editorial material in James Moore and M. A. Stewart, eds., *The correspondence and occasional writings of Francis Hutcheson* (Indianapolis, IN, forthcoming).

[5] [Anonymous], *Shaftesbury's ghost conjur'd; or, A letter to Mr. Francis Hutcheson Professor of Moral Philosophy in the University of Glasgow, wherein several gross and dangerous errors, vented by him in the course of his teaching, are brought to light, and refuted* (n.p.., 1738). The pamphlet is signed 'Euzelus Philalethes', i.e., 'Righteous lover of truth'.

sets about demonstrating their wide discrepancy with both Scripture and the Westminster Confession. The first allegedly Hutchesonian proposition is, 'We could have the Knowledge of Moral Good and Evil, altho' we knew nothing of the Being of God',[6] and the second is that the 'Tendency to promote the Happiness of others, is the Standard of Moral Goodness'.[7] This publication was instantly countered proposition for proposition and in tones of outrage and contempt in *A vindication of Mr. Hutcheson from the calumnious aspersions of a late pamphlet. By several of his scholars*, as the title page has it, and those scholars were fourteen colleagues and students (who could, they say, 'have mentioned many more').[8] There followed another epistolary pamphlet addressed to a prominent orthodox clergyman under the same pseudonym as that of the disgruntled former student and accuser of Hutcheson, but clearly written as a scabrous and in places scatological spoof on Hutcheson's orthodox opponents.[9] The Synod of Glasgow and Ayr did not take any action on the accusations against Hutcheson. In fact, it listened to one of his friends give an eloquent statement of Hutchesonian sentiments about the proper—that is to say, educational—role of clergymen.[10] Hutcheson himself appears to have been somewhat bemused by the controversy, mentioning to his friend Thomas Drennan that '[t]here has been some whimsical Buffoonry about my Heresy of which I will send you a copy'.[11] However, he was not exactly passive, for he found yet another pamphlet so useful that he recommended it to his friends and disciples in Ireland, explaining to one of them, that it 'has run like lightening here [that is, in Glasgow]; and is producing some Effect[;] the author is unknown, tis wrote with anger and contempt of the Kirk and Confession, but it has a Set of Objections against the Confession which I imagine few will have the Brow [that is, effrontery] to answer'.[12] This piece was entitled *A serious address to the Church of Scotland, with relation to the growth of deism and immorality: examining some parts of their discipline and constitution*, and it was written by an anonymous critic who claimed to be a former Edinburgh student, now a minister somewhere in England. It is an

[6] [Anon.], *Shaftesbury's ghost conjur'd*, p. 6.
[7] Ibid., p. 8.
[8] [Anon.], *A vindication of Mr. Hutcheson from the calumnious aspersions of a late pamphlet. By several of his scholars* (n.p., 1738), p. 20.
[9] *A letter to the valiant and undaunted champion of our broken covenants, the reverend and renowned Mr. Ebenezer Erskine; in relation to the present heresies, backslidings, defections, and lukewarmness of the times, and his apostolical testimonies against them, by a bold soldier under his banner, Euzelus Philalethes, author of Shaftesbury's Ghost conjur'd* (London, 1738).
[10] Robert Paton, *The main duty of bishops: a sermon preached before the Synod of Glasgow and Air, October 1738* (Edinburgh, 1739).
[11] Hutcheson to Thomas Drennan, 5 March 1738/9: letter no. 27 in Moore and Stewart, eds., *Correspondence and occasional writings*.
[12] Hutcheson to Thomas Drennan, ibid.

extraordinarily blunt and radical attack on the orthodoxy of the Church of Scotland as presented, for example, in William Dunlop's large *Collection of confessions of faith, catechisms, directories, books of discipline, &c.* At the same time, the author ridicules the Edinburgh clergy whose sermons he had listened to while a student there.[13] Also in this pamphlet we encounter in central place the issue of whether we can have morality independently of religion; indeed, the point is accentuated by the firm assertion that we can be saved simply by living according to the law of nature.

By 1738 Hutcheson was of course no stranger to theological controversy. As a student, he had been taught divinity by John Simson, himself a victim of heresy charges in his time;[14] all his life he was close friends with several of the leading non-subscribers among Irish Presbyterians, and although he himself subscribed twice to the Westminster confession, it should be noted that friends considered him to have—as one of them put it—a 'Superior Latitude with respect to compliances of this Sort'.[15] The flurry of activity in 1738 is of particular interest because of the clarity with which it brought out the central issues and because of its timing. It was sufficiently late in Hutcheson's career for him to have become an established figure and an intellectual leader with a discipleship that was panting to come to his defence at the first sign of any criticism. Yet there remained quite enough of an established orthodox order for Hutchesonianism to be seen as radical, novel, and dangerous. At the same time, as mentioned earlier, the Moderate interest in the Church of Scotland was in the process of formation, and it would be only another sixteen or seventeen years before the Moderates as a 'party' won their decisive victory to take over the establishment. The polemical efforts of Hutcheson and his associates undoubtedly played an important role in preparing the way for a moderate party interest, and one may see this process as continuing until the mid-1750s. At that time, nine years after Hutcheson's death, the discipleship published his *System of moral philosophy* (1755), a large work which he himself had given up on and left in manuscript soon after the pamphlet

[13] Anon., *A collection of confessions of faith, catechisms, directories, books of discipline, &c. Of publick authority in Scotland* (2 vols., Edinburgh, 1719, 1722).

[14] See Anne Skoczylas, *Mr. Simson's knotty case: divinity, politics, and due process in early 18th-century Scotland* (Montreal, 2001).

[15] William Bruce to Hutcheson, 16 December 1738: letter no. 25 in Moore and Stewart, eds., *Correspondence and occasional writings*. Compare Ian McBride, *Scripture politics: Ulster Presbyterians and Irish radicalism in the late eighteenth century* (Oxford, 1998), p. 58; also idem, 'The school of virtue: Francis Hutcheson, Irish Presbyterians and the Scottish Enlightenment', in D. George Boyce, Robert Eccleshall, and Vincent Geoghegan, eds., *Political thought in Ireland since the seventeenth century* (London and New York, 1993), pp. 73–99, and 'Ulster Presbyterians and the confessional state, *c.* 1688–1733', in D. George Boyce, Robert Eccleshall, and Vincent Geoghegan, eds., *Political discourse in seventeenth- and eighteenth-century Ireland* (Basingstoke and New York, 2001), pp. 169–92.

controversy in the late 1730s, but which was eventually published with the support of a large list of subscribers.[16] However, both the image of Hutcheson as a radical and our understanding of the relationship between his thought and the outlook of the Moderates need to be considered in light of some basic features of his philosophy, and it is to those that I now turn.

II

As we have seen, a central issue in the polemical pieces was the old question of whether humanity can discern moral good and evil without knowledge of God, or whether we can live by natural law alone. It was impossible to deny that this was not only Hutcheson's teaching but *central* to that teaching. While he did not deny that original sin had—as he put it in his inaugural lecture—caused a 'weakness of our nature', his concern was to show that 'all our innate desires strive against that weakness and declare that such weakness is not the end of our duties, much less the goal which nature has set for our actions'.[17] From his first work, he had tried to establish that it is part of the natural constitution of the human mind to have a moral faculty that is best thought of as a power of perception, that is, a moral sense. Hutcheson thought that the evidence for this sense is empirical, and a great deal of his work, early and late, is taken up with providing such evidence by showing the ubiquity of benevolent behaviour in human life and, not least, by refuting reductive accounts of such behaviour in terms of self-interest, accounts which he found in the modern heirs to Epicureanism, especially Hobbes, Mandeville, and, eventually, Hume.[18] However, while our nature gives us access to some knowledge of good and evil, this is only the more elementary form of moral insight, and to get any further we do need to go via the divinity. As the disciples defending Hutcheson put it on his behalf,

> We may approve or condemn some Sorts of Virtues and Vices, even tho' we had not known God, or had any Persuasion, that, by his Laws, he required the one, and prohibited the other: We should, for Instance, approve humane, friendly,

[16] Francis Hutcheson, *A system of moral philosophy* (2 vols., Glasgow, 1755); new edition in preparation by the present author.

[17] Francis Hutcheson, *On the natural sociability of mankind* (1730), in James Moore and Michael Silverthorne, eds., *Logic, metaphysics, and the natural sociability of mankind* (Indianapolis, IN, 2006), pp. 191–216, at p. 197. As the editors point out, Hutcheson's orthodox Presbyterian contemporaries would have seen this as Pelagian heterodoxy.

[18] Compare James Moore, 'Utility and humanity: the quest for the *honestum* in Cicero, Hutcheson and Hume', *Utilitas*, 14 (2002), pp. 365–86, and John Robertson, *The case for the Enlightenment: Scotland and Naples, 1680–1760* (Cambridge, 2005), pp. 283–9.

> grateful Actions toward our Fellows, and condemn the contrary; the very *Epicureans* did so, who believed no Providence or Laws of God.[19]

If we are to go beyond what even Epicureans can know, we need to be acquainted with divine providence and its laws. Only thus will we appreciate that individual good acts fit into a system by contributing to the overall happiness of the moral creation and that this is the intention of the Great Benevolist above all benevolists.[20] It is through reference to the universal moral system that we may shore up our moral sense in its weakness when making individual moral judgements. Not least, it is insight into the workings of the divine corporation, as it has usefully been called, that is the object of moral education for the individual and enlightenment for the public.[21] In fact, to provide such education and enlightenment is the task of moral philosophy, a task that Hutcheson saw as the core of his own teaching.

The division of morality into two layers, an elemental passionate response to the stimulus of our surroundings, and a judgemental appreciation of an overarching system of actions and agents, was an idea for which Hutcheson himself found some precursor in Grotius's idea of natural rights as based upon prima facie claims or needs that had to be harmonized by the legal system.[22] And it was surely a line of argument to interest the young David Hume when drawing his distinction between natural and artificial virtues, his basic task being to shape the idea of artifice by showing that providence was surplus to requirement for an understanding of a system of moral relations.

For Hutcheson, however, the teleological view of morality, or moral providence as he called it,[23] was crucial and as important to his theory as the moral sense. It explains why he always considered the moral life as an ongoing project. This is well reflected in the way in which he dealt with Pierre Bayle's two questions. First, the question of 'whether a society of Atheists could subsist?' is, he suggested, simply 'a needless inquiry', not a question to be answered yes or no. Secondly, to inquire 'whether their [the atheists'] state would be better or worse than that of men possessed with some wicked superstition?' is a question 'of no importance'.[24] The point is that the moral life is

[19] [Anon.], *A vindication*, p. 7.

[20] Among many passages, see Hutcheson, *A system*, I, pp. 248–9.

[21] Jerome B. Schneewind, 'The divine corporation and the history of ethics', in Richard Rorty, Jerome B. Schneewind, and Quentin Skinner, eds., *Philosophy and history* (Cambridge, 1984), pp. 173–92. Compare Harris, 'Religion in Hutcheson's moral philosophy'.

[22] Francis Hutcheson, *A short introduction to moral philosophy, in three books* (Glasgow, 1747), II.4.ii, pp. 128–9, and idem, *A system*, I, p. 255; note, in both places, with reference to Hugo Grotius's *De jure belli ac pacis*, I.2.i.

[23] Hutcheson, *A system*, II, p. 313.

[24] Hutcheson, *A system*, I, pp. 219–20. Bayle's discussion of the two questions weaves through many parts of his *Pensées diverses … a l'occasion de la comète qui parut au mois de Decembre 1680*

always in transition, and the *truly valuable* moral life has a direction that can only be supplied by a providential outlook upon the overall happiness that the system is capable of. Neither atheism nor corrupted religion can give us this justifying vision, and this deficiency makes it irrelevant whether the former—atheism—could sustain some sort of sociability here or there, and whether this would be less bad than the practices of superstition.

It is humanity equipped in this way, with a natural moral sense and the capacity and need for understanding the moral providence within which that sense operates—it is humanity thus equipped that makes up both church and civil society. However, given Hutcheson's theological background and ecclesiastical context, we would expect *conscience* to play a central role as far as church membership is concerned; and considering his philosophical provenance and political engagement, we have reason for looking to *natural rights* as the foundation of political association. Accordingly, we have to investigate the relationship between the moral sense and conscience, and between the moral sense and rights in Hutcheson's thought.

III

Conscience seems to be relatively unimportant as a distinctive concept in Hutcheson's work. In the early publications, it barely occurs at all. In his later work, beginning with the inaugural lecture as professor at Glasgow in 1730, Hutcheson does introduce the concept, but then he often identifies it with the moral sense, as when he echoes Joseph Butler and talks of the 'moral sense which we may also call natural conscience'.[25] Alternatively, he makes conscience out to encompass the moral sense but with the added power of judgement about motives and consequences of actions, and about the relationship between actions and moral rules (meaning the natural law issuing from God). The latter more considered concept thus reflects the two sides of Hutcheson's account of moral understanding, the perception of moral qualities and the judgement in accordance with the laws that are constitutive of the overall moral system. It might be thought that this idea of conscience was being used by Hutcheson in his academical writings—here especially the Latin moral compend—where he might need to operate within a traditional curriculum

(1682, 2nd enlarged edn 1684). Hutcheson translates Bayle's language of idolatry into talk about superstition. For an incisive discussion of Scottish, including Hutcheson's, reactions to Bayle on this point, see James Harris, 'Answering Bayle's question: religious belief in the moral philosophy of the Scottish Enlightenment', *Oxford studies in early modern philosophy*, I (2003), pp. 229–53.

[25] Hutcheson, *Natural sociability*, p. 199. Compare Joseph Butler, *Fifteen sermons preached at the Rolls chapel* (London, 1729, Sermon II).

and use its conceptual apparatus, which was largely derived from Reformed or Presbyterian scholasticism. This seems unlikely. Those whose heresy accusations Hutcheson so cavalierly courted were trained in this curriculum, and hardly anyone had been as effective in bringing classroom teaching to bear upon public debates as Hutcheson.[26] So it would have been odd if he had gone out of his way to distort basic features of his original philosophy in order to conform to the traditional teaching whose theological and political implications he was combatting. In the present case of his idea of conscience another explanation is available in the texts. In both *A short introduction to moral philosophy* (1747) and the *System of moral philosophy*, he introduces this concept in the context of the technical discussion of conscience that was demanded by the systematics of natural law in order to explain the imputability of actions; at the same time, he employs the key concept of his earliest and most original work, the moral sense. He puts it like this:

> That inward power called *Conscience*, so much talked of, is either this very moral sense or faculty we have explained, or includes it as its most essential part; since without this sense we could discern no moral qualities. But when this is presupposed, our reason will shew what external actions are laudable or censurable according as they evidence good or evil affections of soul. *Conscience* is commonly defined to be a man's … judgment about his actions as to their conformity or contrariety to the law.[27]

The philosophical issue of the relationship between the perceptive and the judgemental side of conscience or our moral power was transformed by Thomas Reid and became a central theme in his Common Sense theory of morals, but it is not my concern here. The point I want to draw attention to is that Hutcheson accounts for conscience as a feature of the mind that is subject to empirically ascertainable factors and consequently is open to cultivation and education, depending on the circumstances of the individual person. In particular, conscience is never seen as a metaphysically or religiously privileged power that stands outside of the ordinary mental life of people. It is true that Hutcheson grows fond of applying the Stoic designation of *to hegemonikon*, the ruling principle or part, to the moral power; this is especially so in his

[26] This was a continuing effort. When the Latin compend was being made more widely accessible through a translation, Hutcheson was at first reluctant but then clearly sought control over the work. See 'Advertisement' by the translator, in Francis Hutcheson, *Philosophiae moralis institutio compendiaria, with A short introduction to moral philosophy*, ed. Luigi Turco (Indianapolis, IN, 2007), p. 2. Whoever did the actual translation, the work was very close to Hutcheson himself during his final years; it appeared the year after his death. The translator's 'editing' (see the editorial apparatus in Turco's parallel Latin–English text edition) does therefore seem of some significance. In the present context we note that the translator actually turned the generally used Ciceronian phrase 'sensus recti et honesti' and its equivalents into 'conscience'.

[27] Hutcheson, *A short introduction*, p. 116. Similarly idem, *A system*, II, pp. 234n.

annotated translation of the *Meditations of the Emperor Marcus Aurelius*.[28] And it is also the case that he often echoes Platonist language in this connection, but there is never any question of him elevating conscience into an autonomous preserve exempt from the basic characteristics of our desires and judgements in general. Not least, Hutcheson never gives conscience the unassailable status that it had in orthodox Calvinist theology and which is clearly conveyed in the Westminster Confession of Faith as adopted by the Church of Scotland. Here it is put like this:

> God alone is Lord of the Conscience, and hath left it free from the Doctrines and Commandments of Men, which are in any thing contrary to his Word, or beside it, in Matters of Faith or Worship. So that to believe such Doctrines, or to obey such Commandments out of Conscience, is to betray true Liberty of Conscience; and the requiring of an implicite Faith, and an absolute and blind Obedience, is to destroy Liberty of Conscience and Reason also.[29]

However, my suggestion that conscience, for Hutcheson, is to be approached as a matter of empirical psychology and of moral education and character cultivation may appear to be contradicted by his well-known theory that we have an inalienable *right* to a free conscience. This might be taken to suggest that conscience has a foundation beyond that of human nature and its social malleability—a special status, the character of which must be investigated.

In enumerating our natural rights, Hutcheson includes a person's right to 'act according to his own choice … [and] this right we call natural liberty, of which liberty of conscience is not only an essential but an unalienable branch'.[30] But what is meant by inalienability, and what is a natural right? Rights are *alienable*, says Hutcheson, where the alienation can actually be carried out effectively, and where some interest of society may often require such translations. Both these qualities have to concur for a right to be alienable, and since neither of them appertains to our religious opinions or other 'affections and devotions', the 'right of private judgment is … unalienable'. As he explains, 'No man can avoid judging according to the evidence which appears to him; nor can any interest of society require one to profess hypocritically contrary to his inward sentiments.'

In comparison with the pure Calvinist idea of the free conscience, this is clearly a weaker notion. Hutchesonian conscience is explicitly open for social education and moral training, and he points out that weak minds may accept the opinion of those who are wiser as the evidence upon which to form their

[28] *Meditations of the emperor Marcus Aurelius Antoninus*, trans. Francis Hutcheson and James Moor (1742), ed. James Moore and Michael Silverthorne (Indianapolis, IN, 2008).

[29] Chapter xx of the Westminster Confession; quoted here from *A collection of confessions of faith*, I, pp. 102–3.

[30] Hutcheson, *A system*, I, p. 257; cf. idem, *A short introduction*, p. 129. The following quotations in this paragraph are from the brief discussions in *A short introduction*, pp. 114–15, and *A system*, I, pp. 259–60.

own private judgement.[31] What is more, the second criterion for inalienability seems to be a patently false suggestion, namely, that it cannot be in the public interest to force insincere compliance in matters of belief. The explanation for the latter claim is, of course, that Hutcheson does not intend it as an empirical statement about historical societies but about the properly constituted future society, that is, he means it as an implicitly normative proposition to the effect that it would be unjust for a society to force beliefs and opinions. However, for him justice is a matter of the common good, which in individual societies means the public interest. And so, as he says, to compel people 'to profess contrary to their opinions … must always be unjust, as no interest of society can require it'.[32] Nevertheless, although the inalienability of the right to a free conscience in effect is turned into a matter of civil prudence, this argumentative approach does of course serve to emphasize that the liberty of conscience is distinct in nature from the freedom of action exactly because of its inwardness, and Hutcheson is always very forceful about the futility of using coercion in matters of belief.

My characterization of the notion of the right to a free conscience as a matter of civil prudence can be extended to the Hutchesonian notion of natural rights in general. This may seem a surprising suggestion, for Hutcheson is well known to be a genuine theorist of rights for whom these are the basis for all significant interpersonal relationships, including civil society itself, and for the ascription of rights also to animals.[33] What is more, it has often been argued that his theory of rights had some practical influence on the political process, especially in America. Having put forward such ideas myself, I am not now going to deny them;[34] rather, I am suggesting that the practical success of rights theories such as Hutcheson's was due not least to the watered-down concept of rights involved.

Pointing to Grotius as a precursor, Hutcheson poses the idea that rights have a pre-moral source in our desires, as I mentioned earlier. That is to say, the very fact that our moral sense approves of certain actions and disapproves of others leads us to a natural presumption that the agent in question, whether oneself or another, is right in doing the former and wrong in doing the latter. But this is only turned into the position of having a right, in the sense of being able rightfully to exclude others from interference, once the presumptive judgement has passed the test of the common good, that is to say, the test of being derived from the basic natural law that prescribes the preservation or augmentation of the maximum happiness.

[31] Hutcheson, *A system*, I, pp. 295–6.
[32] Ibid., p. 296.
[33] See Aaron Garrett, 'Francis Hutcheson and the origins of animal rights', *Journal of the History of Philosophy*, 45 (2007), pp. 243–65.
[34] Haakonssen, *Natural law and moral philosophy*, ch. 10, and references given there.

> A man hath a *right* to do, possess, or demand any thing when his acting, possessing, or obtaining from another in these circumstances tends to the good of society, or to the interest of the individual consistently with the rights of others and the general good of society, and the obstructing him would have the contrary tendency.[35]

Thus understood a right is 'a faculty or claim established by law', natural law or positive law, depending on one's situation, and this is underscored by constant insistence upon the subordinate nature of rights. Natural rights 'should be maintained to all men', he says, but only 'when no more general interest of mankind requires any abridgement of them'. For,

> no private right can hold against the general interest of all. For a regard to the most extensive advantage of the whole system ought to controll and limit all the rights of individuals or of particular societies.

> Indeed if any grand interest of a community requires [a man] being deprived of some part of his acquisitions, then we see a superior moral form; a publick interest, which a good mind must more regard.[36]

The entire dependency of rights upon the notion of the common good understood as the maximum happiness is further underlined by the fact that Hutcheson insists that the traditional distinction between perfect and imperfect rights is one of degree not of kind.[37]

In short, despite appearances to the contrary, Hutcheson does not provide a theory of rights as spheres of individual autonomy, metaphysically or theologically secured absolutes outside of the empirical, historical existence of individual persons and social groups. On the contrary, rights are creatures of other factors in our moral lives, mainly the moral sense, and although there is a basic general pattern to the way in which rights, as he says, 'ensue upon' the moral sense's perception of morally good behaviour, the recognition of rights, even the most basic and so-called inalienable ones, is always defeasible by considerations of the common good. Just how flexible this makes our basic natural liberty is indicated in the following passage:

> as one may be said to act freely when he follows willingly the direction of another, having a firm dependance on his superior wisdom and kind intentions; it may be justly said, that in the strictest polity, where there are very exact regulations of manners, and a constant discipline over all the people, there still remains to them abundant liberty, if they are fully assured of the wisdom and good intention of the laws, and heartily acquiesce in them, tho they can never

[35] Hutcheson, *A system*, I, p. 253. Compare ibid., pp. 285–6 and idem, *A short introduction*, pp. 110–12.
[36] Hutcheson, *A short introduction*, p. 112; idem, *A system*, I, p. 254.
[37] Compare Haakonssen, *Natural law and moral philosophy*, pp. 81–2.

> counteract them without incurring punishment, and are in a great part of their conduct confined by them to that certain manner which the law prescribes.[38]

This is not to deny, of course, that Hutcheson was what we would call a 'liberal' influence in his time; nor is it to belittle the rhetorical force of the language of rights he applied in his cause. However, a clear view of the nature of his rights theory does help underscore the never-to-be-forgotten, but apparently ever-to-be-repeated point that the elements of liberality had a very different constellation in the early eighteenth century from that of the early twenty-first, and that Hutcheson's ideas exhibit features that are distinctly illiberal by modern standards. Not least, it clarifies the shifting applications of the theory within a short span of time. I concentrate here on matters pertaining to toleration, albeit broadly conceived.

IV

The onslaught by the disgruntled student on Hutcheson's teaching, mentioned earlier, ends with a lengthy charge that the professor subscribed to a strongly Erastian view of the relationship between church and state. In this the student was quite right. Hutcheson always made the overall institution and control of the church part of sovereignty.[39] True, he stressed the *prudence* of leaving the internal governance of church matters to the clergy, but this was entirely subject to the public interest. Thus church property and church income were subject to public control, and while much of what he had to say on this point was part of standard anti-Catholic polemics, he made sure to use such general terms that all organized churches, also his own, were included.[40] Vice versa,

[38] Hutcheson, *A system*, II, pp. 281–2.

[39] In *A short introduction*, p. 266, Hutcheson makes it a matter of the form of the basic constitution whether the church falls within a state's sovereignty: 'if in the very constitution of the civil polity, the sovereign or chief magistrate is only entrusted with such power as is requisite for the preservation of the secular rights of men; then they cannot exert any sort of coercive power about the means of forming mens minds to religion and inward virtue. But when they are entrusted with certain revenues, to be employed for the publick utility at their discretion; and where they are not expressly restricted to the care of the secular rights of men; since human happiness chiefly depends upon virtue, the civil governors must think it belonging to their office, to instill into the minds of their subjects the true sentiments of religion and virtue, and to influence their hearts to relish them, by the best instruction and discipline from their infancy, that they may be furnished for all the honourable offices of life.' As far as I can see, Hutcheson does not take up this quite fundamental thought in *A system*.

[40] e.g. Hutcheson, *A system*, I, pp. 334–5. It is important to distinguish between anti-Catholicism as a doctrinal matter and anti-popery, a political matter. This was not uncommon in Hutcheson's ideological circles; see for example Robert Molesworth in his preface to François Hotman, *Francogallia, or an account of the ancient free state of France* (1721), in Molesworth, *An account of Denmark, with Francogallia and Some considerations for the promoting of agriculture and employing the poor*, ed. Justin Champion (Indianapolis, IN 2011), pp. 176–7. But Hutcheson goes out on a limb by his openness to Catholicism in morals.

the clergy could not act legitimately in the secular sphere except on delegation from the sovereign, 'be they popes, colleges of cardinals, high priests and elders, convocations or assemblies of any kind: and let them inforce their sentences by what artifices they please: if they derive not their power from the state, they assume [illegitimately] a civil sovereignty'.[41]

Hutcheson patently did not think the form of church government very important in itself, as long as it did not transgress on civil sovereignty and thus was to the detriment of the common good. Of course, he knew what he was talking about. In his native Ireland, the Presbyterian church, to which he belonged through family tradition and by very explicit and repeated choice, was a dissenting sect that laboured under considerable legal constraints. In his adopted country, Scotland, Presbyterianism was established as the state church by the same government that checked it across the water. It is hardly surprising that he always urged that as little fuss as possible should be made about clerical arrangements and especially that compulsion should be avoided as far as possible, since this just encouraged fundamentalism of either the enthusiastic or the superstitious kind. But he was equally clear that this was a matter purely of political prudence, not of right. Similarly, he thought it imprudent to suppress alternative confessions to the established church, whichever this might be, as long as they did not threaten the security of the state. Even with dangerous opinions, it is often, he says, 'better to leave such tenets to be exploded by the juster reasonings of wise men, than to proceed to any severities on account of the tenets themselves'.[42] The question is, however, whether such suppression was also immoral, namely an unjust transgression on the right of conscience of such dissenting religionists. The simple answer is yes; for while a *church* could exclude dissenters, the *state* should practise universal toleration. However, the simple answer becomes complicated once we appreciate that Hutcheson also wanted to show, as his disciples put it, 'how [universal toleration] is reconcileable with the Magistrate's Care of Religion'.[43]

For despite his remarkably inclusive tolerationism, Hutcheson certainly thought that the state should have care of religion, not just to avoid trouble but as an essential part of its rationale. Like all other human associations, civil society had as its primary goal the promotion and security of maximum happiness, and just as each state was a contributing part of the universal system of moral creatures, so subpolitical associations were tributaries of the political society. In this hierarchy, the church was a central tool for the state, and Hutcheson's outlook upon the church is dominated by this political role—which is, not surprisingly, that of moral educator:

[41] Hutcheson, *A system*, II, p. 326.

[42] Hutcheson, *A short introduction*, p. 267; the latter half of the passage was added in the translation.

[43] [Anon.], *A vindication*, p. 19.

> As pious dispositions toward God, a firm persuasion of his goodness, and of his providence governing the world, and administering justice in a future state by rewarding justice, temperance, and all social dispositions, and punishing the contrary, are the sources of the most sublime happiness, so they are the strongest incitements to all social, friendly and heroick offices. The civil power should take care that the people be well instructed in these points, and have all arguments presented to their understandings, and all rational inducements proposed which can raise these persuasions, and confirm these dispositions.[44]

Such education should be offered with all respect for the people's 'sacred right of judging for themselves' and hence without any compulsion.[45] But while this principle of right is of greatest moral importance, there is a serious problem of a different moral hue:

> as the far greater part of every people will not use this right [of judging for themselves]; but induced by specious appearances of sanctity, and ostentation of superior wisdom in some designing men, will incautiously give up themselves to be led by them; it must plainly be the business of the magistrate to get this *leading* into his own hands; by appointing men of character and learning to teach the people the just sentiments of religion and virtue, and to confirm them by the most effectual reasonings; that they may not be perverted by the wicked arts of others.[46]

This is from *A short introduction to moral philosophy*. In the corresponding discussion in the *System*, Hutcheson suggests that 'scarce one in an hundred will ever exercise this right of private judgment vigorously'.[47] Hutcheson is obviously not suggesting that the ninety-nine per cent of the population who do not exercise their right to judge for themselves *lose* this right. But he is certainly making good use of the other side of his theory, highlighted above; namely, that the power of judging—conscience, the moral sense—to which people have a right is a socially malleable feature of human nature, not an untouchable individual preserve.

The magistrate's co-called '*leading*' in moral-religious matters is not, however, a purely educational exercise in all circumstances. As already indicated earlier, there are three absolute minimum requirements for all morality, namely 'pious dispositions toward God, a firm persuasion of his goodness, and of his providence governing the world, and administering justice in a future state'. When people deny these, they will 'tend to hurt the state in its most important interests: and the persons who directly publish such tenets

[44] Hutcheson, *A system*, II, pp. 310–11. The political role of the church is well presented in the discussion of Bayle's questions, ibid., I, pp. 219–20; see above at note 24.
[45] Hutcheson, *A short introduction*, p. 266.
[46] Ibid., p. 267.
[47] Hutcheson, *A system*, II, pp. 311–12.

cannot well pretend any obligation in conscience to do so'.[48] The explanation is that without the three core beliefs, you do not *have* a conscience; you are missing the judgement side of conscience that should relate individual behaviour to the overall moral system regulated by the deity's natural law. As we have seen, Hutcheson thought that this was a necessary presupposition for being able to impute actions to agents. Without it, a person would not be a full moral agent, for he would lack the ability to recognize the moral world's basic orderliness, namely coherence between motives, actions, and reactions. Such a person would be living in a moral world that is analogous to a material world in which the laws of physics do not hold. 'The magistrate may … justly restrain [such people] by force, as he might any deluded fool or enthusiasts who pretended conscience in invading the rights or properties of others.'[49] However, even here Hutcheson suggests that force should be a last resort in cases where 'principles are discovered [= revealed] by wicked actions', for 'there is little danger that such tenets will ever prevail in a civilized nation where knowledge and arts are encouraged',[50] and besides there is again the danger that enforcement will be counterproductive.

Hutcheson's scepticism about the ability or will of the great majority of the population to exercise their right of free conscience expressed itself in another way, namely in his view of the relationship between church and state in his own adopted country. As is well known, Scotland in the eighteenth century was largely governed by a member of the highest nobility who acted as agent for the ministry in London and exercised power through an intricate network of patronage. Against the 1690 act that established Presbyterian church government in Scotland, the Patronage Act of 1712 had formalized a similar patronage arrangement for the kirk, which meant that livings were filled either by the Crown or by a small number of nobles or by the merchant elite running town councils, and when these people did not take sufficient interest in church matters—and often they did not—considerable influence was de facto left with the lower and uneducated orders. In the eyes of people such as Hutcheson, this cut out the broader band of natural civic leaders, namely the gentry, from their due influence in the church.

In 1736 the General Assembly of the Church of Scotland passed an act to abolish the existing patronage system, and a bill was introduced in Parliament to the same purpose, but it was defeated and the debate rumbled on during the following decades.[51] Hutcheson wrote his pamphlet *Considerations on*

[48] Ibid., pp. 310 and 313 (emphasis added).

[49] Ibid., p. 313.

[50] Ibid., p. 314.

[51] Richard Sher and Alexander Murdoch, 'Patronage and party in the Church of Scotland, 1750–1800', in Norman Macdougall, ed., *Church, politics and society in Scotland 1408–1929* (Edinburgh, 1983), pp. 197–220.

patronages as a fervent appeal to the Scottish gentry to back the bill before parliament.[52] But while he wanted the abolition of the existing patronage system, he did not wish Scotland to revert to popular selection of ministers. Instead he wanted a system whereby ministers were elected by the local patron of the church and the elders of the presbytery, subject to approval by all male householders. The basis for this argument was that the gentry had the means of education and needed to appreciate that moral education of the Hutchesonian kind was key to both personal and social happiness.[53]

The reason for bringing Hutcheson's ideas about church patronage into the present discussion is that this provides a further variation on my theme that despite its juridical trappings, Hutcheson's theory of toleration and the right to a free conscience is in fact a theory of political prudence and moral pedagogy. To this we can now add an aesthetic dimension. It is well known that Hutcheson thought that our sense of moral goodness was closely similar to our sense of beauty, but what I have in mind here is that the education of our moral judgement itself has an aesthetic aspect. By conscience,

> we discern what is graceful, becoming, beautiful and honourable in the affections of the soul, in our conduct of life, our words and actions … Upon observing the like honourable actions and designs in others, we naturally favour and praise them; and have an high esteem, and goodwill, and endearment toward all in whom we discern such excellent dispositions: and condemn and detest those who take a contrary course. What is approved by this sense we count *right* and *beautiful*, and call it *virtue*; what is condemned, we count *base* and *deformed* and *vitious*.[54]

Similarly, in his inaugural lecture, Hutcheson talked of 'natural conscience, that sense of the beautiful and the fitting'.[55]

This is the basis for Hutcheson's central argument about patronage in the kirk. Here he invokes a moral idyll for the gentlemen of Scotland to behold, one in which the educated, cultured, theologically moderate minister is conversation partner for the laird, pastor to his family, tutor for their children, moral leader and educator to the community, conciliator of conflict, and

[52] Francis Hutcheson, *Considerations on patronages addressed to the gentlemen of Scotland* (London, 1735), in Moore and Stewart, eds., *Correspondence and occasional writings*. The editors of the new edition adduce evidence that in this campaign Hutcheson worked with the lawyer William Grant, later Lord Prestongrange, who—also anonymously—published a closely allied pamphlet that sets out the legal side of the argument with great clarity: *The present state of the Church of Scotland: with respect to patronages; and the Bill now depending before the Parliament* (London, 1736).
[53] Richard B. Sher, *Church and university in the Scottish Enlightenment: the moderate literati of Edinburgh* (Princeton, NJ, and Edinburgh, 1985), pp. 153–4.
[54] Hutcheson, *A short introduction*, p. 35 (original emphasis).
[55] Hutcheson, *Natural sociability*, p. 211.

promoter of communal love, peace, and harmony.[56] Reaching a crescendo in his appeal to the sheer beauty of it all, he asks: 'Abstracting even from Christianity and a future State, don't these things well deserve the Care and Attention of any Gentleman of Thought and Conduct [?]' Hutcheson is describing morally beautiful people leading a life that simply is not possible for the general populace who, in consequence, should be kept out of church matters, not least the choice of ministers. He makes no bones about the negative side of his case:

> what kind of Preachers are they whom the Vulgar chiefly admire? Why chiefly those who strike their outward Senses in the strongest manner, such as have the most noisy and strange Vociferation, use the most violent Action and Gestures; or such as declaim against Superiors in Church and State, and shew the warmest Zeal about little things … [S]uch Clergymen as these … will be generally the greatest Idols of the Populace, though they are possessed of little Learning, Sense, or Moderation, or any other good Qualities.[57]

This was undoubtedly how Hutcheson saw the situation of much of the Church of Scotland in the 1730s. He had to acknowledge that both clergy and laity of such lamentable qualities had a natural right to their free conscience in matters of religion, but at the same time, he saw it as a moral and political necessity to negate the consequences of this right being exercised in the way it was. This was one of the points in his combination of moral sense theory and natural jurisprudence.

V

From a post-Enlightenment perspective, one cannot help but suggest that Hutcheson was that supposed contradiction in terms, a Scotsman without a strong historical sense. In fact, considering all the understandable talk of the historicism of the Scottish Enlightenment, it is a remarkable fact that the main thinker of the early Enlightenment, Hutcheson, and the main thinker of the late Enlightenment, Thomas Reid, were both largely untouched by serious historiographical concerns. Leaving Reid out of consideration on this occasion, we may conclude with a couple of thoughts about Hutcheson and history.

His uncomfortable idea of natural rights that are defeasible by political prudence looks very different, if it is historicized into the idea that rights are dependent upon what spectators at any given historical stage are able to recognize as legitimate preserves of behaviour. Similarly, the static moral

[56] Hutcheson, *Considerations on patronages*, p. 16.
[57] Ibid., p. 20.

psychology of the ideal balance between particular moral perception and systemic moral judgement is virtually begging to be turned into a historical dynamics of moral progress. In extension of this, the truth value of the creedal doctrines could be seen as a matter of historically conditioned understanding, thus sidestepping the either-or situation of, for instance, the subscription debates. As Colin Kidd has argued, this last move was central to Moderatism, and it is a suggestion that may be generalized.[58] This does highlight that the most striking deficiency in Hutcheson's claim to paternity of the Scottish Enlightenment is his lack of historical sense and interest. Nevertheless, he certainly paved the way for the high Enlightenment's historicism by the role he gave to political prudence and by undermining the transcendent force of natural rights. This prudential philosophy owed a great deal to the polemical needs of Hutcheson's immediate circumstances, and it was only made intellectually and morally acceptable through another form of transcendent justification, namely that of providence. But the further move of connecting the history of humanity's future to the history of its past, in the manner of William Robertson, was simply not part of Hutcheson's agenda.

[58] Colin Kidd, 'Subscription, the Scottish Enlightenment and the Moderate interpretation of history', *Journal of Ecclesiastical History*, 55 (2004), pp. 502–19.

Postface

The Grounds for Toleration and the Capacity to Tolerate

JOHN DUNN

ALL HUMAN BEINGS FIND ASPECTS OF ONE another offensive or revolting. The practical challenge of living with others is a strain in the first instance on the dispositional virtue of tolerance, the gracious endurance of exposure to the numerous aspects of others that disturb and distress. That challenge is deepened and complicated wherever what disturbs and distresses is also an occasion for deep and considered disapproval (strong negative evaluation).[1] In these circumstances it is no longer clear that tolerance is guaranteed to remain a virtue. Instead it shades readily and uncontrollably into complicity. Without considerable further interpretation complicity in the deeply disapproved must be a vice, not a virtue. The polite consensus of the modern West values tolerance highly as a virtue, viewing it as something altogether worthier than an engaging and emollient dispositional trait, and gravely overestimating its capacity to serve as a principle of political ordering. Coercion and tolerance are as mutually exclusive at the point of impact as commanding and forbidding. The limits of tolerance are set by the duty to prevent, or more hectically by the duty to try to compel. Either subjectively or objectively, the contours of tolerance and complaisance are inherently vague and heavily context-dependent. They cannot furnish a stable basis on which to judge how to act, still less how to exercise the power to coerce. Instead they presuppose and depend upon just such judgements. One beguiling conception of liberalism is that it enthrones the dispositional virtue of tolerance as the master principle of social (and therefore political) existence, equating it in practice with a deep and equal respect for the autonomy of all human agents.[2] It is hard to combine a respect for the autonomy of all with a vivid disapproval of the uses to which

[1] For the human centrality of strong evaluation see Charles Taylor, 'What is human agency?', in idem, *Philosophical papers 1: human agency and language* (Cambridge, 1985), pp. 15–44, esp. 15–28, and 'The validity of transcendental arguments', in idem, *Philosophical arguments* (Cambridge, MA, 1995), pp. 20–33, esp. 22–8.

[2] For an eloquent defence see the work of Ronald Dworkin, especially *Sovereign virtue: the theory and practice of equality* (Cambridge, MA, 2000).

Proceedings of the British Academy, **186**, 201–209.

many elect to put such autonomy as they can muster. A society in which the great majority endure one another's offences with nonchalance or resolute fortitude is altogether more agreeable than one that yearns to punish every departure from the seemly and reassuring. A society at ease at a particular time with the multiplicity of its constituent cultures would be a happier society in which to live than one where their respective bearers suffer one another's company in acute discomfort and with gritted teeth. But the contrast between them so conceived would be one of historical felicity, not political principle or institutional form.

It is not clear that there are any clear principles to be drawn from the elusive dispositional contours of tolerance and intolerance, or any reliable way of knowing how far or how these characteristics or propensities can be deliberately enhanced or depleted by individuals, aspirant social engineers, or competing political leaders. What is clear is that the spiritual and political struggle to sustain or refashion them goes on competitively virtually everywhere almost all the time.

The political problem of toleration for Western Europe from the sixteenth century to the present is not well seen as a cumulative and increasingly secure triumph of the dispositional virtue of tolerance towards the offensive or disturbing religious beliefs and practices of others over its antithetical vice: still less as its more comprehensive triumph in relation to the far wider range of offence and disturbance emanating from their sexual orientations and exploits or their modes of cultural self-expression.[3] In its Western European setting, the toleration of others' religious beliefs and practices emerged in due course as an intellectual solution to a very hard puzzle: how should a Christian ruler use their power? More particularly, how far did he or she have a peremptory and supervening religious duty to enforce their own assessment of Christianity's requirements on those who saw and felt them very differently, or did not discernibly feel them at all? It was a question, evidently, about the scope of authority and the responsibilities of power. But it was also a question about the structures and content of Christian duty; and it was the latter that set the question to the former. The key shift in establishing religious toleration as a political principle and not a religious dereliction was the blocking of the hallowed Augustinian judgement that forceful assertion of Christian truth towards the obtuse or recalcitrant was a clear religious duty. What subverted that judgement above all was the sapping of the plausibility of the assumption

[3] Compare the teleological criterion of Perez Zagorin, *How the idea of religious toleration came to the West* (Princeton, 2003) with the more exigent requirements of Jonathan Israel, *Radical enlightenment: philosophy and the making of modernity, 1650–1750* (Oxford, 2001) and idem, *Enlightenment contested: philosophy, modernity, and the emancipation of man 1670–1752* (Oxford, 2006).

that those in political authority had any secure means of distinguishing Christian truth from personal misapprehension: *quisque sibi orthodoxus*.[4] At that point the conception of revelation-based authority dissolved before an epistemological scepticism which has served over time as an effective solvent for very many other forms of authority. What its dissolution left behind was not a set of coherent and intellectually orderly regimes with varying degrees of homogenizing ambition, but a set of varyingly explicit accommodations to heterogeneity and intellectual dissent.[5] For all its practical disarray, however, and despite all the political vicissitudes that subsequently befell it, the intellectual dissolution was to prove permanent, and its political implications are hard to miss. To reverse it durably, it would first be necessary to reforge a new and comprehensive structure of epistemic authority.

The shifting balance of tolerance and intolerance within a particular population is a continuing challenge to benign rule, intelligent social cooperation, and prudently limited but necessary conflict: close to the core of politics anywhere that recognizes that it has politics.[6] It is a delusion to suppose that the history of the West (wherever and whenever you care to situate it) has yielded a reliable stock of wisdom (social capital, liberal political philosophy, Chicago School economics, civilization) on how to live this ongoing fate. Where it did in a sense reach a conclusion of a kind, in some exhaustion and very late in the seventeenth century, was to a narrower, shapelier, and fiercer issue set by its own history: the specifically religious duties of Christian rule.

The conclusion it reached was hard won and purely negative. As yet it is far from obvious to what extent it generalizes beyond the Christian *oecumene* and its lingering aftermath—to the lands conquered by Islam instead, to China, to Japan, to South Asia. The problem of religious toleration was set by a jealous God. It does not arise, as eighteenth-century sceptics noted,[7] where gods are comfortably plural and unperturbed by one another's devotional receipts. But the Christian God was an explicit heir to an older counterpart; and there have been, and very much remain, other jealous gods (as well as programmes of authoritarian secularization with equally monopolistic claims to creedal submission). In these respects it is reasonable to believe that some core element in that purely negative conclusion may still hold force even in the face of acute civilizational animosity.[8] Commanding Right and

[4] John Locke, *Epistola de tolerantia / A letter on toleration*, ed. Raymond Klibansky, trans. J. W. Gough (Oxford, 1968), p. 58 (and see p. 112).

[5] Compare John McManners, *Church and society in eighteenth century France* (2 vols., Oxford, 1998) with J. C. W. Clark, *English society 1688–1832* (Cambridge, 1985).

[6] For an explanation and defence of this conception of politics see John Dunn, *The cunning of unreason: making sense of politics* (London, 2000).

[7] Frank Manuel, *The eighteenth century confronts the gods* (Cambridge, MA, 1958).

[8] Compare Samuel Huntington, *The clash of civilisations and the remaking of world order* (New York, 1996).

Forbidding Wrong sound salutary enough commitments for political authority;[9] but to implement them it is first necessary to discern what is right and what is wrong, and where a population is already in sharp disagreement on this score (as virtually every contemporary population manifestly is), a degree of epistemological scepticism on this point is hard to avoid. At the very least it carries, conceptually and analytically, as a distinct and salient shape, a principle of prudential rationality, into any assessment of how best to handle the shifting contours of tolerance and intolerance within existing populations.

The historical experience of Christian intolerance has varied greatly across the European continent in time and space. Viewed as a bloc, what stands out about it is its extraordinary pervasiveness and longevity. To view it as an interminable and gratuitously obstructed journey towards the decent and obvious is as historically insensitive as it is politically inane. A whig history of the dawning of toleration is well enough placed to register cruelty;[10] but it is a clumsy instrument for capturing the movement of either thinking or political judgement. The contributors to this volume are united in presuming the indispensability of understanding both thought and political judgement in the past within the dense historical contexts in which each necessarily occurred. None shows much sympathy with the presumptions of whig historiography or its liberal descendants. They differ, naturally, in some measure in their sense of what these contexts were, and differ too, more importantly, in their conceptions of what in that dense past is most worthwhile to understand. The imperative to understand political or religious thinking in context favours biography or local history as genres over the effort to trace the vicissitudes of concepts or arguments across time and space. It underlines the acuity of the epistemic challenge which even biography or local history need to meet, and casts some doubt by doing so on whether inquiries that range much further in time or wider in space could ever hope to reach those standards. Whether the professional outcome is seen as an index of a more prepossessing and duly self-critical epistemic modesty, or a damagingly comfortable accommodation to epistemic pusillanimity is no doubt largely a matter of personal taste and temperament; but it does also determine how far historical inquiry can bear on the puzzles and dilemmas of the present or the future, and history itself serve as a medium of political reflection. There are two very different possible outcomes of radical historicization of Europe's long painful travails with religious intolerance: one sealing that past off decisively from present and future, and the other equally dense and particular

[9] Compare Michael Cook, *Commanding right and forbidding wrong in Islamic thought* (Cambridge, 2000).

[10] Zagorin, *Idea of religious toleration*, or more demotically A. C. Grayling, *Towards the light: the story of the struggles for liberty and rights that made the modern West* (London, 2007).

in content but orientated, however unsteadily, to grasping why exactly that outcome has been as it has, and what has been learnt and forgotten in the course of reaching it.

An especially sensitive issue between these two historical readings is the salience or otherwise of the distinction between hard and soft thought (or sheer nescience), consequential and inconsequential thinking. This is not a distinction required by the more austerely historicist vision, and may well be one that the former cannot even afford. For the latter, plainly, it is indispensable and arguably central. Both forms of radical historicization require historical analysis of the density and care presented here; but they need it in very different ways. For the former it is in effect sufficient: an assemblage, necessarily unsystematic (for what epistemic authority could any system hold?), of disparate items of value. For the latter, less buoyantly, it is merely necessary. Viewed from either angle, accordingly, the context of the history of casuistry over the justification of religious intolerance or tolerance will come out predominantly as a tissue of fairly soft thought, more a milieu of existence, however quarrelsome, than a purposeful programme of inquiry, and buffered throughout by the accumulated repertoire of self-approbation available to its denizens. For the former vision, nothing more is required (or to be hoped for) than a faithful and vivid ethnographic record of that context. For the latter, the most faithful and scintillating of ethnographies could be only a prelude to the effort to grasp what has been at stake and how the game has come out.

The issue of how to rule as a Christian became acute as soon as Christians acquired responsibility to try to direct the cruel and increasingly shaky authority of the Roman state, and the necessarily in part cruel and always potentially shaky authority of any possible rival or successor. As a question addressed to Christians it was epistemically extreme and imaginatively unnerving from the outset, for all the aplomb that some mustered in responding to it. From the Conversion of Constantine onwards, it overlapped and interacted continuously with the older, and perhaps more fundamental, Christian question of what attitude it was spiritually prepossessing to adopt towards the religious intuitions, interpretations, and practices of fellow Christians of whom you vividly disapproved. Both questions were at issue subsequently in any sustained inquiry into the nature and proper scope of the Christian church, the latter arguably so, once again, from the outset. It was a natural construal of Christianity to view the second question as prior to the first not merely chronologically but also categorically, and to conceive the church itself through the attempt to answer it (as well as viewing the church in practice as its personally preferred answer). In the present volume Maria Rosa Antognazza's sensitive and compelling exploration of Leibniz's response to these challenges presents him as not merely a particularly lucid and generous reader of the claims of tolerance as a Christian virtue, but also as single-mindedly committed to viewing the nature of the Christian church itself and the imperatives that must guide it through the prism of tolerance as a constitutive virtue. As a political programme, the reunification of the Western churches may have had limited political prospects at this (or any other) time; and Leibniz himself made no apparent effort to assess the prudential requirements for dealing with contemporaries self-righteously bent on correcting one another's errors with all the power they could muster. But for all its evident political futility, it showed some real imaginative recognition of the scale of the challenge to Christianity of the cruelty and mutual contempt that had made up so much of its history in the world.

For most of the thinkers discussed in these pages the issue of toleration was addressed less ambitiously, not by a synoptic reading of Christianity's demands, but through more contextually specific assessments of the duties that it imposed, or the entitlements that it conferred, upon the holders of authority in particular settings in church or state. Unlike Bossuet, none of them claimed to derive their conclusions intact from the pages of Scripture alone,[11] and most did not aspire to vindicate the claims to locally exclusive authority advanced by either church or state. They took these claims largely as given and adjusted their theoretical views to the requirements for presenting them as coherently as their content permitted. The result was often unexacting as a piece of thinking: little more than a rationalization of the demands of context. In some settings, however, and for reasons we still very imperfectly comprehend, at least a handful of thinkers clearly came to view these rationalizations as indefensible, and in the most extreme cases even to see and feel their own contexts as a whole as beyond rationalization. That outcome, of course, was not necessarily a product of hard thought: it was as much a matter of attitude and disposition as of strenuous intellectual effort.[12] As the religious histories of different areas of the world press more painfully and hazardously on one another, there is growing urgency to the need to understand how these two very different styles of historicization articulate with one another. Until we are better placed to judge that, however much miscellaneous information we accumulate on how these questions were viewed and felt in the past, we will not necessarily enhance our own judgement of where the hazards that now face us are coming from, or which approaches to meeting them even recognize the lessons of that painful and confusing past. We will fall short of our own past achievements just when we most require their aid, and trap ourselves in a parochialism of time every bit as disabling as the parochialisms

[11] Jacques-Benigne Bossuet, *Politics drawn from the very words of Holy Scripture*, ed. Patrick Riley (Cambridge, 1999).
[12] Compare Israel, *Radical enlightenment* and *Enlightenment contested.*

of space and existential confinement which any human can alleviate only by sustained effort and personal good fortune.

Read by John Rawls, the experience of Europe's wars of religion and the intellectual searchings to which they gave rise eventuated in the liberal world view:[13] the recognition that tolerance is both a requirement of justice, and the source of the key intuition that underlies its primacy as a political goal. But Rawls was scarcely an average reader even in his own day, and very few earlier Christians read their implications in a similar fashion.

In these pages Ian Harris and Timothy Stanton have each made very clear that the deepest Christian interpreter of the political implications of the duty to tolerate the religious convictions of others in the closing decades of the seventeenth century saw those implications far more narrowly. For all the marked divergences between John Locke's commitments and those of contemporary liberals,[14] it may well be true that he also saw them somewhat more clearly. As Harris and Stanton both demonstrate,[15] what enabled him to do so was less a passage of strenuous political under-labouring at the behest of the leader of a major political faction (powerful though that incentive certainly was),[16] than a sustained period of very hard thought, prompted by intellectual difficulties which had come to his attention considerably earlier in life. The lesson that Locke drew from these reflections did not pretend to direct a Christian (or Muslim, or Jewish) ruler on how to rule; and it conspicuously

[13] John Rawls, 'Justice as fairness: political not metaphysical', *Philosophy and Public Affairs*, 14 (1985), pp. 223–51, and idem, *Political liberalism* (New York, 1993).

[14] John Dunn, 'The claim to freedom of conscience: freedom of speech, freedom of thought, freedom of worship', in idem, *The history of political theory and other essays* (Cambridge, 1996), pp. 100–20.

[15] Drawing in each case on much of their earlier work—see especially Timothy Stanton, 'The name and nature of Locke's "Defence of nonconformity"', *Locke Studies*, 6 (2006), pp. 143–72; 'Locke and the politics and theology of toleration', *Political Studies*, 54 (2006), pp. 84–102; 'Locke the thinker', *Locke Studies*, 8 (2008), pp. 23–58; 'Authority and freedom in the interpretation of Locke's political theory', *Political Theory*, 39 (2011), pp. 6–30; 'Christian foundations; or some loose stones? Toleration and the philosophy of Locke's politics', *Critical Review of International Social and Political Theory*, 14 (2011), pp. 323–47; and Ian Harris, *The mind of John Locke: a study of political theory in its intellectual setting* (Cambridge, 1994); 'The politics of Christianity', in G. A. J. Rogers, ed., *Locke's philosophy: content and context* (Oxford, 1994), pp. 193–216; 'Tolérance, église et état chez Locke', in Yves Charles Zarka, Franck Lessay, and G. A. J. Rogers, eds., *Les fondements philosophiques de la tolérance* (3 vols., Paris, 2002), I, pp. 175–218; and compare Harris's careful placing of Pierre Bayle's approach to toleration in idem, 'Toleration and its place: a study of Pierre Bayle in his *Commentaire Philosophique*', in Sarah Hutton and Paul Schuurman, eds., *Studies on Locke: sources, contemporaries, and legacy* (Dordrecht, 2008), pp. 225–43.

[16] See, classically, Peter Laslett, 'Introduction', in John Locke, *Two treatises of government*, ed. Peter Laslett (Cambridge, 1960), pp. 37–79; K. H. D. Haley, *The first earl of Shaftesbury* (Oxford, 1968); Richard Ashcraft, *Revolutionary politics & Locke's Two treatises of government* (Princeton, 1986), with varying degrees of reduction.

failed to suggest how an atheist ruler would be well advised to set about doing so. All it vindicated was a single clear limit to any ruler's authority: the content of other human beings' religious beliefs. Holding political authority could not (and plainly did not) equip rulers to direct the religious conduct of their human fellows. When rulers sought to do so on the presumption that they enjoyed such an entitlement, they menaced those lives in this world, and jeopardized their own prospects along with multitudes of others in any world to come. This simple restriction aligned the scope of political authority neatly with its responsibilities through a common territorial and demographic scope,[17] and separated each from the murkier question of any ruler's practical power to achieve intended effects in the world. It defined both authority and responsibility through a single structure of duties and rights issuing from a law common to both, and equally binding on ruler and subject. It did not tell anyone how to rule as a Christian (or Muslim, or Jew): it just identified one form of conduct that they must eschew whilst attempting to do so.

The question of how to rule as a liberal is unlikely to prove any more tractable than that of how to rule as a Christian.[18] Compelling answers to it (if there are any) will scarcely prove shapelier or more comprehensive in scope than they did in the Christian case. What a liberal must or must not do in governing a political community of their own is hard to separate clearly from what they must or must not attempt to do in seeking to exert such power as it possesses beyond its borders.[19] Neither dispositional tolerance nor respect for the autonomy of others draws clear lines through these spaces. The right to coerce and the duty to rescue are very opaquely related here. Fantasies of beneficence through the exercise of coercive power readily divert attention from the starkness of the first presumption and impair judgement of the recalcitrance of the setting that requires rescue in the first place. Splitting the Far Abroad into sheep and goats, with the former presumed impotent and standing in need of rescue, and the latter viewed as permanently eligible targets for the executive power of the Law of Nature, is an unsound guide to moulding the human world for the better. Rawls's retreat from *A theory of justice* to *the law of peoples*, much deplored by more self-consciously cosmopolitan partisans of the duty to implement justice throughout the world, certainly blurred the outlines of his ethical theory and somewhat lessened its imaginative allure for some groups of readers.[20] But it also, unmistakably,

[17] For this purpose Locke's *Two treatises* fills out *Epistola*, despite the asymmetries between the two lines of thought. Compare Locke, *Two treatises* and idem, *Epistola de tolerantia / A letter on toleration*, ed. Raymond Klibansky, trans. J. W. Gough (Oxford, 1968)

[18] Unsurprisingly, this unclarity is at least as salient for utilitarian aspirants.

[19] Compare John Dunn, 'The dilemma of humanitarian intervention: the executive power of the law of nature, after God', in *History of political theory*, pp. 136–47.

[20] Compare John Rawls, *A theory of justice* (Cambridge, MA, 1971), pp. 378–79, 457–58.

marked a deeply serious effort to recognize the recalcitrance of the world of politics to civilizing missions from any quarter of the world: a forlorn prophylactic warning.

As a dispositional virtue tolerance largely consists of good intentions. As a hard won Christian conclusion toleration is better seen not as a mildly pusillanimous modus vivendi, but as a peremptory barrier to the very best of intentions exerted in the wrong place: a tart reminder that coercive intentions which their victims do not share can scarcely be expected to seem good at the receiving end. Self-righteous coercion is no more ingratiating than its most cynical counterpart—just provocative in at least one additional respect. In the politics of toleration the importunities of the spirit at its most exhilaratingly inspirational still meet the practical accommodations of human coexistence with a violence that is as disconcerting and disorientating as it has ever been. The challenges that they pose to political and ethical judgement are as stark today as they were in 1689. There is more to learn from Europe's long and often hideous past than the denizens of its increasingly shallow present have yet begun to realize.

Index